Acclaim for *Till Death Do Us Part*

"Salvatore G. Cilella Jr. has done a marvelous job editing the letters of Emily and Emory Upton. Readers interested in life in the Army following the Civil War, as well as those seeking to learn about romantic relationships of Victorian Americans, how Americans toured Europe, and Reconstruction from the vantage point of an Army officer will find much in this book. The vibrancy of these letters renders even more poignant Emily's tragic early death in 1870 and Emory's suicide in 1881."

Peter C. Luebke
editor of *The Autobiography of Rear Admiral John A. Dahlgren* and Albion Tourgée's *The Story of a Thousand*

"*Till Death Do Us Part* brings together letters written between 1868 and 1870 by Emory Upton and his wife, Emily. Their correspondence provides valuable detail on army life after the Civil War, keen observations on Europe, and insight into Emory and Emily's loving relationship. In his thorough and comprehensive editing and annotations, Salvatore Cilella Jr. provides the setting for these letters and elaborates on the various characters who appear in them."

Carl H. Moneyhon
author of *Edmund J. Davis of Texas: Civil War General, Republican Leader, Reconstruction Governor*

Till Death
Do Us Part

Till Death Do Us Part

The Letters of
Emory and Emily Upton,
1868–1870

Edited by
Salvatore G. Cilella Jr.

University of Oklahoma Press : Norman

Publication of this book is made possible through the generosity of Edith Kinney Gaylord.

Library of Congress Cataloging-in-Publication Data

Names: Upton, Emory, 1839–1881, author. | Cilella, Salvatore G., editor.
Title: Till death do us part : the letters of Emory and Emily Upton, 1868–1870 / Salvatore G. Cilella Jr.
Other titles: Letters of Emory and Emily Upton, 1868–1870
Description: Norman : University of Oklahoma Press, 2020. | Includes bibliographical references and index. | Summary: "An edited collection of personal correspondence of Major General Emory Upton and his wife, Emily Norwood Martin, forming a poignant narrative of love and affection as they attempted to create a normal life together despite her declining health"— Provided by publisher.
Identifiers: LCCN 2019042722 | ISBN 978-0-8061-6489-2 (paperback)
Subjects: LCSH: Upton, Emory, 1839–1881—Correspondence. | Upton, Emily Norwood, 1846–1870—Correspondence. | Married people—United States—Correspondence. | Tuberculosis—Patients—Biography. | Generals—United States—Biography.
Classification: LCC E181.U73 U67 2020 | DDC 355.0092—dc23
LC record available at https://lccn.loc.gov/2019042722

The paper in this book meets the guidelines for permanence and durability of the Committee on Production Guidelines for Book Longevity of the Council on Library Resources, Inc. ∞

Copyright © 2020 by the University of Oklahoma Press, Norman, Publishing Division of the University. Manufactured in the U.S.A.

All rights reserved. No part of this publication may be reproduced, stored in a retrieval system, or transmitted, in any form or by any means, electronic, mechanical, photocopying, recording, or otherwise—except as permitted under Section 107 or 108 of the United States Copyright Act—without the prior written permission of the University of Oklahoma Press. To request permission to reproduce selections from this book, write to Permissions, University of Oklahoma Press, 2800 Venture Drive, Norman, OK 73069, or email rights.oupress@ou.edu.

CONTENTS

Editorial Statement and Acknowledgments vii

    Introduction 1
1 European Honeymoon 21
2 Paris to Key West 54
3 Christmas in Havana 82
4 Emory to Memphis 111
5 Nassau 138
6 Ordered to Atlanta 179
7 Return to Nassau 197
    Epilogue 236

Appendix: Emory and Emily Timeline 253
Notes 257
Bibliography 307
Index 319

EDITORIAL STATEMENT AND ACKNOWLEDGMENTS

WHEN editing Emory Upton's correspondence for a previous publication, I came across more than sixty letters he wrote to his wife, Emily, in late 1868 and early 1869, which are held by the Princeton University Library. They are among the more than five hundred letters he wrote during his lifetime that are now scattered across the country in public institutions and in private hands from the Library of Congress to the Holland Land Office Museum in Upton's hometown of Batavia, New York. Using these personal letters would have expanded my original project beyond manageable length (which turned out to be two volumes). Instead, I decided to omit the personal letters and to publish them separately. In addition, Emily's letter book and some original letters, all to her parents and siblings, are held at Princeton as well. Unfortunately, the letters she wrote to Emory, if extant, have not surfaced.

The Throop and Martin Family Papers at Princeton are a gold mine of more than three hundred years of history. The entire collection runs from 1693 to 1951 and includes manuscripts, documents, photographs, and, of course, numerous pieces of correspondence. Letters are preserved from nearly every member of the family. The archive includes correspondence to family members from Francis Preston Blair, Martin Van Buren, Montgomery Blair, and William H. Seward, among others.

The collection is contained in twelve boxes totaling 4.2 linear feet. It is divided into eight "series": (1) Works, (2) Correspondence, (3) Autograph Collection, (4) Documents, (5) Miscellaneous Papers, (6) Pictures,

Photographs, Clippings, and Ephemera, (7) Albums and Diaries, and (8) Additional Papers. Each series is broken down into subseries. The majority of the letters, documents, and correspondence transcribed in this book have come from Princeton. They are from Series 7—Emily's Letterbook, and Series 2—Emory's Correspondence to Emily. When from a different source, the document is annotated appropriately. I have taken the liberty of including a few other letters, especially to James Wilson, whom Upton wrote concerning his relation with Emily. These reside in the Wilson Papers at the Library of Congress and at the U.S. Military Academy at West Point.

Unfortunately, none of Emily's letters to Emory have come to light. The Martin family, probably Mrs. Martin, preserved all of his letters to Emily. Emily's letter book and "Albums and Diaries" contain voluminous material Emily wrote to her mother and father while on her honeymoon and from Key West, Nassau, and Atlanta in the summer of 1869 but again, none to Emory. Her diary ranges from 1847 until her death in 1870, but also has Throop-Martin material well into the 1880s. Emory's existing letters to Emily end in 1869, although in 1869 Emily returned a second time to Key West and Nassau, where she stayed until her death in March 1870. None of Emory's letters have surfaced from that latter period.

For readability, I have chosen to present the letters as written with little intrusion into their content or meaning. Both correspondents occasionally used made-up words, which I have left alone. I have created paragraphs where none existed, enabling the reader to more easily understand the text. Where possible, I have inserted punctuation where needed, as most of the letters ignored common grammar and punctuation rules. *Sic* has been used sparingly when absolutely needed for clarity. Where possible, words requiring italics, such as ships' names, have been italicized. The most frustrating aspects of these intimate missives are the occasional "illegibles," which I have assiduously attempted to minimize with strong educated guesses. Emory's handwriting is miserable; Emily's is much more legible, but when she was feeling poorly, her script betrayed her condition. The majority of her letters are copies in a letter book, which appears to have been kept by her mother. Her original letters, most of which were sent from Atlanta, are comparably legible, and from their slant, indicate that she may have been left-handed.

Together, both sets of letters form a poignant narrative of one very strong general's tender love for a woman and her reciprocal affection. They are the remnants of a romantic, passionate relationship mildly surprising for a combat hero who survived a brutal war, was wounded three times, and served in all three branches of the military. They provide a glimpse into post–Civil War America and the military, which was drastically reduced to nearly its prewar strength. The letters speak to the roles each were to play in the mid-nineteenth century, the daily lives of participants of a postwar occupying army in Reconstruction Atlanta and Memphis, and the dashed hopes of a young married couple attempting to create a normal life together.

My heartfelt thanks to AnnaLee Pauls, reference assistant, and Squirrel Walsh, imaging services coordinator, both at the Princeton University Library, who helped me ferret out important documents and photographs from the Throop-Martin files and deliver them in a timely manner. I would be remiss in not thanking Kent Calder of the University of Oklahoma Press for taking a chance on the manuscript by believing in it from the beginning and offering excellent suggestions, which strengthened the tragic love story of Emory and Emily.

Introduction

> You, my dear sister know better than anyone else the trial it is to me to be departed from my dear husband so many, many months especially when the cause is ill health. I have felt at times as if I could not bear it and it takes all my courage to be contented and patient.
> —Emily Upton to her sister, Eveline Alexander, January 3, 1869

Emily Norwood Martin and Emory Upton were married for a little more than two years, from February 19, 1868, until she died March 29, 1870. Almost immediately after their wedding, Emily contracted what appears to have been tuberculosis.[1] We know about Upton (and less about Emily) from three biographies. Peter Smith Michie, a professor of natural philosophy (biology) at West Point, wrote *The Life and Letters of Emory Upton, Colonel of the Fourth Regiment of Artillery, and Brevet Major General, U.S. Army* in 1885, four years after Upton's death. In 1964, Stephen E. Ambrose, relying heavily on Michie's hagiography, wrote *Upton and the Army*. Most recently, David Fitzpatrick's new biography, *Emory Upton: Misunderstood Reformer*, has largely reexamined Upton and his impact on army reform well into this century. Michie devotes an entire chapter to Emily and Emory; Ambrose, only four and a half pages. Fitzpatrick, armed with a few of Upton's letters, offers a more complete picture of their relationship.[2]

All three biographers agree on Upton's arc in history. He was born on a farm in Batavia, Genesee County, New York, on August 27, 1839, one of eleven children of Daniel and Electa Upton. He experienced a strict family life. The Burned Over District of upstate New York shaped his outlook on life and his views on abolition, slavery, emancipation, and ultimately the war. The district, so named for the religious revival of the Second Awakening, became a cauldron of religious and social fervor. After a year at Oberlin College, he began a five-year term in 1856 at West Point, where he graduated in May 1861, eighth in a class of forty-five. Upton served from May 1861 through October 1862 as a second lieutenant in the 4th U.S. Artillery.

During the first year of the Civil War he accepted assignment to the defenses of Washington. He participated in the Battle of Bull Run, where he supposedly fired the first shot, and received his first war wound, a minor one. He commanded his battery during the early part of 1862 in the Virginia Peninsula Campaign and subsequently commanded a regiment and brigade of artillery in the Maryland Campaign.

Upton's infantry experience began as colonel of the 121st New York Volunteers in October 1862. Given command of the 2nd Brigade of the 6th Corps, Army of the Potomac at Gettysburg, he later participated in the battles of Rappahannock Station, Virginia, November 8, 1863, and the Wilderness Campaign of 1864. At Spotsylvania on May 10, he received a second minor wound while leading the assaulting column of twelve regiments on the Confederate salient. Present during the siege of Petersburg, he went north with the 6th Corps in defense of the capital in July 1864 when Jubal Early threatened it. Later, in the Shenandoah Campaign, while commanding a division of infantry at the Battle of the Opequan (Third Winchester), Upton received his third war wound, which put him out of action. As he recuperated, he accepted the command of the 4th Cavalry Division under Gen. James Harrison Wilson during the closing operations in Alabama and Georgia in March through April 1865. After the war he became captain in the 5th Regiment of Artillery in February 1865. He mustered out of the volunteer service April 30, 1866.

Between July 1865 and September 1867, Upton served in the West in administrative posts where he researched and wrote an original system of infantry tactics, which the army adopted in 1867. There, the most formidable opponents he faced were unscrupulous army agents and fraudulent vendors. Despite threats against him, Upton refused to pay for worthless bundles of straw and fraudulent claims of Indian depredations against the government.[3] In one of the first of many army reorganizations, he became a lieutenant colonel in the 25th Infantry, stationed at Paducah, Kentucky, from September 27 to November 12, 1867. That autumn, he met Emily Norwood Martin, the grandniece of a former governor of New York. He proposed to her that fall, and they were married early the next year.

Like Emory, Emily came from a large upstate New York family of eleven children. Her granduncle, Enos T. Throop, migrated, impoverished, to Auburn, New York in 1806. Through shrewd alliances and calculated business deals and investments, Throop eventually served in Congress, served as lieutenant governor to Martin Van Buren, and then became governor of New York (1838–42) when Andrew Jackson named Van Buren his secretary of state.[4] French writer and observer of all things American, Alexis de Tocqueville, visited Auburn in 1831 to inspect its prison. He also paid a call on Throop on July 12, 1831. He wrote later that he found Throop in a "very small wooden" one-story farmhouse "personally supervising the cultivation of his fields." De Tocqueville's traveling companion, Gustave de Beaumont, described Throop as one of "simple manners . . . little money." He noted that Throop spent "only five or six months of the year at Albany." The rest of his time he nurtured his investments in Auburn.[5]

Emily's mother, Cornelia, with whom she corresponded regularly, intensely involved herself in her daughter's development and growth. Their letters reveal a close relationship freighted with religious overtones. The letters reveal an overprotective mother and a sheltered daughter. Emily was only twenty-one when she was married and twenty-three when she died. Tellingly, she signed nearly every letter to her mother, "your loving child." At first, her mother inserted herself into Emily's new life, but as Emily's health became *the* topic of concern, her mother's letters became anguished missives attempting to gauge the severity of her daughter's illness.[6]

Cornelia Martin nevertheless welcomed Emory Upton into the family. Upon the announcement of their engagement, she wrote to Emily a long missive with guidelines and advice for the young future bride, much of it of a religious nature. But she said of Upton: "In General Upton, I already see those sterling qualities of head and heart, which with the blessing of God, must ensure *his* success in life and *your happiness*. He has a tender and genuine heart, great delicacy of feeling, an unusual perception of what is due to those around him and a very manifest spirit, which is apparent in all his actions. To those admirable qualities he adds a thorough education not only in his profession."[7]

Intellectually, the two seemed well matched. Emory's educational journey is well known. For one year, he imbibed the waters of abolitionism at Oberlin College in Ohio. He began his army career at West Point, where he ranked eighth in his graduating class of 1861. The academy exposed him to all the necessary military knowledge needed to function as an officer of the United States Army. Emily, on the other hand, according to extant documentation, did not receive a formal education, so it is unclear where or how she gained her learnedness. Her references in her letters home from Europe indicate knowledge of ancient history and some art history, as well as general worldly intelligence. Her letters mention the major Italian artists and visits to the graves of Keats and Shelley in Rome. She did receive rigorous religious direction from her mother. Her early diary entries and letters to and from her mother give the appearance of a young woman preparing more for a life in the convent rather than a life in the world.

Perhaps a disagreement over religion kept the two apart at first. Emory's letters from West Point (1857–61) are filled with religious references. During the war, through four brutal years, his opinions on God and religion changed radically. They were reinforced with postwar service in the West. Once married he admitted: "My strength . . . is past and bitter though it was, I have at last been taught to say 'Thy will be done.'"[8] It appears from a letter dated December 29, 1868, the two separated for a time and perhaps had dalliances with others. Send him a piece of the wedding cake of a mutual friend, he wrote to Emily, "then we could bury the memory of flirtations we both struck up in the 'winter of our discontent made glorious summer' when I took you in my arms in the 'back car' Nov. 17th, 1867."

Emily's writings throughout are fervently devout. Once he accepted her zeal and reverence, the two reconciled and were married on the shores of Lake Owasco at Sand Beach Church in the afternoon of February 19, 1868. The night before, guests arrived by train to the depot at Auburn, where they were met by horse-drawn sleighs. Traveling through increasingly colder gusts of snow and wind, the parties arrived at the "warm, wood fires" of Willowbrook. Guests included Gen. James H. Wilson, fellow West Pointer Gen. Alfred Thomas Torbert, and classmates Adelbert Ames and Samuel Benjamin. The next day dawned bright and bitter cold: "the snow lay thick upon the roads" as the guests were treated to a breakfast feast at the main house. The arrival of Phil Sheridan and his aide-de-camp, Col. John Schuyler Crosby, was cause for more excitement among the guests. Horse-drawn sleighs whisked the entire wedding party and guests to the three o'clock ceremony at the church. According to soon-to-be brother-in-law Grenville Tremain, the church was filled to overflowing. The white wedding dresses of the bridal party made the dark blue uniforms and gleaming epaulets "more striking." Emily's sisters were in attendance. After the ceremony, the newlyweds were whisked over a fresh blanket of snow in a sleigh to a gala reception at Willowbrook.[9]

The family quickly embraced Emory as a member of the family. Her brother George enthusiastically wrote her, "I know now that you have the love of an earnest man."¹⁰ She was seven years his junior; he was a battle-hardened veteran of the war, she a sheltered, privileged young woman with little world experience. Emily memorialized her engagement in her diary: "November seventeenth [1867]. A day never to be forgotten saw the fulfillment of my dearest hopes. On that day, I promised General Upton that I would be to him forever, a loving wife. That nothing but death should ever part us in spirit and when we had kneeled and asked God's blessing on the solemn step we had taken, I felt the peace I had longed for take possession of my heart."¹¹

The newlyweds faced a decidedly new nation in postwar America. Within the previous few years, the country had been altered significantly and dramatically. George Ticknor, a retired Harvard professor, succinctly summed it up when he wrote to a contemporary that the war "created a gulf between what happened before in our country and what has happened since, or what is likely to happen hereafter. It does not seem to me as if I were living in the country in which I was born."¹² Southern aristocracy vanished, and four million enslaved blacks were freed with little or no immediate methods of integrating them into the social, cultural, economic, or political nineteenth-century world. While northern cities escaped the ravages of war, Charleston, Nashville, Atlanta, Memphis, New Orleans, Charleston, Columbia, and Richmond did not enjoy the benefits of a "Marshall Plan." Depending on recent scholarship, between 650,000 and 700,000 Americans were killed on the battlefield from disease and combat. Civilian casualties, particularly in the South, are unknowable.

The South's agrarian economy had been devastated. In contrast, the rapidly developing industrial north with its paid labor "hurtled forward eagerly toward a future of industrial capitalism that many southerners found distasteful."¹³ Overnight, the Southern elite could not—would not—reject their traditions of family, heritage, and patriarchy. With its agrarian society in tatters and illiteracy rates approaching 50 percent of the population, the South obstinately refused to accept the America that

George Ticknor described. It was to be a "white" reunified country, which, as Shelby Foote has chronicled, "In formal as in common speech, abroad as well as on this side of its oceans, once the nation emerged" from the war, "'the United States *are*' became 'the United States *is*.'"[14]

The changes affected nearly all aspects of life, and the army was no exception. Prior to the war, the United States Regular Army numbered about 17,000. Pushing American Indians farther west became its primary mission. During wartime it swelled to millions with volunteers and conscripts. After the war, Congress reduced the army to nearly its former size of 50,000, then 37,000, and finally, by 1868–69, to 25,000. It returned to its constabulary mission, and under Gen. Phil Sheridan, replaced "displacement" of American Indians with "annihilation." The army witnessed elimination and consolidation of regiments and other units deemed redundant or surplus to the mission. A Republican Congress, loathe to spend money, and minority Democrats, fearful of a strengthened Reconstruction "occupying army," cut appropriations drastically.[15]

The uncertainty provoked anxiety among those regular officers who had remained in the service. Orders from Washington were slow, contradictory, and disruptive. One moment a transfer west was imminent, only to be rescinded with the next dispatch. Regiments were consolidated, disbanded, reformed, and reconfigured. In the postwar milieu, officers who had attained high ranks during "exciting" times were now required to man isolated posts in a constabulary role. Gen. Irvin McDowell, of First Bull Run notoriety, wrote that those men who had experienced intense military action now wanted "rest, and the service in Arizona [was] particularly fatiguing and disagreeable. Many look upon the very act of being sent there as a punishment," he wrote.[16]

Wives and dependents were equally affected. Ada Vogdes wrote in her diary, "Easter Sunday, [March 28, 1869] . . . I wait with intense anxiety to know what will become of us after we are consolidated with the 30th [Regiment]."[17] According to historian Edward Coffman, General

Sherman "urged wives to accompany their officer husbands to the frontier." Although Emily benefited from Emory's rank and standing, her illness prevented her from performing her expected duties as other wives when it came to official and unofficial events. As Coffman writes: "The image of genteel ladies who sacrificed the comforts of eastern homes to ameliorate the lives of their husbands in primitive western posts permeated the writings of those gentlewomen."[18] Recent research has provided a subtler narrative, as historians Anne Bruner Eales, Anni Baker, Sandra Myres, Mary L. Williams, and Verity McInnis have argued. Wives were not merely social baubles on the periphery of their husband's lives, but at the center. Emily was to be the center of that world.[19]

By the turn of the twentieth century, women's narratives of life on the frontier began to appear, although they were hardly competition for muscular army reminiscences of daring-do fighting the Indians on the plains. As Sandra Myres points out, the ladies' stories were not best sellers or financial successes. Myres goes on to quote military historian Robert Utley, who has written extensively on the frontier, that there existed "no strong constituency or interest group in the East" for women's tales of home life. Rather, larger-than-life occurrences sparked the American imagination after Wounded Knee and Custer's last stand. Utley argues that American readers "preferred the stories of Bret Harte and Mary Hallock Foote or the lurid and exciting accounts of Indian warfare in the popular press to the books by officers and their wives who wrote realistically and sympathetically of army life."[20]

Mary Williams has "analyzed the presence of women on the frontier posts" including "types of food and products carried at the post sutlers and traders to the social life and activities, to the very real influence exerted on their husbands." She concludes that "the story of the frontier army can no longer be told without" women's presence and "contributions recognized."[21] As Verity McInnis points out, wives were not only expected but required to understand that "their roles, status, and identities were . . . inseparably entwined to the mission and responsibilities of their officer husbands."[22]

Emily's short-lived marriage and army life could in no way resemble those of her "sister" officer's wives. Their first-person narratives reveal harrowing moments followed by hours of boredom. The threats were real, sometimes life-threatening. The weather alone could wreak havoc on a trek across the prairie. Soldiers and their families faced heavy torrential rains; blinding whiteout blizzards; and unrelenting, scorching sun and heat. Then there were rattlesnakes, insects, wolves, stampeding buffalo, spiders, centipedes; lack of water or too much water; bad food; cholera, malaria, and yellow fever. By 1880, 8 percent of the army had a venereal disease.[23] Fellow human perils were hostile Indians, rebellious and alcohol-fueled cavalry troopers, dishonest sutlers, loneliness, and depression. As one wife described army life on the frontier: the participants were "a handful of people . . . afloat upon an unchartered sea of desolation, miles and miles from civilization—and the shared hardships of a bleak climate with its privations, and the daily perils they faced together."[24]

Emily was crestfallen when she learned of Emory's potential posting to California. She had set her vision and future in Memphis, where as she pointed out, her father, mother, and husband had labored to provide a comfortable home for her. She and Emory set their immediate future on a place of rest and recuperation, not a continent apart from her extended family at Willowbrook. Before she happily learned that Emory's orders were changed once again, this time to Atlanta, she told her father "It is about time that I should commence my soldier life and take some of the hardships like the rest."[25]

When able, Emily performed the role of the officer's wife during the few short months they were together in Atlanta. Because of her illness and long separations from her husband, her experience was not typical. Other wives were more active and influential, if their diaries and reminiscences are to be believed. Like many wives of New England and eastern aesthetics, she was the product of a warm, culturally aware environment. Her parents were responsible for making the family home and compound known as Willowbrook, on Lake Owasco, a center of social and cultural activity. Additionally, she lived only a short time in two relatively quiet postings—Memphis and Atlanta. Moreover, her husband assumed the role of house furnisher and interior decorator in her absence, working tirelessly to provide a safe, warm, and secure environment for his wife and her fragile condition.

Emily Martin Upton understood her role as an army wife. Dignitaries and military personalities, drawn to Willowbrook's comfortable ambience, exposed Emily to the wider world. She remarked on at least one occasion when her brother Jack planned to attend West Point, "We are really becoming an army family and Willowbrook will indeed be 'Army Headquarters.'"[26] Reputedly, notable visitors included President Andrew Johnson, Phillip Sheridan, Ulysses Grant, and Washington Irving.[27] Myles Keogh and George Custer were guests, as were Andrew Alexander and Emory Upton. The latter two men married into the family. Coincidentally, Andrew had served with Upton in the last days of the Civil War in Georgia under Wilson. It is not clear who introduced Emily to Emory—it may have been Alexander—but the initial meetings were not fruitful. Alexander eventually married Eveline or "Evy," as her family called her. Keogh perished with Custer at the Little Big Horn in 1876. Keogh had grown so close to the family that they brought his body back east and buried him on the Throop-Martin lot in Fort Hill Cemetery in Auburn.[28]

Secretary of state and neighbor William Seward, a close friend, was well aware of Emily's condition and thought, along with most of his contemporaries, that Nassau would make an ideal location for her to heal. Seward told his daughter-in-law in September 1868 that he was grieved to hear of Emily's condition, but knowing how well Nassau had served Mary Martin, Emily's oldest sister, known to the family as "Molly," in a similar situation, he hoped "it would be equally beneficial to Mrs. Upton."

He signed off offering to "do anything to contribute to Mrs. Upton's comfort at Nassau." A month later, Janet asked her father-in-law to intercede on the Uptons' behalf to have the American consul at Havana act as a conduit for the couple's mail, which Seward not only did, but offered to ask the same of the British Minister at Nassau.[29]

In order to enjoy a leisurely honeymoon in Europe, Emory received a ten-month leave until December 1, 1868. It may have been one of the more unusual honeymoons in recent memory. Remarkably, both found the time to write home to their siblings and parents during their five-month sojourn. Emily, beginning on the steamer, wrote her parents and siblings religiously from March 15 to August 3, 1868—some twenty-five letters. Her letter books contain in detail a young bride's wonder at an entirely different world. Emory, on the other hand, found time to visit military installations and attend military reviews. He found the time to write to his brother in May to express his strong dislike for the Catholic Church. Emily's letter books also chronicle her struggle with tuberculosis, detailing fatigue and coughing spells. They are replete with lengthy periods of malaise and attempts to gain her strength. She said of Sorrento: "I never breathed such delicious air."[30]

As they left the shores of New York and the mainland slipped from view, they saw Old Glory flying from John Appleton's home on Staten Island. They quickly made friends with other Americans on board. A Mrs. Boardman became solicitous of Emily, but Emory took "the best of care of me," she told her mother.[31] Dr. and Mrs. Boardman and their niece; Mrs. Cooke and the misses Cooke from New York; Dr. Boardman's sister Mrs. Boman; and Mrs. and Miss Robinson from Boston were all shipmates. Emily described the Boardmans as "very intellectual people." Dr. Boardman had been a minister and author of several books. They spent time together, and Emily found them most "agreeable." At the evening meal, Colonel Floyd-Jones joined them.[32]

In Marseilles, they met General and Mrs. George McClellan, whom Emily liked immediately. The McClellans, for an unknown reason, recommended that the Uptons visit Sorrento and stay at an unnamed hotel before seeing Rome. "Though he had praised it very highly," she wrote to her sister Lily (also spelled Leily or Lylie), "he had not overrated its beauties."[33] During a tour of St. Paul's Church in Rome, Emory encountered Dr. Silas Atherton Holman, a surgeon who served in the 6th Corps during the war. The two immediately fell into reminiscences of the war as Emily mused: "It seems strange that they should part in the din and smoke of battle to meet in the solemn stillness of this grand old church." They "fought their battles over until the small hours of the morning."[34]

Almost from the beginning of the trip, and perhaps earlier, Emily had exhibited signs of physical stress. When she felt ill, Emily stayed behind at their hotel, a prisoner in her own room, with her window her only conduit to the outer world, where she surveyed the local inhabitants as they went out about their business. Emory attended to her every need. She wrote her sister at the end of the trip that he had carried her upstairs for at least three months. "He is just a darling," she wrote. He "has been so good to me. He has given up everything and just nurses me like a woman, only it seems as if he had done more for me than anyone else could."[35]

Her mother's words, attempting to be solicitous and empathetic, strike the modern ear as a "helicopter parent." She wrote Emily on her honeymoon that she sympathized with her in "all that [she] suffer[ed] mentally and physically." She also worried about her other daughter Eveline (Evy), stationed with her husband, Andrew Alexander, in far off Arizona.[36] She took comfort from friends and acquaintances that Emily had "married a true man and a gentleman. I am truly happy that sweet Emily shall have married so well."[37]

Emory, on the other hand, indulged his professional interests, often heading out alone. In Brest, he took "an hour or two to see some military schools."[38] At Reims, a day or two later, together the newlyweds visited "the large artillery school." There, Emily discovered that she could understand the French officers "owing to the French book of tactics, I used to read to Emory this winter."³⁹ At Lyons, Emory, armed with letters of introduction, paid a visit to the cavalry school. The school provided a horse for Upton as he accompanied the officer in charge through the inspection.⁴⁰ Twice he left her for military observations. When the couple stopped at Marseilles, Emory visited the military installation at Toulon. Emily's reaction to his leave taking, besides revealing his steadfast pursuit of military knowledge, demonstrates his lifelong determination and drive for perfection.

> This morning, Emory left me quite early for Toulan. He was quite anxious to see Napoleon's first battlefield as well as other military matter there collected, which is very interesting. He had letters and permits from the Commanding Officer here and I have no doubt he will have a day both of instruction and amusement. I declined to go as I thought a day's rest was better for me and I should only interfere with the 'study of war,' which is being carried on so vigorously. I laugh at Emory a good deal. He is determined to make the most of everything and see and learn as much as possible and the way he questions, and cross-examines the poor unfortunates he happens to converse with is too amusing, whether soldiers or civilians, he generally finds out much that they know. He has even visited in Marseilles all the little narrow streets and hospitals so as to see both sides of the picture. This is the first time I have been without my husband for more than three hours since we were married.⁴¹

At the end of the summer, Emory left Emily to visit Chalon to observe the French army, where he wrote her (see chapter 2, Emory to Emily, August 3, 1868). He climbed to the top of the Colosseum in Rome and up Mt. Vesuvius above Pompeii, climbing the volcano's side while it spewed ash and lava. When he turned his eyes away from the heat and dust, "in another direction—the view was magnificent," but he later admitted the danger of the situation. In a surviving remnant of a letter, he detailed the inner workings of the volcano, including a drawing showing various stages of eruptions. [42] Emily chose to stay behind.

He proved a devoted and solicitous newlywed. On his sojourns away from Emily, he would return with fresh fruit or an indigenous flower. She lauded her mother for having "judged so truly that Emory would make the tenderest [sic] and most devoted of husbands."[43] They were probably the first honeymoon couple to read together the *Army Navy Journal* they had discovered in Rome. "There was so much news."[44]

In Rome, they visited all the usual tourist spots. Rome appealed to Emily, but Emory's staunch anti-Catholicism became apparent. Emily especially enjoyed the evening vespers sung by the nuns in the chapel at Sacred Heart convent, but Emory would have none of it. He found the Italian people "detestable, and their condition deplorable," a condition he blamed on the Catholic Church and the government. One "kept them in complete ignorance," and the other "has wrung all their hard earnings." He allowed that the people's condition had improved since the reign of Victor Emanuel, who Emory thought would "rise up and demand Rome for her Capitol . . . and . . . expel the Pope and St. Peter's," relegating both to the same fate as the Colosseum, "one of the grandest ruins of the world." He described Easter Sunday mass: "The sight was magnificent, but to call it religion, one must be beside himself."[45]

Their honeymoon ended that August after visiting Milan, Tuscany, Florence, Venice, and Lake Como. Emily enjoyed the museums and historic sites; Emory prized the "fine fortifications and arsenals" of the "Austrian stronghold" in Verona. At Paris, the two visited the *Invalides*, where they saw Napoleon's old soldiers and "Emory enjoyed talking with them about the Great General. . . . His admiration for Napoleon is unbounded and anything associated with him is interesting."[46]

By October Emily had traveled to Key West and parts south to deal with her increasingly perilous condition. They spent the month of

November 1868 together in Key West. Emily maintained a love-hate relationship with her new surroundings. She fell under the romantic spell of the moonlight as she and Emory came home in their carriage. Ships at anchor in the harbor bobbed around "rocking to and fro in the moonlight . . . standing out so clear and sharp against the sky." She described the island as "queer," and "measuring only six miles wide." She estimated the population as between "four and five thousand," the minority of which were "agreeable people." The rest were either "conks" (Conchs—original settlers) or "Negroes"—"a dreadfully stupid lot." She characterized Key West's accommodations as "frightful" and warned her mother against travel there.[47]

In November, Emory returned to Memphis, and Emily remained in Key West. The separations, according to letters from both of them, were agonizing. His extant letters to Emily are replete with instances of longing. His experience reminds one of the cliché that "absence makes the heart grow fonder." His letters are unabashedly romantic and increasingly anxious. Hers to her mother, father, and siblings are obviously less forthcoming. If we only had her letters to Emory.

Memphis had escaped the harsh realities of war despite two battles taking place there. One of the first major cities to fall into Union hands, it became a hospital town where more than five thousand wounded were treated. As the western terminus for the Memphis and Charleston Railroad, it also served as an important supply depot for Union troops. It is unclear where Upton stayed and attempted to set up household. Many federal officers stayed at Peabody Place, built in 1844, and the Gayoso House. Fort Pickering, originally a Confederate fort seized by federal troops, occupied the bluff above the river and was demolished in 1866.[48]

Emily's sister Cornelia, called Nelly, accompanied Emily to Key West. The two spent Christmas on the steamer and gunboat *Gettysburg*, and the crew treated them with respect and much deference. Emily told her sister Evy how much she enjoyed the voyage, wishing only that her Emory could be with her. She wrote of the "many funny things" that happened and of being overwhelmed with joy: "I was not able to endure the fatigue and excitement" of the day.[49]

During the winter of 1869, the newlyweds corresponded extensively, Emory almost daily. Emily expressed her longing for him to her father. She and Nelly spent their time riding, reading, and talking. She told her father that the days flew by, but that she missed her husband very much and optimistically hoped that the time spent apart would end quickly.[50] But she seemed to adjust to her new life. At one point she wrote her mother that she had become "quite familiar with army matters," and she told her brother that she enjoyed being in barracks very much: "the drills, the bugle calls, and various service of the soldiers interest me exceedingly."[51]

By the end of January 1869, Emily had tired of the social scene in Key West. More important, she became convinced that the climate did her more harm than good. She had resisted the idea of going to Nassau, where Emory and others persuaded her that the climate would be better for her. Each week marked a new undertaking that upset her health. She felt "assured two months at Nassau will do me a great deal of good and I am anxious to get there."[52] There, Emily and Nelly connected with Dr. and Mrs. Kirkwood, old Martin family friends, who insisted they stay with them rather than at a hotel. Nelly quickly became Dr. Kirkwood's favorite, "for she plays billiards and backgammon to his full satisfaction."[53] Emory, on the other hand, remained tormented by Emily's illness and absence. In one telling sentence in his letter to her in February 1869, he summed up the essence of the conflict he dealt with on a daily basis: "My breast is a battleground between hope and fear."[54]

In March, Emory became convinced that they were to be ordered to Arizona, where he hoped the dry climate would help Emily regain her strength. His own words in his letters to her indicate that he understood that a drier climate was more beneficial than the Caribbean. Instead, his orders sent him to Atlanta, where the two set up household at

McPherson Barracks from April to June 1869. February marked their anniversary; still separated, neither could abide the estrangement. Emily told her mother "it was rather sad." But Emory had not forgotten the date. Through Dr. Kirkwood, he "presented a token of" his "thoughtful love—a beautiful amethyst ring like yours, which he had sent down sometime before to be presented on that day."[55]

She began her time in Atlanta as healthy and well rested as possible. She confided in her mother as she traveled to New Orleans to meet Emory, "I must take care and not get cold when I meet my husband for I want him to see me looking as" before.[56] Despite her persistent health issues, she threw herself into a busy social schedule demanded of an officer's wife. Emily continued her work handing out Bibles to officers and men, 108 at one count. She went so far as to inscribe each soldier's name in the front page, giving the Bible a more tangible importance for each man.

The two made every attempt to settle down to a normal routine. Emory began reading John Livingston Nevius's *China and the Chinese* (Harper, 1869). Emily remarked "I have not seen him so much interested in a book for a long time. Every moment he can spare, he takes it up. The care of this large post and the revision of his book, keep Emory at work constantly."[57] A Methodist minister petitioned Emory to set up a center to preach. He responded by offering them a building. Although Upton had been raised a Methodist, the Uptons attended what Emily described as "the little Episcopal church." She reported that it had been "repaired and in part supported by General Meade and his officers, so that it has become the Army church here and it's the only one where officers are not liable to meet with disrespect. The hard feeling here in Atlanta has not in any way dimmed, I am sorry to say."[58]

Unfortunately, the warm, humid Atlanta weather proved as injurious to her health as the Caribbean. At the end of April, she complained of contracting another cold while holding out hope that as soon as the "weather [seemed] more settled" she would "feel better." In June she reported that the coolest room in their quarters registered ninety degrees during the day and eighty at night. Throughout her ordeal, she vacillated between telling her parents her true current condition versus not saying anything, leaving them to wonder and worry. Emory had to write the last few paragraphs of one of Emily's last Atlanta letters, dated June 12, 1869. She wrote: "I am pretty well but not as strong or free from coughing as my impatient spirit would wish." To which he added: "Nevertheless, my courage is good and we hope for the time when I shall be well, I do not recollect what I have written in the first of this letter, but believe me ever, my dear mother, Love affectionately, Emily. PS Emory sent in his application to be ordered to Washington several days ago, we hope for an answer this week and to be home by the 26th or 27th."[59]

Thinking that the cooler climate would be beneficial, she went home to Willowbrook, in Auburn, New York. She met up with her husband for five weeks in New York, where he was attending a reunion of the Army of the Potomac. When recovery proved elusive at Willowbrook, she returned in November 1869 to Nassau and the Bahamas, this time with Emory and Nelly. He had been granted leave again to be with Emily through Christmas 1869. A month later, leaving Emily in Nelly's care, Emory returned to Atlanta, where he remained until the end of May awaiting reassignment. His official duties in Atlanta had concluded in October. He never saw Emily again.[60]

Emily admitted to her sister Evy that another stay in the Bahamas would be her only chance of survival, and she dreaded the thought of being away from her family and Emory. She held out hope that she could return to Willowbrook in the spring and be with Evy and her new daughter Midge. In December 1869, just a few months before her death, Emily predicted that this time around would be even more difficult. But her letters from Emory would console her when she felt lonely.

Emily's letters are a window into the psychological roller coaster she experienced as she battled her fluctuating physical condition. Nelly recorded Emily's conflicting moods in a remarkable letter to her mother in January of the new year. Nelly expressed happiness that her mother "had such a satisfactory visit from Upton. I knew it would be a comfort to you, to see him," she wrote. "I am surprised to see how well Emily gets on without him. She [Emily] was nervous and restless all the time when he was here and unhappy when he was away from her. Now she has made up her mind to do without him and she told me the other day that she behaved better with me than with him."[61]

Ominously, toward the end, Emily penned a letter to her mother apologizing for not writing more often and not writing longer letters "as I have not been feeling at all well lately." She complained of extreme fatigue and lack of appetite. She had the strength to finish an afghan she had been crocheting for Emory as an anniversary gift.[62] Emily wrote her last extant letter to her mother February 19, 1870, wherein she thanked her for remembering her wedding anniversary and showing courage. She told her mother that she was "very happy" and that she "sorely missed [her] dear husband." She had received a camel hair shawl that day accompanied by a letter from Emory, and several acquaintances had dropped by to share the day with her. She remained too weak to venture from her room.[63]

A. D. Kirkwood, the wife of Emily's doctor, expressed pessimism about Emily's condition. She wrote Mrs. Martin in early March: "I feel greatly perplexed to know exactly what to write to you for you all are so much distressed at any unfavorable news of dear Mrs. Upton. I only wish that it was in my power to say that she had improved the last month or two and yet there is nothing to occasion any immediate alarm. About the time of the sailing of the last steamer, she was feeling very miserable and very much nauseated and of course could eat but very little since then. The Dr. has made some change in her medicine and that has passed away." Additionally, he saw "little change in Mrs. Upton's general appearance. She may be a little thinner as well as a little weaker, but her spirits are remarkably good and she is still very hopeful and talks of what she will do next summer."[64] Emily died March 29, 1870, just two years and forty days after her wedding. Emory wrote one last letter to her, which arrived after her death. Her body was returned to her home, where she was buried at Willowbrook.[65]

Emily's affliction is never named, but from her symptoms—excessive coughing, frequent colds, fatigue, lack of appetite, and the fact that two of her siblings had died of tuberculosis—assuredly she had "consumption" or respiratory tuberculosis. Unwittingly, she and Emory chose the worst places for her to recover—Key West and Nassau, two places with high humidity and heat. Tuberculosis thrives in damp conditions; an army posting to Arizona with its dry air, provided, for one brief moment, a distinct possibility that would have prolonged her life and possibly saved it. Unfortunately, Emory's assignment to McPherson Barracks in Atlanta undoubtedly exacerbated her condition. In February 1869, he told his father-in-law that he would request a posting to New Mexico for two years, an idea that never materialized, but perhaps would have saved her life or at least might have postponed the inevitable.

1   European Honeymoon

Emory

Willowbrook, Auburn, N.Y. November 21st 1867[1]

General:

I have the honor to report that the troops of my command broke camp at Paducah, Ky Nov. 11, and in light marching orders commenced a decisive campaign, of which Auburn was the objective point.[2] The march was conducted with great precision and singularity; the different commands submitting cheerfully to the hardships incident to a campaign so late in the season and displaying not a little eagerness to meet the enemy, no matter what his position or numbers. Conscious of the supreme morale of my troops, I advanced [steadily?] till my skirmishers reached the foot of Owasco Lake where it was discovered that the enemy was in position a mile in our front.

To define fully this position would require more topographical knowledge than I possess, but I will hope to give some idea by stating that the flanks were well protected and that a heavy line of skirmishers concealed all available points in front. Though provided with an efficient staff I could gain no reliable information of the enemy, I was compelled at great personal risk to reconnoiter the line myself and after thorough examination I confess [that] I returned to my command not a little demoralized.

The sham enthusiasm of my troops revealed itself at the first whistle of the enemy's bullets; neither did it seem possible to re-inspire them. What was to be done? To retreat was to incur ignominy. To advance, who could divine the issue of the battle? Time was short—I made up my mind. I resolved to make a direct attack, and placing myself at the head of the troops, colors in my hands, I led them to the assault. The sight was sublime, every member of that devoted band vied with his General in deeds of daring, death being preferable to defeat. The struggle was short and sharp and decisive; treason was in the enemy camp "il nuit bas ses armes" and when the smoke lifted from this memorable battlefield, I found myself engaged to the lovely Miss Emily Martin.

The campaign, which opened under doubtful auspices, was brought to a successful close. The troops are now quietly in camp enjoying that repose to which their eminent services and glorious victory entitle them.

Trusting that my operations within the last few days will meet with your approval, I have the honor to be your obed. Servt., E. Upton

PS My Dear Wilson. I expect to apply at once for a year's leave—go to Europe and upon my return get married. My kindest regards to Mrs. W. [and] Alexander told me that he met you. I wish I might have had the same good fortune. E. U.

Emily

Steamer *Napoleon III*, March 15, 1868

My dearest Mother

This is really the first time I have felt equal to the exertion of writing and while it is a little quiet this noon, I must improve the opportunity. We have been at sea one week and I have a good taste of "life on the ocean wide." "I don't think I am going to like it." The days here are so much alike that I can find little of interest to tell you. But I will make the attempt, commencing from the time when I bade good-bye to you my dear mother and the friends whose kindness we can never forget.

I sat on deck with Emory until the last trace of land had almost disappeared and night forced us to say "My Motherland 'Good Night.'" One of the last things we saw was a flag, which Mr. John Appleton[3] had promised should wave from his house on Staten Island as a parting salute to us. Then we were summoned to dinner, notwithstanding your admonition to the contrary. I must say a word about the fare on this steamer. We sit down to a table each day, which is certainly surprisingly well spread for a dinner party. We have generally about fifteen courses. No pains are spared and the variety of soups, fish, meats and confectionary, as well as fresh vegetables is remarkable. We have five meals a day. Coffee and rolls at half past six (in bed); breakfast at ten; lunch at one, dinner at four and half, and supper at eight. I content myself with three meals a day.

My occupations are not very varied, but I hope to feel more active next week. I felt the reaction after trying to keep up in New York, for this is the first day I have sat up to do anything. I generally lie all day on the sofa upstairs, except when it is pleasant, and then Emory wraps me up and lie on the deck in the sun, which I enjoy very much. We have had very rough weather since Wednesday and I have had full opportunity of seeing mountain waves. One or two nights we were constantly knocked from one side to the other of our berths and it required no small amount of maneuvering to keep one's plate or glasses out of one's lap, but I think it is now growing a little quieter. We have seen but one or two vessels since we left New York. Those we passed. The voyage thus far has been very prosperous and we have made excellent time.

March 17th

I must now tell you something of the passengers on board. There are very few. Those I am with the most and like the best are Dr. and Mrs. Boardman,[4] Mrs. Boman [*possibly Bowman*] who is an invalid and niece. Then Mrs. Cooke and the Miss Cooke from New York, Mrs. and Miss Robinson from Boston.[5] We are together a great deal and I have found them very agreeable. I do not know why it is, but everyone has been so particularly kind to me. I have felt rather miserable most of the time for I was so tired when I came on board and the constant motion tires me a good deal still.

Mrs. Boardman has taken as much interest in me and has done as much for me as though I had been her own child. She and her husband as well as his sister, Mrs. Boman, are very intellectual people and Dr. Boardman has written several books. He has also been a minister.

I have not been really seasick. For the first few days I felt quite uncomfortable but gradually I have gotten over it, and have been at every meal since we started. Emory, I think, has felt much more uncomfortable than I but he has been really sick but one day. I believe however, that he finds studying French at sea, [he] is pursuing knowledge under difficulties but still perseveres in the attempt.

Colonel Floyd Jones is quite an acquisition to our party.[6] He sits opposite me at table. I am the only lady at our table and am therefore quite a belle: being treated with distinguished attention. We are all in the best of spirits today as we hope to reach land on Thursday. We shall leave the steamer at Brest and go by railroad to Paris. Yesterday we had quite a serious incident on board. A box of crackers, which were being hoisted from the hold, fell on a little sailor and almost crushed him. Was it not sad? They do not think he will live. The *femme de chambre* was fully impressed by your talk and has come to me night and morning to do all that I wished. If you could hear the animated conversations we carry on. My French in ordinary cases is very much better than I supposed and I manage always to make myself understood. It seems strange to hear as much French and Spanish. Last Sunday we spent in quite a Christian manner. At one, all the passengers assembled in the cabin and Dr. Boardman had service making some excellent remarks. In the afternoon, I read and took a rest. During the evening we had a good deal of singing. The Misses Cooke sing a great deal, which is very pleasant.

March 18th

Yesterday we made greater progress than any day before; two hundred and seventy-five miles and we are now within two hundred and eighty miles of Brest. For the last three days, the steamer has been surrounded with numbers of "Mother Carry's Chickens."[7] They are such graceful pretty creatures that it is quite fascinating to lean over the ship and watch them. Last night I saw what I have always had a great curiosity to witness: the phosphorescent light on the water. It was very beautiful. All the foam and the tips of the waves were covered with this beautiful golden light.

Yesterday I felt better and stronger than any day since I started. I think when I can once more be on land and get thoroughly rested; I shall find the voyage has been of great benefit to me. I will write again after we land but shall send this from Brest. I have not seen Madame Davenport[8] since the day we sailed. She has been seasick ever since, but I have not had the slightest need of her services. The little sailor boy who was hurt is better. A purse was made up for him yesterday of over two hundred francs. I fear dear mother you will have difficulty reading this letter but the vessel rocks so constantly that I cannot make a straight letter. The whole is but a "sickly attempt" but you must pardon the lack of interesting material. I shall await with great impatience my first letter from home. I am anxious to know how long you remained in New York and all about your visit. Give my love to everyone at dear Willowbrook and with a large share for yourself, believe me,

Your loving daughter, Emily

PS Emory sends a great deal of love to all. He is a splendid nurse and has taken the best of care of me.

Brest, March 19th 1868

My dear Father,

I am left alone for an hour or two and can think of no better way of employing my time than in giving you an account of my landing in France. This morning we were awakened by the joyful intelligence that land was in sight. After arranging my things for going on shore, I went up on deck where all the passengers were assembled to see our entrance into the harbor of Brest. I cannot tell you how pleasant it looked to me. The shores at this point are very abrupt and crowned by forts, which look very formidable, the side toward the sea bristling with guns of all sizes. One of the most refreshing things that met our eyes were the fields and hillsides green with corn and wheat. We had some grand views of the country in all directions, which was with exception, hilly and even at this early season was quite fresh and beautiful. We passed numbers of ships of war and other vessels and finally arrived at our destination. We went from the vessel to the customhouse, where I remained quietly seated with my friends the Boardman's until the operation of examining our trunks was over. It was quite amusing to see them poking in all the corners, and under all the trays for something wrong. The only thing that they objected to in my trunk was the bottle of Madeira, but they gave it back at last.

Our next move was to the Hotel de la Marquis where I am now writing. From what I have seen, I think it is a dirty, horrible place. My room looked cold and uncomfortable, but a bright little open fire now gives it a cheerful look and I have been sitting by its side reading for the last hour. Emory has gone for an hour or two to see some military schools, etc., which are here and when he returns I am to take a drive over the city, which has several places of note.

Do you remember the interesting account we read this winter of a tour through Brittany and the queer places and people described? That is just the tour we shall take from here to Paris. This is a queer old place. Everything looks so ancient and dirty. Nearly everyone wears wooden shoes and all are dressed in the most unremarkable way. It is hard to realize that one only hears the wooden shoes instead of horses trampling in the street below. I have just had my dinner served to me in my room and have eaten my numerous courses in solitary grandeur. Yesterday being our last day at sea we had the "Captain's Dinner," a superb affair—twenty-three courses.

Later

Well, I just have now been all over this strange, old place and am more than ever impressed with its oddity. One feels as if they had stepped back several centuries and were living in the times of the ancient Britons for the people have scarcely changed. They wear the same dress, and speak the same language, as when they took refuge here ages ago. The women look so strangely [sic] with their high crowned, pointed caps, short black dresses and wooden shoes. Even the smallest children and babies have close, white caps as that I saw not a vestige of hair. The men are quite as strange. Nearly all the buildings look as though they were ready to fall and many parts of the town are in ruins. The whole town is surrounded by a wall and is strongly fortified and contains numbers of soldiers for its defense.

March 20th Hotel de France, Reims

We have now settled down for the evening in our room so I will take this time to give you the benefit of my observations for today. We left Brest this morning at six and took our places for the first time in a

French railway coach, which we found very comfortable and pleasant. The country through which we passed was interesting from its being so entirely new to me in every respect. It was very hilly and large portions of it were moors covered with yellow broom and Plantagenet.⁹ Other parts were under good cultivation and the land looked rich but the manner of cultivation and the dress of the peasants amused us. The houses are all built of stone with thatched roofs extending over them. We saw numbers of ruined castles and old churches, all built in a very quaint style. The fields are divided by little walls of mud, which are crowned with grass. Fine trees are scarcely to be seen and wood seems to be wanting. Nearly all the trees are scarred stumps as they cut off all the limbs every year or two for faggots.

But I have not time at present to go into more particulars. We reached Reims at three and after a short rest; I went out with for a drive with Emory, as we both wished to see as much as possible of the place. One of the chief attractions for my soldier was, of course, the large artillery school, which is here, so I went with him to see it. After a little difficulty, we were admitted and the French officers showed us everything with the utmost politeness. I was quite interested, but what pleased me most was to find that I understood all the officers in French. I think it was owing to the French book of tactics I used to read to Emory this winter. The remainder of the afternoon we spent in seeing the other curiosities and wonders of the place, all of which interested me exceedingly.

March 21st

We left this morning for Paris where we arrived about three. The journey today has been very interesting for most of the places we passed through were of historical interest. Levat, Le Mans, Chartres, Maintenon, Versailles were those of the most importance. We found the country very much-improved in every way, more trees, the land under more perfect cultivation and a gradual advancement in everything as we neared Paris. It was hard to realize when Paris came in sight that it was really the place of which I had read and heard so much about for so long a time. We were soon on our way to the Westminster Hotel where by five [o'clock]; I was comfortably settled and resting from the fatigue of the day. I stand traveling much better than I thought I should. I am improving every day I think, but as my cold still holds on and troubles me a good deal, we shall only stay in Paris long to make a few necessary purchases and shall then go directly to Italy, leaving most of the sight-seeing for our return when I shall be stronger and better able to enjoy all the wonders of Paris.

March 22nd

We went to church today at the American Chapel and heard a most excellent sermon from Dr. Eldridge.[10] On our way to and from the church we saw numerous magnificent buildings as well as most beautiful parks and squares, the Champs Elysees, Tuileries, etc.

March 23rd

This morning at ten, Madame Davenport came for me and we started out on a shopping expedition, first to the dressmakers, and then to the numerous other places. It would tire you to follow us in and out of stores, upstairs, through narrow alleys, broad squares, and magnificent streets, so I will spare you further detail and only say I got through the day very well. You know this is the first time I have been called upon to use my own taste, or discretion in dress, but I found no difficulty in deciding and did a great deal.

At half past three I returned to the hotel and as we were to change our quarters, I packed my things and we came to the "Hotel de l'Athenie" Rue Scribe,[11] which we like much better. After dinner this evening, Emory told me he had a surprise for me and imagine my delight when he gave me mother's letter from New York. My first letter from home and I had not thought of one for weeks yet. We have had a great deal of amusement this evening over the arrival of my numerous purchases, gloves, laces, shawls, shoes, etc. etc. We are very comfortably settled here and I feel very well and happy tonight, though I am tired and must close my letter.

Gen'l Dix[12] received Emory very cordially and handsomely and has invited us to dine with them on Wednesday, which we shall do. I shall keep most of my letters of introduction until we return to Paris. I find Mr. and Mrs. Austin[13] are in Rome and I think we shall join them.

Good night dear father. I know you will follow us on all our journey and only wish you were here to enjoy everything with us. Give my love to Grandma, Uncle, Aunty, and all the family not forgetting Mrs. Harbison.[14]

I am ever your loving child, Emily

Paris, March 26th, 1868

My Dear Nelly,
Yesterday I went with Emory for a drive. We went, before our return to the "Boi de Bologne."[15]

It was every way beautiful and on a grand scale, but has not nearly as many natural advantages as Central Park and is not as pretty. I have hardly yet a clear idea of Paris, for I have hurriedly seen so many things, but on our return, I hope to do justice to the many grand and beautiful objects to be seen there.

We dined with General Dix and had a very pleasant time. Mr. Peabody[16] was expected but did not come: Miss Dix is to be married in three weeks. I had a conversation with the gentleman to whom she is engaged. He has a mercantile house in Japan; he knows all the Browns. Robert Brown[17] is in his employ.

I have not tried to see anyone in Paris this time, for I have all I can do to get through the necessary shopping. I have just been to the window to see some soldiers pass, it seems as if half the men here were soldiers; as far as the eye can reach now in both directions, there is nothing but rows of infantry till I have given up all hope of seeing the end of them and have come back to my writing.

We telegraphed to Mr. Austin at Rome, that if they could find us rooms we would be there for Holy Week and he has taken rooms for us at the same hotel, will it not be pleasant to be with them?

Lyons, March 28th

We left Paris yesterday at eleven and reached Lyons last night at ten. All the way we passed through a most interesting country and we found the scenery much more beautiful and imposing than anything we have seen before. We first passed near Fountain Bleu, which was an object of great interest to us, being so closely connected with Napoleon. Most of the country is a vine-growing region and at Lyon, where we dined, we tasted the fine Burgundy for which this part of the country is celebrated.

We passed several of the battlefields of Napoleon as well as one, which is celebrated as being fought over by Caesar. Lyons is full of historical interest. Claudius and Caligula were both born here. It was almost demolished by order of the national convention during the French Revolution and everywhere bears traces of what it then suffered. One of the most curious things I have seen here is the celebrated clock in the old cathedral made in 1508, it has about a dozen different figures which perform a number of remarkable exploits. The city is very beautiful and is built on a peninsula between the Rhone and Saone [Rivers],[18] so that in all directions you see the pretty arched bridges.

Emory has been to a review of cavalry, in which he was very much interested. He has letters from the minister of war, which will admit him almost anywhere. The General this morning gave him a horse and he accompanied him through the whole inspection.

Monday, we leave for Marseilles, where we shall remain one day only. I have only been out one day since I came here. The houses are very cold here. They are dark and damp. The most expensive thing is wood. We have to pay nine cents for every small stick we burn; the poor must freeze. So far, we have had constant cold weather but the peach trees are in bloom and the streets are filled with spring flowers. Yesterday and today Emory has brought me delicious violets. Love to all at home.

I am your aff. sister, Emily

Marseilles, April 3rd [1868]

My dear Molly,

I must write you next though my letters seem hardly worth sending so far. For I have not had sufficient courage to write a good letter since I left home. But still I shall go on in a stupid way hoping for some improvement, by and by.

Our stay in Paris was very [short] but I enjoyed it very much and was delighted with the multitude of pretty things I saw there. I did not deliver the letter to Mrs. Riggs[19] but hope on our return to find her still in Paris. I did not feel like seeing anyone during our short visit. I hardly rested enough in Paris though I was as careful as possible. I think I must have taken a little more cold for when I reached Lyons, I felt quite sick. But after two resting days, I came on here. I was very anxious to get into a warm climate and so made quite an exertion to reach Marseilles for which I feel repaid, for we found it so much warmer and pleasanter [sic]. As I was not at all well when I got here, Emory insisted that Dr. Sieur[20] should come and see me, which he did and said I only wanted rest and I must not leave Marseilles for more than a week. This I was quite content to do as we had a delightful, large room overlooking out upon the main street; bright and pleasant and I was tired enough to keep still for a few days.

I have been resting with a will ever since. The first days I lay in bed all day with the window open enjoying the warm air and perfect repose and above all the lovely flowers, which my room is always filled. I have just lived in an atmosphere of orange flowers ever since I came here. Emory brings me a lovely bouquet every morning, each one more beautiful than the last. I never saw such flowers so large and so fragrant. This morning my bouquet is first a row of bunches of white geraniums, then heliotrope, twice the size of ours; crimson and white rosebuds, and such wonder of pansies. Then I had another heliotrope, pink carnations and orange flowers. The weather is warm and delightful and yesterday I went out for a drive down to the seashore, which I enjoyed very much.

We went through the Prado to the Chateau Bourales,[21] one of the loveliest places I have ever seen. It is owned by the city and is three miles from it. It is a beautiful park with ponds, high waterfalls, little streams, flowerbeds in great profusion and the most beautiful trees and shrubs of all kinds. There are several handsome houses in it. One containing pictures and statuary can be visited. But the loveliest part is the situation. On one side you see the Mediterranean in all its loveliness and on the others, the mountains rising almost to the clouds. It makes the most perfect picture background for the most lovely picture. I have scarcely, since I left home, seen a place more perfectly beautiful since I left home and I shall never forget it.

After leaving the Chateaux, we came out on the Corniche road,[22] which follows the sea at this place for miles and then I had my first real view of the Mediterranean and lovely it was indeed. The water was the richest shade of blue growing more intense in the distance and was dotted here and there by the boats of the fishermen and other larger vessels whose white sails glistening in the sun added much to the beautiful view. Not far across the waters we could see the high rocks surmounted by forts for the defense of the city. The celebrated Corniche road is one of the best I have ever seen. It is cut out of the solid rock and is as hard and smooth as a floor. On one side rises [sic] the high rocks and on the other you look down into the sea. Near the shore the water is full of light green spots, which we found were caused by the white rocks under the water in these places. It is almost twelve and as I have promised to be ready for a drive at half past one, I must close my letter and get up. Give my love to Grandmother, Auntie, Aunt Evy and all the rest of the family and believe me,

   Your most affectionate sister, Emily

   PS Emory sends his love to all.

Marseilles, April 6th 1868

My dearest Mother,

I had hoped long ere this to have answered your letters, which I received at Paris, but thus far all my attempts have been in vain. Your last letter I stopped at Monroe's for on our way to the cars for Lyons and I sat down in the depot to read it while Emory was attending to the baggage. I can assure you I enjoyed every word and thank you for giving me such a detailed account of your visit in New York. I am glad you enjoyed it and hope that you will feel the benefit of it after you return home. I received your letter too late to avail myself of Mr. Johnson's[23] offer but I think I have gotten all that [I] wanted quite reasonably. If I have not, I might as well learn by experience and do better next time.

   Madame Davenport was very kind and obliging. I did not see her on the steamer until the last day as she was seasick the whole voyage. She asked if I would like her to come to me on Monday in Paris and show me where to make my purchases. I gladly assented and Monday, Tuesday and Thursday she spent half the day with me in shopping.

As I would not return for four months, I was obliged to get all I wanted for the summer; dresses, shoes, hat, bonnet, linen, and many little things. So, it was a great comfort to have Madame Davenport go with me.

I am enjoying Marseilles very much and we are staying here so long that I shall have seen everything of importance before I leave. On Saturday I went with Emory to the Zoological Gardens[24] and was very much interested by the number of strange animals and birds we saw as well as by the great beauty and order of the place.

Last week General and Mrs. McClellan were here. I like them both very much. They were exceedingly polite and kind and I am very glad we met them. They both advise me strongly not to go to Rome at present but to go first to Sorrento (a lovely quiet place near Naples). I think we shall do this in the end, but I am anxious to stop one day in Rome to get our letters and to see the Austins. I have of course, heard nothing since I left Paris and am longing for letters. I think we shall leave here Wednesday on the steamer and shall reach Rome about Friday.

Last night Mr. Conway (the American consul) and his wife called on us. They were very pleasant people and we found it quite pleasant to see some Americans after all the foreigners we have met.

This morning Emory left me quite early for Toulon. He was quite anxious to see Napoleon's first battlefield as well as other military matter there collected, which is very interesting. He had letters and permits from the commanding officer here and I have no doubt he will have a day both of instruction and amusement. I declined to go as I thought a day's rest was better for me and I should only interfere with the "study of war," which is being carried on so vigorously. I laugh at Emory a good deal. He is determined to make the most of everything and see and learn as much as possible and the way he questions and cross-examines the poor unfortunates he happens to converse with is too amusing, whether soldiers or civilians, he generally finds out much that they know. He has even visited in Marseilles all the little narrow streets and hospitals so as to see both sides of the picture. This is the first time I have been without my husband for more than three hours since we were married.

So, I have kept very busy all day. This noon, I went out for the first time for a walk and I really enjoyed it very much. As I was alone, I walked along the street looking into every shop window that was interesting, as long as I pleased and stopping once in a while to make some small purchase. I can assure [you] it was very interesting. One of my amusements here is sitting by the window and watching the people pass. You see such a variety of costume as well as a variety of people of all nations. This morning I met Turks, Greeks, Spaniards, Italians, etc. The great commerce of the city brings every nation into her ports. Since we have been here we have seen all our steamer friends who have stopped here en route for Rome. It was very pleasant for us.

I shall have to be content with this much of a letter today, as I want to write to Evy. I am anxious to hear from her. I am better and stronger today than I have been for two weeks. I fear you think my letters very illegible, but my favorite gold pen refuses to write and I am forced to use what I find in the room.

With a great deal of love, I am dearest mother, your loving child, Emily

Rome, Hotel de Londres, April 10th 1868[25]

My dear Mother,

Here we are at last in Rome and it is hard for me as yet to realize that this is really the world-renowned city, where so many acts of historical interest have taken place and that we are constantly treading and viewing classic ground, but so it is and when I have had time [to] see where I am, I shall become used to the idea. It is very pleasant, after all, that we can be here Easter Sunday for we had given up the idea and had written to Mr. Austin to give up our rooms for this week as we intended going direct to Naples and Sorrento but our letters being here and my desire to see the Austins induced us to stop for a day or two on our way. We left Marseilles Wednesday evening in a little steamer and on Friday found ourselves at Civita Vecchia.[26] We had a very disagreeable passage and nearly all the passengers were sick and confined to their staterooms. Emory was frightfully seasick. From the time the boat started I never saw anyone more wretched. I was sorry for him from the bottom of my heart and was thankful for his sake when the boat reached Civita Vecchia. This morning he had his color back again and feels quite like himself. The short waves and horrid little boats are much more trying than the Atlantic. I was not very well that day, but was not at all seasick being the only lady at the table during the voyage.

We passed, during the day, the islands of Corsica and Elba both of which were very mountainous. It was quite interesting to see the birthplace and place of banishment of Napoleon. We remained at Civita Vecchia until the train for Rome left, at three o'clock. Emory and I went to the hotel where we slept most of the time. The place is small and all that particularly impressed us was the wind and dust. In the afternoon, our passport and trunks having been examined. we started for Rome. Most of [the] journey was through the wild uncultivated land near the sea, which in some parts was covered by immense herds of horses, mules and cows. They look entirely different from ours, are much larger, all dark grey and have very handsome large horns, branching back from their heads. The people look quite unlike the French we have just left. Some I saw were about the color of an Indian with the blackest hair imaginable. It was not hard to believe every man we saw by the roadside [was] a brigand, for their dark fierce faces and high hats, they seemed ready for anything.

We did not arrive at Rome until after dark when we had to wait an hour for our trunks to be gotten out. At last we started for a hotel with but little chance of finding rooms for all the hotels had refused the day before to take any more people and all the first ones at which we stopped were full to overflowing. We went with much doubting to the "Hotel de Londres" where the Austins were. We found them gone for a week, but their rooms had been reserved for us since last Monday as they had gone before our last dispatch giving up the rooms, reached them. We were thankful enough to have a room to come to for at this late day, money will not procure lodgings and we have very handsome rooms and are comfortably settled.

This morning immediately after breakfast Emory went to the bankers and soon returned with twelve letters, which I can assure, we fully appreciated. Among them was your letter from New York written just before you started and two from Nelly with their enclosures. You and Julia Rankins must have enjoyed the journey home together.

This morning is wet and cold so I have remained at home while Emory has gone out to make some explorations. He has been to Mr. Cushman's (the American Consul) who has promised to get us if possible, [a] seat at St. Peter's for tomorrow. It is almost an impossibility and can only be done by applying to some distinguished person. Emory is obliged to be in full uniform and I have to wear a long black veil. I hope we can go for it is a very imposing ceremony and worth seeing.

I am going to content myself with looking out of the windows for today and save my energy for tomorrow. Almost under my window is a very old basin with several fountains in it and it is quite interesting to watch the men and women coming there every few minutes for water with their pitchers and pails all looking queer and foreign to me.

Emory went this morning all over St. Peters and was surprised and delighted with all he saw. My letter from Miss Le Clerc[27] to Mrs. Cushman[28] came this morning. If we stay more than one a day or two, I shall present it, if not I will wait till our return. I was quite disappointed not to find Mrs. Austin here as we shall not see her at all now, but I found letters from her and Mr. Austin, which was very pleasant.

I think I am steadily improving now and hope a week or two at Sorrento will do wonders for me. My neuralgia is much better, which is a great relief and I hope, one by one, all my pains and aches will cease. You must write me all you hear from Evy. I shall be glad to hear that she has reached Fort McDowell in safety and to know how she likes it. I suppose before this Uncle has gone to New York. I have no doubt he will like [it] better. He has so many friends there and will find more to amuse him. I am glad Col. Keogh is with you and hope his leg will soon be well. Give him my kindest regards and tell him I would like nothing better than to sit down with my work (as I did that fall he was with us) and hear him read Charles O'Malley again. I shall write again on Monday.

With love to father, the girls, Jack, George, Fred and Violet, Grandma and Aunty.[29] I am ever your affectionate child, Emily.

Sorrento, Italy April 16th 1868

My dear Father,

I believe Emory gave you quite a full description of the ceremony at St. Peters on Easter Sunday so I do not know that there is much for me to say.[30] I am so glad that we were able to be there on that particular day, for it was a scene one can never forget. After seating me among the ladies (who by the way were obliged to be dressed in black with long lace veils on their heads) Emory went to his place that had been reserved for him in the gallery of distinguished military men next to the Cardinals, as he had a splendid view of everything that took place. The music was delightful and some of the parts of the ceremony very imposing. The church seemed about half full of soldiers (the Pope's guard) who in their armor and magnificent uniforms, looked like old

Knights and were busied during most of the service in keeping the crowd in order with their halberds. I saw the pope quite distinctly as he was being carried in, but a great part of the time he was hidden from view. As we left the church and looked from the steps down on the square below, as far as the eye could reach in every direction it was just one sea of human heads all looking eagerly for the Pope who by his blessing absolves them all from the sins of the past year. There were thousands and thousands of people and I can assure you it was a very impressive sight when the whole of this great multitude fell on their knees and with bowed heads heard the benediction at the close of which, a shout from the whole rent the air, all the bells sent forth a merry peal, while in all directions were heard the booming of cannon and music by the different bands. The next sight was the illumination of St. Peters, which I saw. It was perfectly magnificent. The whole of this vast building as well as the colonnade leading to it was one blaze of light and enabled one to realize better than in the daytime, the size and grandeur of the building.

Monday morning, we started to see the Coliseum. It was even grander than I supposed. As I sat among the ruins and looked at the great walls and arches within whose bounds for so many hundreds of years, the old Romans witnessed the games and exploits of those days, it required little imagination once more to people the different stories; galleries with the eager crowd gazing down into the arena below where once more the Christian martyrs struggled for their lives with the wild beasts who rushed out from their cells (still visible in the lower wall.)[31] It is undoubtedly the grandest ruin in the world for the very sight brings up whole trains of recollections. Emory ascended to the highest point but I contented myself with wandering about below and only looking up.

Next, we visited the Baths of Caracalla, which were also very interesting and covered a large portion of ground. The only remains of their former magnificence are the beautiful pavements of mosaic all colors and in every imaginable figure. The arches and walls are immense and numbers of them still stand. We passed through the arches of Constantine and Titus, which are very large and highly ornamented with sculpture, parts of which are now so nearly destroyed as to be almost invisible.

Though I had but a short time left for sight-seeing in Rome, I concluded to spend it in seeing as much as possible of St. Peters as we next went there. It seems too grand a place to attempt a description of anything one can say seems tame compared with the reality. One of the most striking things is the perfect unity of everything in regard to size and it makes it difficult for one to realize that the building is so immense. I never imagined anything so magnificently beautiful. The study of the paintings above is a work for days and I felt that I had only had a taste to make me the more anxious to return and finish my view of St. Peters. We left Rome Tuesday morning as I found it would be better for me to wait till I was stronger (for what is really a labor) seeing Rome as it should be seen.

I suppose you will have your hands full this summer in keeping up the gardens. We think and talk of you all very often and I often think longingly of Willowbrook in its spring beauty. I have never yet seen in the world-renowned Italy, a place that compared (in my mind) with it or which I would change for it.

You would have been amused to see with what delight Emory and I read the "Army and Navy Journals" we found at Rome. There was so much news. I hope dear Father that you will write to me sometimes for I am always glad to get your letters.

With love to all, I am ever your loving child, Emily

PS I must tell you about a lemon Emory saw, plucked and brought to me. It is a monster; 7 inches long and over 13 inches in circumference. We are living in an orange and lemon grove.

Sorrento Italy, April 18th, 1868

My dearest Lily,[32]

I received your letter the day before I left Rome and was very glad to hear from you. I must give you an account of our journey to and arrival at Naples and Sorrento.

We left Rome Tuesday morning and one might suppose from the crowds at the depot that most of the other strangers left it at the same time, but at last we were settled and started on one of the most interesting of our day's rides. The country was full of old Roman ruins and we passed through many old towns of which I had often heard.

About eight we arrived at Naples and went to Hotel la Vittoria[33] where we spent the night. I shall never forget it. First a thunderstorm, a carriage-stand under our window, donkeys without number, braying; as well as a herd of cattle who were quartered near us for the night, made sleep almost an impossibility. When we came into breakfast the next morning we found ladies who crossed the steamer with us. We all felt as if we had met old friends and enjoyed the little glimpse very much.

At nine we started for Sorrento taking the train as far as Castellammare where we took an open carriage for the rest of the way, a distance of twenty miles through the most beautiful country I ever imagined. I cannot give you a just description of the ride, but will try with what a few words can do. The road for the whole distance runs near the water and was as smooth as a floor, which overhangs the sea and is built hundreds of feet above it. On the other side of us were hard rocks, whose summits were covered with small shrubs and flowers. The road was very winding and as we darted round the corners at a fast trot, one minute we were looking at the blue Mediterranean with Naples and Mount Vesuvius at our back; before us the little island of Capri and the little villages dotting the cliffs along the bay as far as the eye could reach. Then as we turned we saw on all sides of us the mountains covered with fruit trees and vines terraced up to the very summit, which looked like a beautiful garden. Every spot is so finely cultivated and the same is the case in the ravines below, which are filled with orange, lemon and olive trees.

As we drew near Naples the orange and lemon trees grew less scarce until at last on every side of us we could see nothing but the yellow fruit hanging most temptingly over the walls. We went to the hotel Gen'l McClellan had recommended and though he had praised it very highly he had not overrated its beauties. The road at the entrance runs through an orange, lemon and olive grove, at the end of which is the Villa Rispoli[34] surrounded on all sides by roses in full bloom and other lovely flowers so that at the first view of the house, one is charmed. The garden is filled with beautiful walks of mosaic pavement (or rather tile made to represent it) and seats in the shade of the same material. The other side of the house overlooks the sea and from the balcony we have a beautiful view of the city of Naples looking in the distance with its white houses like a great flock of sheep at the foot of Mount Vesuvius, which rises at the side and mingles day and night its smoke with the clouds. It is a grand sight to see it towering so high above all the other land, and watch the smoke steadily pouring from its mouth. Then on one side are the huge rocks skirting along the shore for miles and dotted here and there with little villages or further villas in the midst of olive groves.

Some of the mountains in the background are covered at the top with snow so that it is hard to tell the snow from the clouds. On the water, which always looks beautiful are numbers of little boats coming and going between here and Naples. One of my amusements is to watch the barefooted women and children, as well as the donkeys, creep up and down the steep road with their heavy burdens to the sea to where their loads are shipped in small sail boats to Naples.

One of the great enjoyments here are the fresh oranges. They are delicious when so fresh I can never get enough.

Emory received today a letter from Molly.[35] I am surprised Col. Keogh goes away so soon! Does he return to Fort Wallace?[36]

I think we shall be here for some time. I want to visit the places in the vicinity of Pompeii, etc. I must close this letter only wishing that I had been most successful in describing this beautiful country.

Give a great deal of love to all at home, and believe me, your loving sister, Emily

Sorrento, April 26th, 1868

My dearest Mother,
I am very sorry I have let so many days slip by since writing home, but I had no idea until I counted this morning. We are enjoying Sorrento very much and the rest and pure warm air is doing me good. I have done little sightseeing since I have been here leaving for Emory most of the hard work such as climbing the mountain and other laborious feats. Though in doing so, I lose a great many fine views. A very pleasant English family are [sic] staying here, Dr. and Mrs. Cosson and their two sons.[37] We see a great deal of them and often take our rides and rows together. The time here flies in a most remarkable manner, for there are four hours about noon when it is too warm to venture out so I read, sleep or sew and at three we generally take a ride or go out with Dr. Cosson in their row boat. I cannot tell you how charming it is. The water such a lovely color, the fresh salt air and such beautiful views of Vesuvius, Naples, the Island of Capri, and all the rocky coast.

The rocks are filled with passages from the ground down to the shore, some of them a quarter of a mile long. There is one in this garden, through which we go down to the shore, which is a quarter of a mile long and built with stone arches. Some of the caves we row into are very beautiful, the rocks and stone are covered with different colored seaweed, and lichens. I have taken one donkey ride but found it too slow for me after "Zayde" but I must confess I never saw such climbing. My donkey went up and down the stairs cut in the rocks and stones as if it was level ground.

Emory went last week to Pompeii and also ascended to the very top of the crater, which has been formed by this last eruption. He was the most burnt looking creature you ever imagined. We have been very fortunate in seeing Vesuvius in action for several evenings. Last week we sat out on the piazza and saw the fire and the mountain cast up red hot stones very distinctly. I have not given up Pompeii but shall try when I go to Naples to see it.

I wanted to write you a long letter, but I cannot do it tonight so rather than wait another day, I will send it as it is.

With much love, your affectionate child, Emily

Sorrento, May 3, 1868

My dearest Mother,

I have just this minute received your letter of the sixth of April and I am so delighted to hear from you that I cannot resist the temptation to answer it immediately. It was the first letter I had had for ten days or more as Emory, thinking we should return to Rome last week, wrote for our letters to be detained there but as I was not at all well and unfit for traveling, we concluded to remain a week or two longer and give Sorrento a fair trial. So, the letters we sent for have just come. It seems really a pity to remain so long in one place when there is so much to see in Italy but I have no doubt that we shall find in the end that we have saved time. For if I stay here till I am stronger, I can move much faster when we start again. The truth is until the last ten days I had hardly improved a bit and was not as well as when I left home, my cough being much worse so that in writing home, as you know, my letters were mere hopes of improvement necessarily than actual accounts of it. But now, thanks to the advice of an English physician here and the warm pure air of Sorrento, I have really improved very much and hope to get really strong before leaving here. I enjoy Sorrento very much. I never breathed such delicious air.

At noon it is very hot but now when we go out for our rides, drives, and rows, it is perfectly delightful, the atmosphere filled with the perfume of roses and other flowers, then the water is always a delight, it is so variable and covered with a variety of boats and ships. Vesuvius too is an object of constant attention. It never looks two days the same, sometimes almost hidden in the clouds of smoke then again looming up clearly against the blue sky with its huge column of smoke and vapor.

Tuesday, we visited the Island of Capri, which is about twelve miles from Sorrento. We went in a small boat with six sailors to row. Mr. and Mrs. Crittenden from St. Louis,[38] Mrs. Hazeldon,[39] Mr. De Cosson, Emory and myself made up the party. We had quite rough weather before we reached the Island but I rather enjoyed the rough water.

We went first to the "Blue Grotto" for which the island is justly celebrated. Here we left the larger boat for a smaller one as the entrance to the cave is only high enough to admit one, crouched down in the boat. It was quite a large cave beautifully arched inside and perfectly blue from the reflection of the water, which was the most exquisite shade of blue I ever saw and clear as crystal. When the oars come out of it, all the water looked like precious stones as it dripped from them. After leaving the grotto, we took our lunch and then landed at Capri. As soon as we were seen from the shore, the women with their donkeys came rushing down the rocks to meet us. The island is just one mountain and from the top, the view is splendid. I fortunately found a little pony and, with a girl at its head to guide and pull it along and a woman behind to beat it, I commenced the ascent of the mountain. Such steep places, such long flights of steps in the rocks, one would consider formidable but with the help of my attendants, my pony made the ascent quite comfortably though I could not help smiling sometimes when I thought how queer it must look to see me going down the steps with a person holding the head of my horse and another holding him up by the tail. The view from the summit was grand and took in a great part of the bay.

Well, I must say Jack's change of plans surprised one, but I am very glad for I know he has wished to go to West Point for some time.[40] I think he showed a good deal of pluck in writing to Mr. Seward.[41] I know he will do well. We are really becoming an army family and Willowbrook will indeed be "Army Headquarters."

So, Frederick Townsend has resigned, indeed I thought he would if there was a change in California.[42] I do hope my next letter will bring news of Evy. It was strange my letter was so long reaching you but I hope you have had others before now. I have written quite often though not interestingly as it has been a great effort for me to write at all. I must close my letter and dress for dinner. I am sitting with all the windows open and in a white dress. I am very glad you liked the bible I sent you. I cannot tell you how often my thoughts wander towards you all at home and how dearly I love to think of each and everyone and most often and lovingly I think of you my dear, dear father. All the trouble which began a year ago today you understood and sympathized so fully in that it brought me nearer to you than ever if possible.

You judged so truly that Emory would make the tenderest [sic] and most devoted of husbands.

With love to all, in which Emory joins, I am ever, your loving child, Emily

Emory

Sorrento, Italy, May 7th, 1868[43]

My dear brother John,
I have a little spare time this evening and shall devote it to you and Julia thinking perhaps that you may like to hear directly as a few

things from Europe. I have directed Sara and Maria to forward my letters regularly to the other members of the family so I hope you have not been entirely ignorant of my movements.

We have now been a month in Italy and are getting a thorough insight into Italian character. The people are detestable, and their condition deplorable from having been for ages the victims of two equally grievous oppressions. The first is the Catholic Church. The priests of which for selfish ends have kept them in complete ignorance. The second is their government, which has wrung from them all their hard earnings. The people all assemble in towns, those who cultivate the soil going to it and returning from it every day. The towns are all very ancient in appearance with streets in most instances not wide enough to permit two carriages to pass.

Shops, stores, groceries, etc., usually occupy the ground floor while in the stores above the rooms are packed with occupants, as many as five of them sleeping in one bed. An immense number of idlers are always to be found in the streets and these are ready to beg of everybody. The begging is characteristic and embraces all sexes, and ages and conditions. A little child will come up to you, perhaps for effect, badly clad but healthy in appearance and will follow you for squares. Should you motion or even push it away, it will nevertheless cling to you still. One naturally has to steel his heart against them for nine-tenths of them are beggars and the rest can live by want if they will.

The condition of the people has improved since Victor Emanuel's reign. He has struck several important blows to the Church, but the great and final one yet remains, and that will be delivered when the present French Emperor[44] quits the throne of France and leaves Italy free. She will then rise up and demand Rome for her Capitol. He'll expel the Pope and St. Peter's,[45] like the coliseum, may at no distant day, be one of the grandest ruins of the world.

I suppose you know that I had the opportunity to attend the ceremonies at St. Peter's on Easter Sunday. Had seat (reserved) just behind the Cardinals, saw the Pope on his throne borne on the shoulders of his men; saw him snuff incense, saw cardinals, priests, and the whole multitude kneel before him, and more around on the altar were stationed sentinels who not let you approach unless you were dressed for an evening party. Long lines of troops were drawn up within the vast edifice to form a part of the pageant. The sight was magnificent, but to call it religion, one must be beside himself.

We have now been here almost a month for Emily's [health], which has little improved since her marriage under skillful treatment. However she is now improving. We shall leave here next week [to] go to Naples, Rome, then to Florence, Venice, Vienna, and so on to Russia. I enjoy my tour very much but everyday makes me prouder of my country, its people, and their enterprise. To come here but for a moment is to admit that the power of the world has moved to another continent and that the U.S., have a destiny no other nation ever had. It however is painful to think that, while all lovers of liberty the world over, look to the United States to host a moral revolution which shall de-throne oppression and elevate mankind. Our leaders should be so corrupt as ever now to jeopardize the liberties we possess.

We hear little from America. I hope Grant will be nominated by the Republicans and elected and that with his election will come profound peace.

Sara writes me that you have been presented with another daughter and I am glad to learn that Julia is doing well.

Don't view this letter critically for I have jotted down whatever has come into my mind and shall not take the trouble to look it over.

Emily sends her love to you and we both shall hope to see you all in September or October.[46]

Your aff. bro. Emory

PS Our address is care of Jno Monroe & Co., Bankers, Rue Scribe, Paris

Let me know about politics.

Emily

Sorrento, May 9th 1868

My dearest Mother,

I had a day or two ago a delightful bundle of letters from home on from Molly, one from George, and two from you besides Emory's from you.[47]

We are leading such a quiet, lazy life just now that I have little to tell you of interest so this will be just a gossipy letter. I am very glad you are reconciled to Jack's going into the army and I have no doubt that he will do well and be very happy. I am so glad he has something he really likes to do.

We leave here Tuesday for Naples where we shall spend only a day or two as the heat and the dust are frightful. It has been very hot here for the last few days and that with the sirocco blowing[48] has made it almost impossible to exert ourselves much. Even the inhabitants find it hard to work while this wind is blowing.

I am glad to hear Nelly has left home for I think the entire change of air and scene will do her good but you will all miss her very much.

Goodbye and believe me, dearest mother, your very affectionate child, Emily

Rome, May 18th, 1868

My dear Molly,

I intended to write you on your birthday but I found it impossible to get time for a letter as I was then in Naples so I had to content myself with mentally sending my good wishes and defer my letter till I reached Rome.

We arrived here Saturday night and came to the same hotel where we were last time in the "Piazza di Spagna."[49] Mr. and Mrs. Walch

(Kitty Dix)⁵⁰ came with us. We met them first at Sorrento and we were together a great deal at Naples. We had a whole carriage to ourselves and had a delightful time. The country the whole way was very beautiful, a perfect feast to the eye. I do not think I have enjoyed any ride as much as this. The last day in Naples we spent in the museum,⁵¹ which interested me very much. We saw an immense amount of curiosities from all quarters of the globe and a large collection of antiquities from Pompeii and Herculaneum, bread with the baker's name still distinct upon it, all varieties of household goods and the most beautiful precious stones. The intaglio carved on some of them was exquisite. But the most interesting part of the museum to me was the picture galleries. Some of the pictures were from the finest Old Masters; Raphael, Titian, Guido, etc.

In your last letter received at Naples you spoke of wanting a flower from the grave of Shelley, so I determined to get [it] for you.⁵² It rained hard all-day Sunday but about five the sun came out. So, we started for the protestant burial ground (which is obliged to be outside the walls). Here we easily found the grave under the Aurelian wall. It had a simple marble slab with this inscription "Percy Byss[h]e Shelley, Cor Cordeum" (the Heart of Hearts) "Natus 1792, obit 1822." The only flowers about the grave were large white roses. I brought you one from the head. I also brought you some things from the grave of Keats, which is in the old cemetery. By his request, his name is not on it only this: "Here lies all that was mortal of a young English poet who on his death bed in the bitterness of his heart at the malicious power of his enemies desired these words to be engraven [sic] on his tombstone." "Here lies one whose name was written in water." This grave touched and interested me very much. It was in the deserted ground and looked so neglected and lonely. I must go to bed now for I am tired from my day's work of sight-seeing. Emory sends you his love.

Your loving sister, Emily

Rome, May 20th 1868

My dearest Mother,

My letter to Molly was too short to send so I have kept it a day that I might write to you also and tell you what we have seen thus far.

Monday, we spent the great part of the day in the Vatican and then saw but a portion of its wonders of art. We first visited the stanze of Raphael, three rooms the sides of which as well as the ceiling were covered with the most beautiful paintings of Raphael.[53] They are all frescoes but have kept their color remarkably and each one is worthy of days of study. We spent a great part of our morning in these rooms and left them at last with great reluctance to visit the museum and other galleries. I saw such a variety and vast amount of curious things that the very thought of enumerating is confusing so I will only speak of those which impressed me the most.

Among the statues, the Apollo Belvedere[54] and the Lacoon[55] were the most striking and I was by no means disappointed in their beauty much as I had always read of them. Of course, the popes having the power to gather all the most celebrated statues and paintings from every quarter into their collection house, made the Vatican the repository of the first gems of art the world contains. We also visited the three galleries containing the tapestries of Raphael. It was for these tapestries, Raphael made his celebrated cartoons of the principal scenes of the life of Christ and his apostles and though they have been manufactured fully three hundred and fifty years, the colors are as bright and beautiful as ever.

The Sistine Chapel interested me very much. The paintings on the ceilings and at the lower end of the chapel are by Michelangelo. The one over the altar being his very celebrated "Last Judgment." I spent a long time here and yet felt but half satisfied so much is there to be seen and studied. The Vatican is perfectly enormous and contains some rooms that are magnificent. In every hall and room, we found members of the pope's guard. Their dress is very peculiar and striking, being a uniform of red, black and yellow. The frescoes and ornamentations of the halls and staircases were very beautiful and the mosaic pavements were also very fine.

The picture gallery we left for another day but after dinner we set out for a drive on the Appian Way.[56] This we found very interesting as we were constantly passing old Roman ruins of churches, houses and a great many tombs.

Sunday on our return from the English cemetery, we visited St. Paul's, which I think is really more beautiful than St. Peter's though not so grand by any means. Here the remains of St. Paul are supposed to rest and the church is filled with pictures of the scenes of his life. I shall try to visit it once more before leaving Rome. Here Emory met an old friend of his—Dr. Holman, medical director of the Sixth Corps.[57] They seemed to be delighted to meet and immediately commenced to rouse old memories. It seems strange that they should part in the din and smoke of battle to meet in the solemn stillness of this grand old church. Dr. Holman spent the evening with us and he and Emory fought their battles over until the small hours of the morning. It reminded me of some of the talks Andrew and Emory used to have. Mr. and Mrs. Walch also spent part of the evening with us.

I am very much better than when I was at Rome before and can enjoy everything much more, still I am very careful not to overtask my strength. I shall hope to find letters from you at Florence. Our letters received here were not of very late date. Emory joins me in love to all at home,

Your very loving, Emily

2 Paris to Key West

Emily

Florence, May 24th 1868

My dear Lily,
We reached Florence last night and now that I am somewhat settled in my new quarters, I must tell you of my movements since last writing. But first I must tell you that I am staying at Mrs. Chapman's boarding house in the via Pandolphini.[1] We had high recommendations of this place from some friends we met and therefore came here. There are only a few boarders here and those are treated as guests. Mrs. Chapman is an American lady who came here for the benefit of her daughters voice and opened the boarding house. It looked so little like a hotel when we arrived here last night. In our little parlor we found the table spread for supper (we were expected) and delicious flowers and fruit in the room as though we were guests and this morning, Mrs. Chapman went with us to church were we met several Americans.

   I did not half finish my account of Rome so I must travel back there (though it is fifteen mortal hours). Tuesday, we renewed our attack on the Vatican from which we only desisted when forced by fatigue and hunger and then carrying off such treasures (of memory) as only time can take from us. This day we devoted to pictures alone and such a feast as it was. The room in which we spent most of our time contained but three pictures, two of them, the finest in the world. Raphael's "Transfiguration" and Domenichino's "Administration of the Sacrament to St. Jerome."[2]

Oh, they were just glorious! And the more you looked at them, the more you wished to look. We were both perfectly fascinated with them looking from one face to another and finishing them only to return for another study. There is no doubt genius will make itself felt. Even those who are not admirers of the fine arts cannot but see and realize the power of a masterpiece. Nearly all the pictures of the collection are the originals, many of them having been purchased by the popes for immense sums from the cities and churches for which they were originally painted.

Wednesday, we went first to the Capitol of painting and sculpture[3]. The most remarkable statues we saw were the "Dying Gladiator"[4] and the "Venus of the Capitol."[5] We visited all the different rooms where the senators still hold their meetings and where various ceremonies and councils take place. From there we went to the Pantheon,[6] a glorious old building, which though it has stood unrecognized for thousands of years looks as though it might stand thousands of years more. It is now filled with shrines and altars and seems to serve as well for the worship of God as it did for the worship of the old Roman deities so many centuries ago. It is almost unchanged and stands there in the midst of ruins in its stern simplicity, the best preserved monument of ancient Rome.

Thursday was a feast day and everything but the churches were closed. The ceremonies took place at the Lateran where the pope[7], all the cardinals, bishops, etc. took part in the service. We went quite early and as I was in the prescribed dress, I had a seat in the gallery for ladies, which I could see most perfectly all the ceremonies. It was, of course, much like Easter. The pope entered on his throne followed by the cardinals, senators, etc. in their long scarlet robes, who when his holiness was seated approached one by one, prostrated themselves and kissed his hands most reverently. The whole service consisted of bowing and kneeling to the pope more than anything else. The church was half filled with soldiers whose brilliant uniforms added to the beauty of the scene. At the close, the pope blessed the people from the balcony of the church.

In the afternoon we visited St. Peters and examined its beauties and wonders with great interest once more. While there we heard the priests chant choral service, which was very fine. But what I enjoyed most was hearing vespers in the little chapel attached to the convent of Sacred Heart. The nuns behind the grating sang the service while those who were not in black veils and the young girls who were scholars at the convent, sat just before the altar. It was one of the most solemn as well as the sweetest services I ever attended. It was just at sunset and the beautiful little chapel was at first bright with its rays, but gradually it assumed a more somber hue and the stillness was broken only by the voice of the priest and the sweet voices of the nuns as they chanted the long responses. It made one forget all else but the scene before them.

Friday was last day at Rome much to our regret but it would take months to really satisfy oneself in regard to all the wonders here and we could not devote any more time to it just now. In the morning we went first to Mr. Hazeltine's studio and saw some exquisite pieces of statuary; from there to the Borghese Palace where we spent several hours in examining the picture galleries, which were very beautiful and contained some very fine pictures.[8] The different rooms also were very fine and fitted up with great beauty. Before returning home, we visited the church of Santa Maria Maggiore,[9] which is one of the most magnificent churches in Rome. The present pope has raised a monument to himself there as he wishes it for his last resting place.

Towards evening, we took a drive and visited the villa Borghese, one of the largest and most lovely villas I have yet seen. The grounds are very extensive and beautiful and are opened to the public. We then drove to the Pincio[10], which being on a very high ground commands a fine view of Rome. Here we saw the sweetest and it was a grand sight, the whole of the eternal city, brilliant with the golden light and looking grander and more impressive than ever before.

The Cushman's and everyone else I knew were out of town so I had not the trouble making or receiving calls. Well, this is a long letter. I must stop.

With love to all, your aff. sister, Emily

PS Emory heard from Throop and Father here.

Venice, June 18th 1868

My dear Father,

I believe I am your debtor for a letter so I shall devote the time remaining before dinner to the pleasant task of writing you. We spent the last two days of our stay in Florence in visiting the principal galleries and churches, which I had not been able to visit before. I found them interesting and some of the pictures were the most beautiful I had yet seen. The last day we dined with Col. Lawrence (Consul General to Italy).[11] We had a charming little dinner, which we both enjoyed very much. Col. Lawrence has been very polite to us. He sent Emory soon after our arrival there, four bottles of old whiskey for me. He has invited us on several occasions to go with him to see unusual things and he sent me last week first a bouquet of superb flowers three feet round then a basket, which was certainly four or five feet. The kindness of Mr. and Mrs. Marsh was unbounded.[12] The last thing they did was to send me a little camp chair, which they had made for me. Mrs. Cooley and her daughter also invited us to dinner and took us to drive several times our only being in Florence too much attention for our time.

Wednesday, we left Florence for Venice and I certainly never saw a more beautiful country than that we were passing through all day.

The wheat and other grain was fully ripe and formed a fine contrast (the bright yellow and the red poppies with which it is interspersed) to the fruit trees and vines, which divide the fields. Nearly all the fields are divided into small lots by fruit trees of all kinds and grapevines are festooned from one tree to another. You cannot imagine how graceful and picturesque they look. But after all the pleasantest incident of the journey was our approach to Venice. Although I had thought of it, I did not realize how strange it would seem to see a city in the midst of the water and the sight of Venice as we crossed an arm of the Adriatic was queer enough. When we arrived at the station instead of the noise of coachmen and rattling of carriages, we found numbers of gondolas in one of which we took our places with our baggage and in perfect quiet, were rowed towards our hotel. I cannot better describe our entrance into this beautiful city than by quoting Roger's beautiful lines "There is a glorious city in the sea. The sea is in the broad, the narrow streets. Ebbing and flowing and the salt seaweed clings to the marble of the palaces. No track of men, no footsteps to and fro lead to her gates. The path lies through the deep, and from the land we went as to a floating city, steering in and gliding up her streets as in a dream."[13]

I cannot describe to you how strange it seemed; the perfect stillness, not a sound but the voice now and then of a boatman as he warned others of his approach in the dusk. We rowed in and out now in the Grand Canal; now in some narrow passage. Where the boatman's utmost skill was needed to avoid running into other boats and at last arrived at our Hotel Barberi where we stepped from the boat to the marble stairs nearly covered at high tide. We had a fine large room over the water and I hurried off my hat to take my place in the window and continue my investigation of the strangest city I had ever seen.

The night was warm but a refreshing breeze rose from the water and every few moments the heavens were lit up by lightning, during the flashes of which I could see land opposite, the most conspicuous objects being a grand old church and several large vessels anchored in the stream. Added to this was the splashing of the water against the house, the noise of distant thunder and a strain now and then of music across the water. No wonder I felt that I was in a dream and almost fretted to move lest the scene before me should vanish and I should wake to ordinary commonplace things. Yes, Venice does give one a new sensation—it differs from all the rest of the world and the novelty is charming.

This morning after breakfast we entered a gondola and set out to explore a part of the city. Of all the lazy, delightful modes of locomotion this is the pleasantest and most luxurious. The boat (about thirty feet long) was jet black and beautifully carved. It was carpeted and covered with an awning and curtains and contained great, comfortable cushioned seats so that one was almost reclining. The gondolier stood up on the covered part of the boat behind us and with one oar, propelled the gondola in the most marvelous manner while we comfortably settled in the interior, enjoyed the sea breeze, and the naval scene before us. We passed boats carrying wood, water, fruit, vegetables, etc. Then fine gondolas containing gentlemen and ladies reading and sewing in their little cabins, some of which inside were very handsome. By the laws of Venice, all gondolas are painted black and are quite similar.

We went to the bankers, then to St. Mark's where we visited the grand old church and saw many wonderful things. The shops are all under cover being the lower stories of the great houses, so we could walk under the cool stone porticos and see as much as we pleased of the curiosities they contained. In the center of the square of St. Mark's is a large clock tower. The hours are struck on a bell at the summit by two great bronze men. As the clock strikes twelve, the pigeons from all parts of the city flock here to be fed. It has been the custom for hundreds of years and is done by the request of a lady of Venice. I saw hundreds in the square just as I was leaving and could almost step on them as I walked.

When we returned, I commenced this letter, the writing of which you must excuse, for the temptation to sit in the window (the broad edge of which extends over the water and is protected from the sun by a curtain) instead of writing properly at a table was too great to be resisted. So, this letter is written on my lap where the breeze now and then makes my paper move not a little.

June 19th

Last evening, we took a most delightful row down the Grand Canal and out into the Adriatic Sea passing on our way numbers of old palaces and churches. As we passed the Rialto, I thought of the Merchant of Venice. On our way back, we called on the consul where we spent a pleasant hour or two. This morning we spent at the academy of Les Belle Arti where we saw numbers of fine pictures and carvings.[14] Then to the treasury of St. Mark's, where today the sacred relics and jewels were to be seen. After that we visited the Palaces of the Doges, which was very magnificent and contained some very celebrated pictures and frescos and which interested us exceedingly.

When you last wrote us, you were just starting for the West. I suppose that long ere this you have returned and the family are once more at rest. I am glad uncle is not to leave us this summer, we should indeed miss him very much. Please tell him with my love that I received his letter while at Florence and will answer it soon. I send mother a copy of the pictures Emory and I had taken at Naples, mine is the best. I am feeling much better than I did while at Florence. I like the salt air very much.

With a great deal of love from Emory and myself, I am ever, your loving child, Emily

Lake Como, Italy June 28th 1868

My dear Mother,

It is some time since I have written home but we have been about so much the last week that I have not found time to write.

Last Monday we left Venice having enjoyed our few days there very much. We went first to Verona where we spent our time looking at the old churches and monuments. Some of the churches dated back to the eleventh century and contained some curious works of art. The particular interest of the place to Emory was the fine fortifications and arsenals for until lately Verona was the stronghold of the Austrians in Italy.

We left Verona Tuesday for Lake Como where we arrived in the evening. Our journey all day was through a most interesting country. We passed by several battlefields of note among others Solferino.[15] At Lecco,[16] we took a diligence[17] and rode to Bellagio on Lake Como where we are now staying. After spending a day or two here we went to Milan as we had made arrangements with General Parsons[18] to meet him at the head of Lake Maggiore on Monday from which place we were to cross the Alps by the Vincent Gotthard Pass[19] in a carriage—a journey of three days. But when I reached Milan I felt too unwell to undertake the trip. This and meeting Dr. de Cosson quite unexpectedly at Milan determined me to give up the trip for a week or ten days for he assured us that with my cough and lack of strength, etc. it would be very unwise to attempt a journey and as he is going to Como, advises us to return with them where he would do what he could for me and try to relieve my cough, which seems to baffle all remedies thus far. We thought this the best plan though with our short time left we can hardly afford it but it may save time elsewhere.

We have had no letters for two weeks but have sent to Geneva to have ours forwarded to us here. Among them I hope to find one from you dear mother for it is nearly two months since I have received more than a page from you. I shall be home in less than two months, but

I can hardly realize it. I am not at all in a letter writing mood this afternoon so I shall send you a short letter and write another soon.

Emory is quite delighted to be with the young de Cossons and will, I have no doubt, find plenty to engage him here with bathing, rowing and fishing.

Give my love to Uncle, Grandma, and Aunty as well as to all of the family and believe me dearest mother, your loving child, Emily

Paris, Aug. 2nd 1868

My dearest Mother,

I wrote you a few lines a day or two ago, telling you when I should be home. Now I will tell you what I have done since I have been here.

We arrived here Tuesday morning and all that day I spent in bed resting. Wednesday, Thursday and Friday, I spent part of the day in shopping and the rest in riding about and resting. I have now about finished all my shopping, which is a great relief for there was really a great deal to do. Madame Davenport has gone out with me every day and has been very kind indeed.

Yesterday I went with Emory to the Invalides. We saw all Napoleon's old soldiers and Emory enjoyed talking with them about the great General exceedingly. His admiration for Napoleon is unbounded and everything associated with him is interesting. We saw Napoleon's tomb and those of his brothers and favorite generals. His tomb is very beautiful and as severely plain as it is grand. I must acknowledge to a feeling of awe when I stood where his remains rested.

Emory left me last night for Chalons where the French army are encamped. He was very anxious to go there before he left Europe and we both thought it would be better for me to rest here in Paris instead of having the fatigue of another journey. Madame Davenport kindly offered to stay with me during his absence, which will only be until

Tuesday so that he left me well taken care of. I went to see Madame Chigarey[20] and had a pleasant call. I also went to see Mrs. Riggs but she was engaged and I did not see her.

I am more delighted than I can tell you when I think that the last of this month will see me settled at home. I am very anxious to see you all and you in particular, my dearest mother and I shall count the hours till I am with you again. Emory seems just as glad to think of being at Willowbrook again as I do. He is most decidedly one of the family. If you did not love him for his own sake, you must love him now if you knew half how good he has been to me. No one but you my dear mother, could have done more for me. I am so glad he has gone to Chalon for it is the first thing he has done for himself and I know he will enjoy it.

I now remember the steamer we go in: The *Cuba*.[21] I hope you will be able to meet me in New York for it will be pleasant to see you a few days before I could otherwise. Madame Davenport tells me that Mrs. Graham[22] is alone in New York for the summer so if it is convenient, we will go there. If we sail the 15th, we ought to be in New York by the 25th. I am feeling better than when I came to Paris and I think I shall enjoy the voyage home.

This is almost the last letter I shall write. Soon I shall be with you and be indeed, your loving child, Emily

Paris, Hotel du Louvre, August 3rd, 68[23]

My dearest Sister,

I trust you have not thought me neglectful of you since I have been away. This is not the first letter I have commenced to you and I hope this will not share the fate of the others and be left unfinished. The truth is I have been so sick since I left home that I have only been able to write to Willowbrook now and then and as they wrote me they send you my letters. I have tried to feel satisfied. The truth is, dear Evy, I have not been well or free from pain one day since I left home. My cough has been much worse and it is only by keeping a blister open that I am sometimes relieved from it.

I am now much better though I cannot walk but a little and thus miss a great deal. Emory has carried me upstairs with but a few exceptions for the last three months. He is just a darling and has been so good to me. He has given up everything and just nurses me like a woman, only it seems as if he had done more for me than anyone else could.

I last wrote to you from Sorrento. Of course, you have heard of my movements since then. I was at Sorrento four weeks, then at Naples, Rome, Florence, Venice, Verona, [and] Lake Como where I spent about a month, as I was quite sick there. Then we went into Switzerland where we only visited a few places, but those we enjoyed very much. I was delighted with our journey across the Alps. The scenery was grand. We were at Geneva several days and left there for Paris.

Monday, I have a good deal of shopping to do for myself and others and I have had to do it very quietly for I am not strong yet. Yesterday Emory and I went to Les invalids where we saw all Napoleon's old soldiers. We saw Napoleon's tomb and other matters of interest. We both were very much interested in all that concerned the great Napoleon and this visit was a great satisfaction. In the afternoon Emory left me for Chalon where the French army are now encamped. I think he will be very much interested in what he will see there.

In the meantime, Madame Davenport (who has been shopping with me) stays with me. Emory and I thought it would be less fatiguing for me to rest here during the few days of his absence.

I received a letter from you a short time ago and Emory one from Andrew since we reached here. I was very glad to know how you were situated though I think you are a little too near the Indians to be comfortable. I trust and pray that by this time you have been gladdened by the fulfillment of your hope for the last few months and that you are well and happy. I shall be very anxious to get home and hear about you.

We leave Paris this week for London and shall sail from Liverpool on the fifteenth on the *Cuba*. I shall be very glad to get home. Though with all my sickness. I have never been really homesick, so contented and happy have I been with my dear husband, who each day, makes me love more. Give a great deal of love to my dear brother [in-law] Andrew. How much I want to kiss him but you must do it for me. I do long often to see you and when I get home, I hope to show my love more [than] by letters.

Your ever-loving sister, Emily

Emory

Mourmelon, August 3, 1868[24]

My dear little wife:

How is it that away from you I feel again like love making? Certain it is that the days of our engagement are again upon me, and I presume were I to be separated from you for several weeks; you would again consider me as your lover rather than your husband. Engagements have their pleasures no less than married life but then we are slow to recognize them preferring rather to anticipate those of which they are but the harbinger. Those days are now over and in place we have that union of hearts and interests whence flow all the real blessings and happiness of life.

This morning at six o'clock I went out to see the maneuvers, a horse being furnished me for the occasion. The coup d'oeil[25] was magnificent but I saw nothing really new or interesting. General La Boeuf[26] received me yesterday very kindly, and tomorrow, I am to have the pleasure of breakfasting with him and his lady.

Tomorrow there will also take place some evolutions of a corps d'Horse, which will be interesting. This letter you will receive tomorrow morning and as I shall be with you in the evening it is not necessary to write more. I do hope my darling that you have been prudent during my absence, and that you will find yourself in good condition for the journey to London, and thence home. May that wish be to you as the "Touchstone" to health as well as happiness. My cold is much better. My regards to Mrs. Davenport.

Your aff. husband, Emory

Bowen's Office, Batavia, September 2nd, 1868[27]

My darling wife,

I arrived home yesterday, having had, as you know, most agreeable occupancy as far as Rochester. Father met me at the depot and at home I found all well, and all anxious to see you. Maria has not yet returned from Battle Creek, but they are hourly expecting her and James, as well as Sara, John's oldest daughter.

I came out to town this morning to have my teeth fixed which I am glad to say has been satisfactorily accomplished. Have not yet seen Mrs. Root who will have forty thousand questions to ask in lieu of shaming me about the girls as she used to. My darling you have put a stop to that practice. I occupied our old room last night.

Maria[28] is going to New York the coming year; and will be with Miss Haines. I am very glad of the arrangement for she will enjoy herself very much, and will be able to see more of society than at Le Roy.[29]

I shall try to bring her to Auburn with me but cannot till she comes. Louisa and Sara[30] were delighted with your presents as well as Mother. They love you devoutly and think you perfection and was seconded of Willowbrook by several photographs, which ornamented the walls.

In looking around I spied also a photograph of the sweet Emily Martin, which I kissed affectionately just as I retired to bed.

I hope my darling that in a few days you will feel much stronger. September must agree with you and I hope will October. I will be down Saturday. Be a good child and know that you are inseparable from the thoughts of your affectionate husband. Emory

Emily

Key West, October 25th 1868

My dearest Mother,
Emory tells me that he is going down town in half an hour and can take my letter to the "*Florida*" before she sails. I will send you a few lines at least.

I suppose Nelly has given you a full account of our five days in New York, which were most satisfactory to us both [*"both" is crossed out*] all. I stayed in the house and so saw all my friends. Aunty Walsh[31] came to see us quite early and sat with me sometime before I was up. She came again in the afternoon and was very kind and pleasant. The Lindley's[32] also came to see me twice, which I enjoyed very much. Cousin Lily came up from Saybrook and we had two good visits from her and Mr. Hart. Mrs. W. E. Dodge[33] also called on me I was very much pleased with her. You have no idea how pleasant it was for Lily and I to be there together and introduce our husbands to so many of our friends. Only it seemed rather absurd to flourish as married women where we had last been as schoolgirls.

I shall not forget how good and kind Mr. and Mrs. Graham were. Mr. Graham took out state rooms on the train for us; sent the carriage and baggage wagon to us and although the night was cold and rainy, [he] went to the cars with us and helped us in every way.

Nelly told you of our voyage; it was not pleasant but our warm greeting here made us feel at home at once. We are very pleasantly settled here and as happy as possible. Emory is waiting for this letter so with love to all at home,

I am ever, your affectionate child, Emily

PS Emory send his love.

Key West, October 30th 1868

My dear Mother,

My last letter to you was ended so abruptly that it but half satisfied me and as we hope a steamer will go north sometime today, I am going to make another attempt.

I am enjoying my life here very much and am as happy as possible. Although the weather is warm, we do not feel it so very much, for a sea breeze is constantly blowing, which is delightful. Our room has seven windows in it so we can have a constant current of air through it day and night.

We live very lazy lives and are rapidly becoming quite Southern in our ways. The soldiers here tho' they are but few are quite a source of interest to me and my attention is so much divided in the morning between dressing and watching guard mounting, that it takes me an endless time to get ready for breakfast. I am already becoming quite "expert" with army matters. We have two charming naval officers here; commanders Wilson and Eastman.[34] They come up to the post quite often and are a great acquisition to the society here. Next week, the admiral and the squadron are expected, which will make it quite gay for a while.

I think Nelly and Emory will go out to Tortugas for a day or two soon. I am afraid of being too much banged about in a sailing vessel. I expect we shall have a delightful time going to Havana with Capt. Eastman next week.

The moonlight here is very beautiful of course, you know from your Nassau experience how very white it is shining off the coral dust and last night, when we were coming home by moonlight from our dinner, I thought I had never seen anything more beautiful than the views we had of the ocean. The harbor filled with ships and boats rocking to and fro in the moonlight and standing out so clear and sharp against the sky and the shores skirted with palms and other foreign looking trees, which gave a strange appearance to the whole scene. The island altogether is queer looking and is only six miles long, the farther end not being inhabited but covered with a dense undergrowth of bushes and small trees. The population is between four and five thousand, but the society of agreeable people is small as most of the citizens are "conks" or Negroes and are dreadfully stupid.[35] I would not advise any one to come down here for the number for the accommodations are frightful. We have the only pleasant place in Key West, three quarters of a mile from town just on the water and green and fresh as possible. I think I am improving in every way and feel more energy and strength than for some time past. I feel perfectly contented to spend the winter here and try to do all I can for my complete restoration to health so that I can be with Emory in the spring.

Just think, we have no letter from home yet though several steamers are due. You ask if you shall send the things I left in my room? No, I think not! I am not in need of them. We are obliged to send home a trunk of things now as the damp did not spoil silks and gloves and the moths eat the woolen things as they hang in the room.

Good-bye dearest mother, your loving child, Emily

Key West, November 5th 1868

My dear Mother,
We have just this moment received quite a package of letters from home; yours to Emory, and me, George's, copies of Evy's, Father's,

Molly's, etc. and I have been enjoying them very much. I am perfectly delighted that Evy thinks of coming in before summer. How lovely it will be to see the dear little baby. The Indian nurse will be quite enough if Evy can civilize her. We had a splendid chance to send letters to Evy by the Santis [?] to Aspinwall, which will bring them to but two or three weeks sooner than otherwise.[36]

I am glad Molly has had such a charming visit and has seen so many of her friends. She will feel better for it all winter. Lily also writes us of her "perfect happiness" in her home. I am glad she is so pleasantly situated. But before I say anything more, I must thank you for your lovely piece of poetry. Nelly and I were very much pleased with it. It was so sweet of you our dear Mother and I shall keep it very safely always. Mrs. Davis' letter I was very glad to see, for it does not make the judge's case seem so very frightful. I will return it by this mail.

I think I have improved a great deal in the two weeks I have been here and already find myself able to do twice as much as I could at home. The first day or two was very hot, but since then it has been charming, a breeze blowing all the time and we have not suffered in the least from the heat. Indeed, one day this week I wore a thick dress and we had a fire all day. It is considered a great luxury to have a fire on the hearth and we admired and enjoyed it very much. [*Illegible*] home is bright and pleasant and we are all as happy as possible. Emory mourns daily that he must leave such delightful quarters. Time fairly flies here and if the days pass as rapidly all month, we shall be home before you know it.

All Emory knows about the sword was to send the one which was in your closet with his hat in Memphis.

Nelly has told you all that we have seen and done since arriving here. As I will close with dearest love to you in which Emory heartily joins, I hope dear grandmother is better. We have been quite anxious about her, but enough.

Love to all, your loving child, Emily

Emory

Havana, November 16, 1868[37]

My darling wife:

Though the pain of parting with you is so recent, I nevertheless feel richer than I ever did before in giving away to duty, for behind me have left a treasure so priceless that its repossession will give me the brightest anticipation till we meet again.

We left Key West almost immediately after the last kiss we threw each other, and although the wind was after us, the vessel rolled heavily, giving me little comfort in my berth, against which my knees and elbows knocked as if in a vain effort to beat it down. The stateroom too was very suffocating, and then supper added a visit to the lee rail[38]—made my night not very comfortable.

Before light we reached the port, which has a fine harbor as I ever saw—Old fortifications like the Morro Castle guarding the entrance, together with the foreign air of architecture made me think almost that I was in Europe, save only I had not you with me. But this magnificent view I did not see without some inconvenience, for instead of being on deck, I thrust my head through the porthole, and soon received a copious discharge of water in my hair and down my neck. I had forgotten that at that hour it was customary at sea to wash the deck. Having cast anchor and dressed myself, I proceeded to board the *Penobscot*, but my boat men, in the attempt came near running over and sinking the Admiral's flag ship, but as he was moving away, I did not think it necessary to apologize. When announced Eastman[39] was taking his morning snooze, from which I did not hesitate to awaken him.

Breakfast—soon followed, to which, having been so generous to the privy tube the night before, I did ample justice. There we took the Captain's gig, and armed with Nelly's memorandum, we made for shore. The shopping, thanks to Eastman's [re]connaissance, was soon done—oranges, cigars, guava were bought and paid for, and the city generally done up.

The place to me is quite unique, the buildings all very low mostly, one story and scarcely never more than two. In addition to the stores Nelly ordered, I send you a barrel of oranges, which I hope you will all enjoy. The guava also is slightly in excess and tell Nelly when she is eating it that I forgive her not having asked me to pass my dish a fourth time for berries. Captain Eastman leaves here tomorrow night for Key West and will deliver all the things. For you, please accept a hammock for the 17th and a fan for the 29th for Nelly and Mrs. Rawles[40] each a fan of sandalwood, and to "Sep" the major, a box of cigars.

You cannot imagine how sorry I am that you and Nelly are not here, for just now I have learned that the *Maryland*[41] will not sail till 4 P.M. tomorrow, and then what an opportunity to get back! But Eastman will be here again in January, and perhaps before that time. Capt. Morse may be able to make a trip. You must see the place. Eastman is a trump. He has been everywhere with me, and having made him a present of a cigar holder, he desires me to say to you that he thinks a great deal of army officers.

I am now writing in his cabin, shall pass the night with him, and probably go to the Opera. You may think I am very gay but through it all you are ever present. I love you dearly, more than I ever thought it possible, but my little pet as I shall have to conclude this tomorrow, I will suspend the flow of thought, for the present, for fear that the supply of paper will give out, the navy having made no special appropriation for this case.

17th. [Of November] Last night my darling we went to the theater[42] but it was so hot that we vamoosed before the conclusion of the first act and then it being a bright moon light night, we sauntered up and down in part of the [*illegible*] and listened to the music of a fine band.

The ladies turned out in force, and with or without protectors, sat in their volantes[43] during all the music. I stayed with Eastman last night and this morning went with him to visit the flagship and came upon Admiral Hoff. Gen. Rosecrans,[44] Minister to Mexico was on board at the same, so we had a very pleasant time. The *Morro Castle* came in this morning from New York and Eastman, after getting the mail, was going direct to Key West, but a few minutes since we learned of the wreck of the *Star of the West*[45] about forty miles from here, so now he has orders to extricate her from difficulty before commencing his cruise, but he will be in Key West in a day or two.

I got the thread this morning, which is as near what you desired as possible. The *Maryland* sails in about two hours. I hope you will be satisfied, as well as Nelly with the execution of your commissions. Vi I have not seen since the night I left when she was very lonely but was well cared for.

I wish, my pet, instead of having to receive this, I hoped to take you tenderly in my arms and kiss you as I would like but this cannot be. Time here will pass speedily and almost before you know it, you will be restored to me. Remember to take care of yourself. And not be imprudent for this winter should see you rightly restored and then you can go wherever I am ordered. If unmindful of your present advantages, you neglect any opportunity to gain strength; it will only separate us the longer. Be therefore a good girl and get well as fast as you can. My love to Nelly & regard to Maj. and Mrs. Rawles. I send also two cigars for Rawles[46] and tell him to help himself.

I regret the appearance of my letter, but overlook everything save the contents. It will be sometime before I receive a letter from you. Be minute in all your letters and I will also in mine.

With much love, your affectionate husband, Emory

PS There is every prospect of fair weather to New Orleans so do not be anxious about me. Accept a kiss.

Emily

Key West, November 19th 1868[47]

My dearest Father,

Your welcome letter of November 10th reached me this morning and I assure you gave me great pleasure. We shall be very glad to get the letter, which I suppose will arrive soon by the *Cuba.* In regard to the mail steamer leaving Baltimore, there are only two, the *Cuba* and the *Maryland,* one leaving every two weeks arriving the fifth day then going to Havana and New Orleans, returning here on the home trip in about two weeks. We have also two vessels a month from New York, but they bring no mail. A regular mail for Key West is brought to Havana every Tuesday by the line of steamers from New York. Here it remains till they have a chance to send it over, often on the same day by some stray fishing smack, steamer, or schooner. The mail we received last night had been waiting some seven days to get over. No matter when you write or how you address your letters, they come by the first opportunity. We had a mail last night and one this morning.

The weather here is very pleasant, tho' we have high winds all this month which everyone says is the most trying of the year, but still I stand it very well though I know I shall improve more when they cease to blow so constantly. This is the dampest place I ever knew. This morning I found a little leather case in my room all covered with green mold but still it does not seem to be hurtful and I find myself better in many respects than when I came.

We are very happy here (tho' I miss my husband every moment) but we ride, sew, read, and talk and the days fairly fly. Five months away from Emory seem like a long time but I suppose it will end before I know it.

Molly did make quite a long visit, but I suppose she is at home now. Evy's letters interest me very much. Andrew's was very funny. I am so glad they will be home in the spring. What a delight the baby will be!

In the letter you sent us from Mr. Simmonds he says the bust was cut in the most spotless marble and was sent thro' the American bankers in Florence sometime in September so I suppose it may come to you any day. I do hope it will be good and that you and mother will be pleased with our present to you.[48]

Nelly looks as well and has grown so fat that you would be astonished to see her. This letter, my dear Father is not fit to send for I have written it in a great hurry to send by this morning's steamer.

Love to all, I am your loving child, Emily

Emory

Steamer *Maryland,* November 20, 1868

My darling wife:
I have unrolled the little writing case for the purpose of telling you that I love you; that I love the little pet who has chosen to share the pleasure and cares of life with me. We are now steaming up the broad Mississippi and with good luck will arrive in New Orleans about 3 P.M. We left Havana the evening of the 17th, with a calm sea and fair wind. I slept soundly the first night but waked up to find quite a high sea and to experience the disagreeable sensations incident there to. From morning to night, I was sick, and quite contented to be so for nothing but bile escaped me showing how bilious I had become at Key West. I now feel altogether better, in fact like a new man, ready for any emergency.

The passage has been without incident. This morning about 4 we arrived off the mouth of the River and found it a good deal colder than with you. By the way, the cold air reminds me that I left my overcoat, which I wish you would wrap up, and send by Capt. Dukehart to N. O. thence to be expressed to me at Memphis. I fear also that I left the little book of Psalms presented me by your mother, which please send with it. I hope that long before this, shall reach you, Eastman will have delivered my letter with the things accompanying. Unconsciously I find my thoughts drifting back to the spot where stays the one I hold most dear, my precious Emily, and then leaping over time and space, I see her again restored to my arms. Keep up good courage, darling. I pray for you, remembering you at all times when I lift my voice to God, asking that you may be given strength to endure all your afflictions and that in His own appointed time and way He may restore you to health. I love you beyond expression. Give Nelly my love and remember me to Mr. & Mrs. Rawles.

Your affectionate husband, Emory.

PS A short letter, but others will follow by same mail.

New Orleans, November 21st 1868

My pet wife:

A very peculiar expression to make, and one, which you may think needs explanation, considering I have never avowed myself a Mormon. Well my darling, by law, you are my wife, a fact of which is my *pride* to remind you, and then also you are my pet, and as both titles are very dear to me, I thought there would be no harm in joining them. I hope therefore dearest, you will excuse me. I intend you shall have a good mail by the return steamer, which leaves here Wednesday next, and hence have determined till that time to write you daily, but because it gives me pleasure to say anything or nothing to one who loving me, criticizes nothing and welcomes my expression of tenderness.

Last night my first on terra firma since leaving you, I missed you very much, and when supper finished and the papers read, I had nothing left to do but betake myself to my room and retire. I was too lonely to be happy in looking at the photograph in the green case, which stole its way under my pillow, its accustomed place till we meet again. But also, my darling, it was not you with your sweet, winning ways, yet it reminded me of you and with that tried to be satisfied.

I have dropped into a regular nest of friends—Gen. Ayres,[49] Neal[50] & Graham[51] of the Army of the Potomac & Hatch[52] of Wilson's Cavalry Corps.[53] I am having a very nice time, as good as under the circumstances I could desire. The Opera is in full blast, and tonight shall attend it with Ayres—"Faust" to be represented. The weather is extremely cold. Have had to put on winter underclothing and winter suits. Last night had [to] order an extra blanket and use all of my coats. I feel it the more from having previously experienced such mild weather.

I commenced yesterday [the] 20th to read the little testament through by summer, one chapter daily, won't you do the same catching up with me when you receive this?

New Orleans is quieter since the election. The people are getting tired of politics, and will soon devote most of their time and attention to filling their pockets, a very sensible resolution.

Accept now my darling, my fondest love, and a shower of kisses,

Your affectionate husband, Emory

PS I don't expect you to write more than once or twice a week and short at that.

New Orleans November 22, 1868

My Darling Emily:

Before retiring, I must write my pet her daily bulletin, but this time not withstanding thoughts of sadness, for all day I have been sorrowing with Judge & Mrs. Tremain[54] over the death of little Lyman, of which you have doubtless heard. I took up "The World" this morning and read in it a dispatch from Albany stating that on the 17th he fell over the bannisters in the second story receiving injuries of which he died that evening.

What a terrible affliction for his parents! Their pride and joy taken from them in an instant, and with him buried so much of hope and promise. How heavily also must it fall upon Evie[55] and Lily, a dark cloud in their hitherto bright sky to remind them that joy and sorrow must ever mingle together.

The face of the dear little fellow has haunted me all day and my pity has gone out toward all the afflicted ones he has left behind. This morning I attended service at Trinity Church and by previous appointment met Gen. & Mrs. Graham of the Artillery, whom I accompanied to Sedgwick Barracks,[56] five miles out, where I spent the afternoon and dined. They are delightfully situated occupying as quarters a former hospital, which cost the Govt. about two millions of dollars. While I was there, a soldier of his command was brought here, mortally wounded by accidental discharge of his gun. He died before we left for town. But I have already chronicled too much of gloomy news. So, I will turn to other things. I am glad my darling to inform you that the 25th is probably fixed in Tennessee for some time to come. I learned today that the 29th Inf. ordered into the state just prior to the election, has been ordered to assemble at Memphis, and thence proceed to *Texas*—these being two regiments you know.

I thought I more than probable that the 25th would be the one for frontier service, but this settles the matter. I shall now go to work gradually to prepare a comfortable nest for my little bird, when she joins [me] in the spring. We shall both have something bright to look forward to and will be all the nearer to each other for our separation. I long to hear from you, but know I must wait nearly two weeks more.

When do you & Nelly think of going to Nassau? Good night my love—I often feel that I am holding you in my arms. Good night, with a kiss, your affectionate, Emory

New Orleans, November 23, 1868

My dear wife

Withdrawing from the bustle and confusion of this active city, I have now a quiet hour to devote to my darling. How I wish that instead of writing, I could steal in gently and kiss your cheek, take you in my arms and hold you in my lap. Wouldn't it be bliss? Do you know that would it not interfere with the leave I shall necessarily want to go to Willowbrook[57] for you next fall? I would like to run down and pay you a visit about the anniversary of our wedding and this notwithstanding sea-sickness and all. Yes, I would swim over if I could and put Leander[58] to the blush.

Today, Gen. Hatch has been putting me through this morning with a good time out, and with Gen. L. C. Hunt[59] & Mr. Casey[60], a brother in law of Gen. Grant, he drove me down to some sugar plantations, where I saw the interesting operation of sugar making. The cane looking just like cornstalks, trimmed of the blades, is passed between two large iron rollers, under such pressure as to extrude all the juice, which falling in a stream, is received in troughs and first carried into vats where it is cleansed with sulphur, and thence run into a series of cauldrons. As it boils and concentrates it is transferred from one cauldron to another, from the last of which it is run off into large vats where it crystalizes. The surplus liquor is then drawn off and the sugar is placed in Hogsheads in the bottoms of which holes are made to enable the molasses to drain through. The sugar is then ready for market; often brown sugar you used to eat on your bread and butter exclaiming "What tood be dooder" ["What could be better?"].

Toward evening, he drove Gen. Croxton[61] and myself out to Lake Ponchartrain, which we enjoyed very much.

I shall leave Wednesday morning for Memphis, and I shall be glad when I cease to go farther from you.

The quinine I have been taking has made me itch so today that I could hardly keep still. It and morphine served me the same trick after my typhoid fever. I learned the *Cuba* had a very bad passage coming in after leaving Key West. Poor Mrs. Weisels'[62] eyes were more bloodshot than ever and the Dr. was entirely *hors-de-combat*.

I enquired about Nelly's friend Miss Davis but she was not seen. Darling do you yearn for me? I yearn for you awfully. Be industrious and the time will pass quickly. With love, your affectionate husband, Emory.

Emily

Key West, November 27, 1868[63]

My dear Jack,

I was very glad to get your letter and was very much amused at your account of the torch light procession. I have no doubt that you and George did good service tho' the election was not all you desired. I am glad that you like Mr. Rice[64] so much. The little I saw of him before we left pleased me very much.

I am charmed that you can take French lessons this winter. You will find it such a help next summer. I have brought down some French books to read here, but as yet I have not found leisure for it. I am working a sofa cushion for Emory's Christmas present, which keeps me very busy. How very lonely you must have been with Father, Mother and Violet gone from your small circle. Uncle and Grandmother too away. Well, that is a change for Willowbrook.

We have had quite an excitement this week among the men. Last week they were paid for the first time in *five* months, consequently most of them got drunk downtown, some deserted, some refused to obey orders and had to be punished in various ways and quite a number are still in the guard house. I enjoy being in barracks very much. The drills, bugle calls and various services of the soldiers interest me exceedingly.

I am glad the Sabbath School are to have a Christmas tree. I think it is the pleasantest thing for them and it does the people good to get it up. I hope, my dear Jack, that you will write to me often this winter for I am so glad to hear from home. Nothing that you write will fail to interest me. How much I would give to have a good ride on Raider. There are nothing but little ponies here and I would not care to ride them.

Love to all, I am ever, your aff. sister, Emily

3   Christmas in Havana

Emory

Memphis, December 1st, 1868[1]

My dear wife:
Yesterday brought me a mail with your dear superscription on the envelopes. The letters were after the 17th and 19th of Nov. You do not know how glad they made me, for now I may look forward to a regular series. I have already written you once from here but have plenty more to say. Yesterday was the last day of my liberty and yesterday I made my debut before the citizens of Memphis. It happened this way. Grays[2] is sick, that is not very lively and yesterday evening when he should have been present at a Citizen's Dinner given at the Overton[3] to Hon. Mr. Leftwich[4] congressman elect, to respond to the toast the "Army and Navy of the United States" he pled ill health and was excused. The committee then pounced upon me as the officer next in rank, whose duty it was to make the response; I was taken by surprise, a cold chill ran all over me; I begged hard to be let off, but they were inexorable and I had to submit. This finally I did with good grace knowing that sooner or later in life I might be called upon frequently to speak, and why not commence now.

At 10 O'clock, the citizens began to assemble. Many had been invited to a number of two hundred and fully two hundred and fifty were present. Among those were judges of the Supreme Court, eloquent members of the Bar, clergymen and the leading businessmen of the city. The spread was elegant. Two long tables extended the entire length of the hall, and these were connected by a semi-circular table constituting the head. Here sat, in the center, the chairman with the guest of the evening on his right. Just on his left came the Episcopal Minister and then your husband. In this position, I felt too conspicuous to be comfortable. A fine band stood near, which when the minister had asked a blessing, struck up "Hail Columbia, Happy Land" and continued to discourse beautiful music during the dinner. Champagne and Sherry flowed quite freely and soon we found ourselves ready for dessert. When the cloth was removed and speaking commenced Fifteen Toasts were to be proposed. 1st "The President of the US," 2 "The President Elect." 3 "Our honored Guest," 4 "The Army and Navy of the United States." The meeting had been called regardless of party, but I could see that both sides desired their sentiments to be understood, so I resolved I would not conceal mine. Cheers had welcomed each of its three speakers who had preceded. I was perfectly cool and why? The last thing I did before leaving my room was to place your photograph in my breast pocket with your face so turned that you could look directly into my heart where I had resolved you should not see one sign of trepidation. The fourth toast was announced; perfect silence reigned, I rose up, and darling for a few moments I spoke to my intense satisfaction, to the delight of the young officers who were attentive listeners, and to all the citizens present. Frequent applause greeted my remarks and today I have been complimented as having delivered the most appropriate speech of the occasion.

    I ought not to have taken up so much of your time dearest, but I feel even that the ice is broken and that hereafter, whatever may be the circumstances, if called upon to speak, I shall have no fear of disgracing myself. I enclose [for] you the bill of fare, which may interest you. I am not yet in my quarters, which are being repaired and put in order.

Today I have been purchasing furniture—bureau, bedstead, and washstand, walnut with marble tops $75.00. Two carpets for bedrooms $65.00, mattress, with spring, $21.00. 7 chairs $24.00—I want you to decide upon the parlor carpet, three ply, pine pattern, made up $2.25 per yard. Russett, $2.00. The first can be turned and wears longer, I think, than last. Shall I get a sofa or a lounge? I saw a lounge today—very handsome which unfolds and makes a perfect double bed, price $45.00. I also found sets of plates and everything complete. French China, $65.00, ironstone china [$]42. These things need not be purchased till a short time before you arrive, but I want to know your ideas, so that the house may be quite ready for your occupancy.[5] My expenses here are going to be very moderate. $40 per month board at Overton, $10 Servant, & $5 for washing, incidental, $20, enabling me easily to save upwards of one hundred per month. These savings will enable us to furnish our house and start even, and then darling, if restored to health, you will have nothing to disturb your happiness.

Benjamin's[6] cards came today, and I forward them.

With ever so much love, your affectionate husband, Emory

Memphis, December 4th, 1868

My dear Pet, My Emily:

Today I received a great big mail from Key West containing several letters from you, one from dear Nelly, and Mrs. Rawles, and numerous ones from various quarters. It delights my heart to hear from you, but occasions pain when I learn that you are not well. So much of our happiness in life depends upon your restoration to health that I cannot believe that you will not, of yourself, take every needful precaution to attain that end. If Key West does not cure you then you will have to seek other climates and all this time we will have to be separated, when life to either of us is scarcely worth having without the other.

I sometimes fear Key West is not as desirable as Nassau. The cold weather you have had rather confirms this belief I wonder if Nassau is as much subject to "Northers" as Key West. Certain it is they are dangerous to you from their sudden changes and should you not be already much stronger than when you left home it may yet be desirable to pass the rest of your time at Nassau. Nelly will be a good counselor and you can decide the matter between yourselves.

It is too bad the soldiers behaved so badly after payday, but it occurs more or less throughout the army and is in a great degree due to our pernicious system of irregular payments.[7]

I am breaking into my new duties and when I get into my new quarters, which will not be for a week to come, I shall be quite contented.

Do not fear my darling that I shall learn to live without you. Every parlor or home that I enter, arranged by the hands of a loving wife, recalls to me how much of this life's happiness I am losing through your absence. I would like for amusement to carry you upstairs three or four times. Let me know darling just how you are. Are your pains diminishing or increasing? Tell me all about yourself. When settled, I shall be five squares from the Overton making for my meals, thirty squares per day, almost enough exercise.[8]

Please give my love to Nelly & remembrances [to] Mrs. Rawles & the Major. With a kiss and an embrace, your affectionate, Emory.

Memphis December 4th, 1868

My dear Emily:

As Lily says, I am a squeezeist [sic] and would just now like to take you in my lap and squeeze you to my satisfaction. I think of you so much, so constantly that I find a difficulty in writing every two days, and feel my duty undone almost if I do not do it every day—a reciprocation

I do not expect; as it would be too much of an effort for you. Only tell me you love me that I am as dear to you as you are to me and a few words about your health, that is all I want.

I pity poor Alexander.[9] He ought to pay Evy off in his own coin, see only "her" talk only of "she" etc. If he loved babies as I think I might, he would have no trouble. Maria[10] wrote me a long letter complaining that I was neglecting her—that for six weeks I had not written to her, but I am sure I wrote to her from Key West. She says Esther Haines[11] is to be married; that she spent last week with them and that "*She is not our Emily.*" The fact is my pet—I think the Upton tribe think you are just right. R is in the hands of the soldiers and is looking well. My quarters are gradually being put in order and every day when I go to look at them, I think of the time when you will join me and we will be together as happy as two doves. But then I think that we will scarcely be settled before you will be off again for Willowbrook. Willowbrook needs a sensation and Evy is bound to make it. Her "Midge" by that time will be barely kissable, but don't tell her. She doubtless thinks her very [*Here a page of the letter is missing. The concluding page is as follows.*]

If you have occasion to write Bettie Blair[12] tell her my admiration of her now, great as it ever has been, knows no bounds. She shows great elevation of soul to have allowed principle to triumph over blood.

Another company has just been ordered back here, which will raise the number to four, making it quite a respectable command. I sent Nelly her fan and your father his box of cigars, but have not yet had time to hear from them. I am looking around for a carriage so that we can drive about as much as we please. It is a big thing to have two horses of your own. Have written to Paducah[13] about "Max" whose Dora was not half so good as the dear Emily is my loving wife.

Your affectionate husband, Emory.

Memphis, December 6th, 1868

My dear Wife:

That is very good writing isn't it? Good enough even to satisfy your good mother, but I can't keep it up long. I never feel myself thoroughly on duty. Today just as Maj. Rawles does every Sunday, I had to attend inspection. Had myself got up in "grand time"—epaulettes and ostrich feathers when rain set in cancelling the inspection to be made in quarters. Too bad was it not? Not to be able to show myself off in my new uniform. I like to wear it so. Your fondest desires in that respect will be gratified when you visit me in the Spring, for now I have to wear it all the time. Wear it even at the hotel when I go for meals.

It has rained nearly all day, and in consequence the attendance at church was small. It being Communion Sunday, I attended Calvary[14] church. Dr. White,[15] a very pious good man–rector. I attended it that I might, although absent from you renew again the pledges of obedience to God, and remembered you, as you doubtless did me, in my prayers.

Tonight, Bishop Quintard[16] administered the rites of confirmation and preaches a sermon. As I am anxious to hear him, I should attend this evening. You remember Mrs. [*Here text is missing. The subsequent text does not follow.*] of Providence, when we met at Florence, and again on his way home, with his daughter Emma, at Paris. During his passage he became erratic, grew rapidly worse, and died a maniac almost within a week after his return home. How terrible and unexpected must have been, this affliction to Mrs. Palmer.[17]

I find, my love, that I am writing you almost every day, and for your sake, lest you be tempted to write more than you are able, I will hereafter write but two or three times a week. Almost a month has passed since we parted. We will soon be together and happy.

Your fond husband, Emory

Memphis, December 9th, 1868

My darling Wife:

I intended to have written you last night, but the sudden appearance of the paymaster thwarted my purpose. Tonight, however, I am free and eagerly seize my pen. This morning I rec'd my darling's present on her 22nd birthday, a lovely gift. It was turkey handkerchiefs, [which] hereafter will have a delicious odor, and of course, every time I place one in or withdraw one from the case, I shall think of the lovely hands that made it.[18]

Today, also I secured back my slippers, which are very beautiful. The shoemakers here, however, are very extravagant in their prices, it having cost six dollars to make them up. They will be a great addition to my comfort and I love you for doing so much for me.

Tomorrow I shall move into my house. The parlor and the room above it which will be our sleeping room, have been carpeted and those only shall I furnish, and rather inadequately at that, till you come. I shall be very comfortable, shall read a great deal and if time slips by the way it has for the last three weeks, I shall hardly think you have been absent. My time is very much divided, which accounts for its lapse.

[I] rise at 7, walk up to and breakfast at the Overton at 8, guard mounting at 9, office hours 9 to 10, dinner 2, Battalion drill, 3 to 4½, supper at 7 to 8. Writing letters and reading till 11. So, you see my precious darling, time cannot hang on my hands. I wish for your sake you were equally well situated but as that is not possible, you will be the more anxious to join and stay with your husband in the spring.

I would like to have Capt. Poole's[19] quarters. He is a very nice man and the kind of company I like to have about me. The officers generally I like very well and I am happy to say, there are no hard drinkers. They all too are very glad that I have joined. The post has suffered much from frequent change of commanders; there has been no one to take a deep interest in affairs, and while the discipline has been very fair, the drill has been entirely neglected. Yesterday battalion drill commenced and will continue during the good weather. There is much room for improvement and I am certain when you report for duty from sick leave, you will learn that much has been made.

In the telegram I sent you, I said "ma cher femme" not what they wrote "My dear Emma." [*Here Upton's letter ends.*]

[*The following fragment of a letter seems to fit chronologically here. It has a drawing of the Uptons' quarters along what is probably the Wolf River Lagoon in Memphis, to the far left. The quarters are separated from the river by "Promenade St." and a row of blocks that Upton identified as "Soldier's quarters," "Old Navy Yard," and " . . . . . ." Upton describes in great detail the living spaces he and Emily would be occupying.*]

There is as you will see, a double house. We shall occupy the one facing the two streets[20] and Col. Christopher[21] will occupy the other. I give you the ground floor. Our room is exactly like the parlor, another of equal size near the dining room and a second servant's room over the one marked so.

In the upper story at the south end of the hall and with the same width is a narrow room suitable for trunks and a closet. The kitchen will be entirely outside.

I send you the foregoing sketch thinking it may interest you. Think darling, of our being in our own dining room entertaining our friends. Hurry up my dear, I can't wait long!

I shall soon subscribe for a New Orleans paper that I may know how to prepare my mail for the steamer. I wish I could now take you into my arms and give you a good squeeze, but once there, you would curl down and be a contented as Mr. Nap is when in your lap. Give my love, pet, to Nelly, the Rawles, Van Reeds, [*Three other names appear here. They are difficult to read but may be Cornichs, Herricks, and Roemer.*] and any inquiring friends.

With an affectionate kiss, your devoted, Emory

[*The following fragment was probably written in December 1868.*]

to love and caress you and once this separation is over, I don't think you can possibly get away from me again. I did not know till you were gone from me how far our existences had become identical, but now realize it perfectly and what a good husband you are going to come to; for I shall do everything possible to make you comfortable and happy. I am tired of Man's society, and want to experience some of the softening, refining influence of a dear good woman like my wife; ever precious, fond, loving and true.

Nelly, I think will be delighted to again see her native soil. She has been very good to you my dear and we must reward her for it. George[22] has commenced a correspondence with me and I shall cultivate him.

All the Upton tribe were well at last accounts and also the family at Willowbrook. Dodge still continues with me, and not withstanding his proximity to New York, I get letters from you about as often as he does from his wife. I don't think she is playing the Christian part to say the least. I know that in his case, I would not suffer myself to be abandoned, but fortunately I am *not*. I have a dear good little wife, who appreciates her husband's happiness and would make any sacrifice [to] insure it. Some women however have no heads and the man is to be pitied who has not the sense to discover it before he marries.

Now my darling with this last letter to you by the mail goes my heart full of love, tenderness and affection for you. It cries for its mate and will not be solaced till its darling arrives to make it happy. Goodby my Pet; with the prayerful hope that you will come to me soon, Your increasingly fond and devoted husband, Emory

PS My regards to Dr. & Mrs. Kirkwood.[23]

Memphis, December 11th, 1868

My darling Emily:

I do pity the poor man so. There he is in a large house all to himself with a parlor containing but a round table, a half dozen chairs, an étagère. The walls are staring at him, no pictures, no thousand and one interesting articles, which a wife could add to his comfort. What a pity it is his lovely wife can't be with him. She would make him so happy! Such, I may suppose are the remarks of the ladies who may know my situation.

So today, my love, I left Capt. Poole's hospitable, comfortable quarters and move into my own. By the time you come, they will be as pleasant as possible, but just now having a cold snap and not as yet being adequately heated, I am suffering slightly from the cold. Last night I anticipated a new luxury-that of sleeping on a board bed. Before this, I had used Nelly's mattress and to keep warm, had to lie on it as stiff as a board and as straight as a sardine. But last night, I was disappointed. Notwithstanding, I slept under three pairs blankets of the heaviest description. I had to curl myself up in fact, get out one of your knots[24] and then could barely keep warm. The cold spell will be over in a day or two and then my situation will be very comfortable. Mrs. Christopher[25] makes the same complaints.

Drills are going on and soon recitations in tactics will begin. Between these duties and others pertaining to the command, I have scarcely the time to write even to my pet. But she always had the lion's share of my thoughts and attention. I am sorry I cannot do anything for you for Christmas, but for your present, when you return to me, you may select a large chromolithograph either for your own room or the parlor. Your sleeping room you will like very much. It is just large enough to be cozy, and every night, as I retire to it I look all around to see if by chance you may not be there. But it can't be so. We will soon turn a very important point in our separation. December [is] past—it is no longer next year, but this year that you are to return to me.

Not next May but May. The days will grow longer, spring will come with its birds and flowers, and in the midst of their songs and perfumes, my love will fly back to me, mutually happy to be in each other's arms.

The Societies of the Armies of the Cumberland, Ohio, and Tennessee met in Chicago on the 15th were it not that I had traveled a little this year, I should attend; the RR fare being reduced one half. Wilson[26] [is] to be there, whom I would like to see very much, but the expense now that I have a wife would be too much.

Sorry to say, [I] did not think of Benjamin on his wedding day. Sent Ball, Black & Co.,[27] check for $80.00 to purchase Miss Fish's present and rec'd reply that the article sent could not fail to please. Benjamin is permitted to delay joining his battery till further orders—a well merited privilege. His prospects may not be so bad after all. Molly writes me on the 15th that your mother is still in New York and that she believes Throop's[28] engagement with Miss O is broken off. I have not heard a word from him. Vi[29] is very lovely and she came to take up her quarters with me till we get to keeping house she will be a genuine elephant. Both of us till that time, will have to go out to take our meals.

You will hear much bugling when you get here and I am trying to raise a band. Wouldn't that be pleasant? It would be almost always at our post. As time wears on, do not, my dear pet, forget that you have ever been in my arms but think as holding you closely to me, and petting you with my usual tenderness. Be a good girl and don't forget to tell me of your health, for if you keep silent of course, I assume that you are not improving, and perhaps getting worse. Tell me everything for you know darling, how deeply I sympathize with you. With a fond embrace.

Your affectionate husband, Emory

Key West, December 13, 1868

My dearest Mother,

Your lovely birthday gift comes too late for me to tell you how much I was pleased by it, but if you had been home soon it was put into use, you would have been sure you had sent me just the thing I most wanted for I really needed a book rack.

On my return from the Tortugas, I found your letter from Saybrook awaiting me, which I was very glad to receive for I was anxious to know about your visit to New York. How pleasant it was for you to take your Thanksgiving dinner with Lily Hart[30] and Aunty and I have no doubt they enjoyed it very much and spared no pains to make the dinner worthy of the day. So, you did see Mrs. Birnby [?][31] again before she sailed for Europe. I should like to see some of her accounts of what she did in Europe, how enthusiastic she will be about everything. I am glad she is going. How much Violet will enjoy all she sees in New York. I know she will be a great comfort to you while you are gone she is so companionable and appreciates all that she sees and hears. I am glad Aunty is better from Lily's account when I was in New York. I feared she was not as well.

I have not heard from Emory since he reached Memphis. My last letters were from New Orleans; indeed, I have not heard a word for two weeks. A steamer from New Orleans has been due for the last five days but no trace is yet heard of it. It is a great discomfort to hear from my husband so seldom when I have nothing to do by think of him in the interval, but one month is now gone and the other will have an end sometime.

We are having quite cold weather just now and as I took cold coming from Fort Jefferson, I have not left the fire in my room for the last day or two. The wind blows so constantly here that I take cold very readily, yet I am much stronger. While at Fort Jefferson, I used to walk round the breakwater, nearly a mile each day besides other shorter walks.[32]

Our visit to Fort Jefferson was a very interesting one and I shall not forget many things I witnessed there. It is a perfect prison. Alone in the ocean and one cannot but feel whenever they go outside how completely the isolation is. The only communication with the world beyond is thru a little schooner, which if wrecked, no one would know of for some time. Mrs. McElrath,[33] whom we stayed with, we liked very much. She is a true lady in every thought and action and made our visit very pleasant.

I must dear mother, content myself with a short letter tonight. With fondest love, I am your loving child, Emily

Memphis, Dec. 13th 1868

My dear Pet:

It seems peculiarly appropriate to write to one's nearest friend on a Sunday evening—how much more then ought a husband to write to his wife, his better self, bone of his bone and flesh of his flesh? I set it aside as a peculiar privilege to enjoy that of communing with you on a Sunday, after all the duties are done. The hardening cares of the world are set aside, and thought in all its purity is allowed to flow till the object toward which it is directed comes into view, even into your very presence. Even so it seems to me that now you sit beside me, so vivid through memory are all your ways and acts. But when I look around cheerful as is the blaze on my grate, I discover a void, for you are not here, you are far away, perhaps sick and suffering, and I have no means of relieving you, no way of cherishing you save by oft-repeating the love I give you, the sympathy I feel for you. But in Providence, let us hope that soon again we may unite, no more to be separated till it shall please God to call one of us home and then through his grace may it be into his presence, to enjoy his glory forever.

This morning I attended Calvary Church, Dr. White, Rector. His sermon was on "Transubstantiation" heeded, I doubt not, by some of his congregation who perhaps are wavering between the Episcopal and Romish faith. A short time since one of the Episcopal ministers in city, of the High Church School, went over to Romanism because [he was] not allowed to carry out his notions in his church. His apostasy created quite a commotion and now with all the energy of a proselyte he is endeavoring to draw others over to his new love.

Could all the high church believers in the Episcopal Church slough off and go over to Rome, they would do the church service and perhaps restore to it that depth and fervor of worship it so much requires.

The military duties of the day were Sunday morning inspection and dress parade. At inspection the condition of the men is not only looked to, but their quarters are also. The hospital is visited, and the general condition of the entire post is looked into. There is one man in the hospital who I fear will not recover. Should you regain your strength, you will not be at a loss for doing good to the command. I am certain that the visit of a lady to the hospital to read tracts, and to show some Christian sympathy, they would do much to cheer and comfort the patients. Military discipline seems devoid of sympathy, and the best of officers are liable to forget this man, with all his interest temporal and spiritual, in the military machine, whose sole duty is to obey orders.

I have had a stove put up into rooms off the parlor and now am no longer troubled with cold. My servant, a colored boy "Ruben" is very attentive to his duties and falls readily into my ways.

Tomorrow we commence the study of Tactics, and your husband will have to be a student equally with his brother officers.

This evening, at Capt. Estes'[34] quarters, I shall listen to some sacred music from Mrs. Pettit,[35] a widowed sister of the Capt. A young Lieutenant is reported to be sweet on her, but I find her over more to be admired than anything else.

Tell Nelly I love her a great deal and that when we get settled, I shall claim the execution of my punishment and insist upon her making her home with us.

Had a letter a day or two since from your father, he was well and very glad to get the cigars. Your mother had not yet returned from N.Y.

Six years ago, today was the bloody Battle of Fredericksburg. How differently the two days have closed—the one mid the flashes of musketry, and the war of attrition, with ten thousand killed and wounded stretched cold upon the plain, or writhing in their agony; the other with a bright sun, the very symbol of peace and happiness. Good night my darling, I press you to me, and kiss you, hoping that you are improving and happy.

With much love, your affectionate husband, Emory

Memphis, December 15th, 1868

My dear pet:

Today I read your two letters of Dec. 1st & 2d and enjoyed then most thoroughly. I am very anxious at all times to hear from you and the more so that I do not know the state of your health. But to this perhaps it is not best too often to allude. Your walking pleases me for when there is no physical reason to prevent you most certainly gain strength by it. A want of exercise leaves all muscles in a weak relaxed condition, the contrary strengthens them and the whole system. Dr. de Cosson told you when you might and when you ought not to walk. The fact therefore that now you are able to take some of that exercise, gives me some encouragement, and I hope you may continue it if not detrimental to your health. Take good care of the cough; are you not careless in dressing? Do you keep your under clothing the same? Remember that it is your duty to watch yourself, and not to rely upon others to do it for you.

A calendar month, my darling, has passed since our last kiss. One twelfth of the time that was to separate us, soon it will be a third and with January past, and the spring near at hand, we will not be for long separated. But I do miss you. Everything is at hand to make you happy were you here and well. Our house can be made a perfect little home. Several ladies have visited our room and pronounced it very cozy. The view both up and down the river will be a source of constant delight. All the steamers pass in sight and look very majestic as they round the point above and come into view. Mrs. Christopher & Mrs. Estis and Mrs. Pettit all visited me today and sympathize with me over the absence of my better self.

I keep as busy as a bee, the battalion having my constant attention. All the officers and the ladies are delighted to have a field officer over them, and it would please you to see already the improvements made in drill and discipline. When you come to me, you will have duties as well as myself to perform. We must keep up a kindly, sociable feeling at the post. You are right—on not taking up any one's quarrels at Key West. Let each party pour their complaints in your ear but let them go no further. Follow old "Shakes" "Take each man's censure, but reserve thy judgment."[36] I am glad to know you have gone to Tortugas as I know you will enjoy it. Enclosed letter from Alex,[37] love to Nelly. Goodnight darling (I haven't had tea yet) I love you and press you fondly to me. Your devoted husband Emory.

PS Keep the studs & coat.

Memphis, Dec 17th, [1868]

My dear wife

I enclose you two letters—one from dear old Dr. de Cosson and the other from your good father. The Dr. seems to be enjoying life and the entire group keeps fit and all come as vividly before my mind as if they were actually here.

Your father seems particularly delighted with the bust; and after what he says; I ought to feel ashamed of ever having felt so poor as to regret the involvement. But at that time there were several things to worry me and I did not know how to make the two ends meet. My financial condition being flourishing, I am most heartily glad that they have. If you want, it is better than any portrait or photograph. Two thousand years hence, this same bust may be exhumed from mighty ruins and then antiquarians reading the name will puzzle their brains perhaps over who was the husband of so noble a woman with such a classic face. I shall send Simmons[38] a good letter quoting from your father.

Yesterday rec'd your first letter from Tortugas and was delighted to learn of your visit there. Hope you thoroughly enjoyed it and saw more of life there as the contracted spheres of Key West. I am now commencing at the foundation of drill and discipline being restored to have a command after my own heart.[39]

Tonight, is the opera and I am *going* but absolutely alone, one ticket and I will [have] no idea who will be my neighbors.

The weather still can at times, be awful. The river is full of floating ice, showing cold weather farther North. A gentleman from Wisconsin told me they had the thermometer 20 degrees below zero. Your slippers and *Newton's* dressing gown[40] make me very comfortable. Have bought a lounger, making in case of emergency, a double bed, which for experiment I slept in last night and I pronounce a success.

Now, my darling what shall I say of you. I love you and I miss you more and more each day. I grieve over your absence from me at a time when everything could be afforded by me. Four months and a half only separate us now. Have you heard of Alice Martin's[41] engagement? *Confidential*. But of course, tell Nelly. My kindest regards to Maj. and Mrs. Rawles and as you are now back at Key West. When you write to Tortugas, remember me to the officers and ladies of that post. Goodbye darling with an affectionate kiss. Your devoted husband.

Emory

Memphis, December 19th 1868

My darling Emily:

This being the tenth monthly anniversary of an event in our memories, I thought I would write you though I did so by last night, to let you know how dear you are to me and how much happiness is yet to flow from our union consummated on that day. Just think my dear, almost a year we have been husband and wife, each everything to the other and with our affections, strong as they were and have been, still growing stronger. I wish that you could be here tonight then, I might kiss you and expressing fond sighs for you, but I must possess my soul; a patience waiting for the happy day when I shall see you again.

Your letter of Dec. 4th from Tortugas came to hand today. It delighted me to learn that you were enjoying yourself so much. The want of privacy you complain of at Key West is rather exceptional. I am quite sure we shall be as private in our household affairs as anyone could desire.

Baldwin[42] seems to be a privileged character, but were he under me he would have to deport himself perfectly or he would soon feel the hand of authority. Drinking disgusts me and when it has once fastened its hold upon an officer, he loses all self-respect, all honor, and sooner or later must go to the dogs. Fortunately, at this post, there are now no hard drinkers; on the contrary, all are temperate.

Today Dr. Tremain[43] and his wife returned to the post. Have not met her but am told she is a very nice lady. Mrs. Christopher is very pleasant, also Mrs. Estes.[44]

The recitations in Tactics are very interesting to the officers and all seem to enjoy them, credit that the post is improving, which I trust is true. Babcock[45] and Porter[46] will arrive here tomorrow and I shall make them my guests if possible. They will give me a great deal of news. Molly sent me the enclosed account of Benjamin's *wedding*, which will prove interesting.

Do you remember my cousin Geo. Randall's[47] marriage in Buffalo about a year ago? He is a Captain in the 4th Inf. I hear that the poor fellow has just lost his wife, who died in childbirth or shortly after. Please remember me to Nelly and believe me,

Your ever-devoted husband, Emory.

Memphis, Tenn. December 21st 1868

My dear Emily:

I am so busy that to even write to you, I have to seize the first spare moments that present themselves.

Babcock and Porter arrived yesterday and came directly to my house where I am entertaining them. We talked so long last night that you were cheated out of your Sunday letter, but doubtless you were thought of fully as many times as if you had been present. I found myself dreaming about you in the night. You complained of being cold, snugged up to me, I placed my arm under your head and then you vanished. But I appreciated even that short enjoyment of your presence and now only hope that the time is coming when we shall know no further separations.

From all accounts, they had a very jolly time at Chicago. More than two thousand officers assembled and as they had not met many of them since their last battle, they were disposed to drink several healths [sic] and became very hilarious. Seats were prepared at the banquet for 1750 persons and the toasts required about thirty responses. But before the speech making commenced so many gallant solders were placed "hors de combat" through the careless popping of champagne bottles that the speakers could make no impressions. The noble fellows could contain themselves only long enough to hear the toast announced and cheer the speaker as he arose when talking and immoderate laughter would break out all over the hall.[48] Porter told me that in about four years, they would try to fix him at West

Point. You know I don't want to go there till you can enjoy it, as otherwise I would have no pleasure in the position.

I enclose you a letter from your mother. Her letters are treasures of love and information. They all seem very delighted with the bust. So, Comstock[49] & Betty Blair[50] have arranged matters at last. Their visit will be an event for you to look forward to with interest.

Goodbye my darling. You know how much I love you. You go with me in all my rides and walks, even in drill. B and Porter send kindest regards.

Your affectionate husband, Emory

Memphis, December 23rd, 1868

My dear little girl:

Today I received two of your sweetest letters; one the last you wrote at Tortugas, the other just after your return to Key West. They seem to have drawn me closer to you for they made me feel more strongly than ever before that I am a necessity to you. By nature, you are loving, constant and confiding. You need a tender care and a strong arm to recline on and if I fill that measure I am only too happy. You are dear good girl, a lovely woman, a noble wife. Ought I not to be a good husband to you, my love? And dear Emily, I always will, beyond inclination before I married you I resolved that nothing I could do would ever make you regret being my wife and I shall ever love you tenderly and watch over you as a shield. I wish I could take you now in my arms and hold you, or at night—feel that for love and protection you had drawn closely to me nestling with sweet confidence on a breast where you may ever find repose.

At night, when I retire, the fire burning brightly in my room, I think last of you, wind my watch, place watch and purse under my pillow, then kiss the photograph and place it with them. My mind then rambles and before I drop to sleep I have to wind myself in my sheets so reclusively so cold and bachelor like, that I almost revolt at my condition. The fact is darling, it is bad to be brevet wife or husband.

Babcock and Porter left yesterday for Little Rock. They enjoyed their visit very much, and so did I. It is very pleasant to be able to entertain ones friends. I was sorry to hear of the state of affairs at Tortugas and you may now realize what a great influence either for good or evil a commanding officer can exert. Your storm must have been frightful and I am only too thankful that you got off as well as you did. You can now, at least, say that you have experienced a storm at sea, although you couldn't quite see it. I wish when you reply to this you would give me "Naps"[51] opinion of Fort Jefferson. I am very glad he is with you and sympathize with him in his seasickness.

Vi and I don't harmonize very well. She has an aversion to me because I chastised her severely whenever she gives herself to the performance of any "Nap"oleonic tricks on my carpet and then my complaint against her is that she is destitute of affection, and prefers Reuben's'[52] society to mine, howling vociferously whenever he leaves her.

Our weather here still continues beautiful, although just now it is cold. Your cold snap was simultaneous with the coldest spell we have had yet.

I am very sorry that you have caught another cold. I wrote you some time since that I thought it might be advisable for you & Nelly to go over and remain at Nassau. That place may be more exempt from northers than Key West. Time *ought not* to be lost. In a large hotel with many new faces, plenty of good society, you might be more contented than at Key West, and the time would probably pass even more rapidly. Remember, my dear, how much depends upon healing your cough. Every cold sets you back and if a Southern climate does not benefit you, you might have to try Minnesota. From what you now write me, I wish we had gone to Nassau in the first place. It cured

Molly[53] and more wonderful still, Gen. McMahon,[54] who had had repeated hemorrhages. If you make up your mind to go, don't stop to write to Willowbrook, but go at once as you have the necessary funds. I shall write Nelly tonight. Keep up your courage, and above all, be careful about catching cold. How much would I not give to see you my darling but absence will only make us dearer when we meet. I am glad you are back to Key West and hope better weather for you.

With much love, your ever-fond husband, Emory

Memphis, December 24th 1868

My Angel

When all I can do for you is to write I ought not to fail in a duty, which gives us both equal pleasure. I love to write to you, for loving you; sweet thoughts ever fill my mind and draw you closer to me. I wonder how it will seem when I have you back again to pet, kiss and caress as long as I desire. I know now that you take to it right kindly and so would I. In my letter of yesterday urging you to go to Nassau, I said nothing of the unpleasantness of your situation, which you alluded in your letter. I did all I could by argument and example, but with little success and therefore was entirely prepared for your statements in regard to it. Should you go, which is still my opinion and desire, the letters to you & Nelly of yesterday should be sufficient explanation for your action. With your sensibilities, your situation may become harrowing and should be avoided; besides in going to Nassau, we shall both feel that as much has been done for you as can be in a Southern Climate.

Next fall you must return here by the 1st of September for from that time till Jan. the weather is beautiful. January & February only are bad. I have confidence that you will yet be a strong woman. I can't believe anything else, I have faith that we shall yet come together and with you in good health, be as happy as two mortals can. Tomorrow is

Christmas. The last I believe I spent, I know I spent at Willowbrook, being at the time a brevet member of the family. You are now stronger than you were then and believe the next Christmas we shall have a still more favorable report.

I enclose you a letter from Henry.[55] He has professed religion, the twelfth of the children and there only remains one son, Parley the eldest brother. God has indeed blessed my parents and given them in this life the reward of the careful training they have bestowed upon their children. To Susan,[56] who is an earnest good Christian may, under the grace of God, be ascribed much influence in bringing this happy result. Good night my darling—you are ever in my thoughts.

Your loving husband, Emory.

Memphis, Christmas 1868[57]

My dear wife

A year ago tonight I could not call you by so dear a name, although with bright anticipations, we looked forward to the time when we should be one in feeling, interest and thought. These anticipations have been realized; my then Pet became my fond loving wife, the being in whom center all of my affection and happiness. We can now see how each could desert fathers and mothers, brothers and sister to cleave to the other our better part. (Our signifying one). How beautiful is our relation, each the complement of the other, and both our whole—One harsh, the other gentle, one ugly, the other beautiful, one worldly the other spiritual. I wish I could take the embodiment of what I call good into my arms this pleasant evening and talk to her even till she might become weary; to feel her weight, once again upon my lap, and receive a kiss from her on my forehead.

The day with me, barring your absence, has been quite pleasantly spent. Attended church at 11 A.M. and dined at Col. Christopher's, Major & Mrs. Floyd[58] being invited. After finishing my letter, I am to go to Capt. Estes where there is a small entertainment, which will conclude the day. The men all had a good dinner, turkey, oysters, plum pudding & mince pies all in abundance. They, no doubt, appreciated such a change from the ordinary corn beef and hard tack. I am anxious to see Jan. 1st. It will seem to bring you nearer to me. I almost feel certain that once more in possession of you, you will find it very difficult to get away from me again. Yet, next summer you will have to go home to see Evy and to this, I will give a reluctant assent provided you come back within two months. Christmas is celebrated in Memphis with fireworks, and by the way, someone presented you today a chromolithograph, a facsimile of the little pups you gave Lily a year ago. I want you, darling to knit a tidy[59] for my lounge. It is very pretty now, and I don't want to soil it.

Accept a kiss my love, and a fond embrace from your devoted husband, Emory.

Memphis, Sunday Dec. 27th, 1868

My darling Emily:

For two-or three-days past, I have felt that peculiar yearning feeling for you, which you have so often experienced toward me when absent from you. I feel that I must have you back and would give the world for one kiss from you, or to feel the soft touch of your cheek against mine. Your ways are so tender and gentle compared with mine and you are so lovely altogether when contrasted with my harshness that I miss you fearfully. I think my love that you are just right, you are my idol and I truly adore you. Wouldn't I go on my hands and knees to [do] anything for you? Wouldn't I pick you up in my arms and run up stairs with you as if you were but a feather? I wish you could but be with me again and you would see how broad, how high, how deep is my tender love for my fond devoted wife. Just opposite to me my love sits Gen. Ayres who is reading Caesars Commentaries,[60] and who breaks out whenever he sees anything which strikes him forcibly. He is here en route to Arkansas to investigate the troubles between the State Militia and citizens,[61] and will remain till tomorrow night. Babcock and Porter will probably return tomorrow and will go on to New Orleans.

This morning, I attended Calvary Church and had a very pleasant service. You would often be in my thoughts; which I must say I encouraged, as we did not have a particularly good sermon. It is a great pleasure my dear, to write you, to give you thoughts, good or bad, knowing that you will receive them with charity.

Christmas passed very quietly and New Year's will be the same. I have made a few calls, and when the day is over, shall make my plans for 1869. That year, I pray God may restore you to me in good health, and witness a marked increase in our usefulness in the World.

Keep up good courage darling, and I will make up your present lapses by increased devotion and love. Gen. Ayres sends his kindest regards and regrets that he does not find you here.

Ma cheri, je vous baise sur le front; les yeux, les levres, la menton et le cou, aussi je obliesai pas votre nez. [*Translation: "My dear, I kiss you on the forehead; the eyes, the lips, the chin, and the neck, so I did not obliterate your nose."*]

Votre affectione Emory

Key West, December 28th, 1868

My dearest Father,
On our arrival here last Sunday, I found among my letters two from you, which I need not assure you delighted me especially as they brought me tidings of the bust. It seems so long since I had seen it that I began to fear that it would not make its appearance. I am just delighted with your account of the bust and now feel repaid for the long many hours I spent sitting for it. I think you will now agree with

me that a bust is really more satisfying than a picture on account of the many views one has of the face. Mr. Simmons[62] was anxious to do himself credit and I have no doubt he has done his best.

I was very glad to get the letters you sent me from Mother and Evy. Nelly and I were so much behind in family news owing to the delay in the mail that we had a perfect feast when it did come.

I have so much to write you of our visit to Havana that I do not know where to commence and shall have to reserve the greater part for some library talk. It was indeed a perfect success, tho' at times we feared we should not get home as soon as we desired. You know we went for five hours and stayed four days. Nelly wrote Throop how we happened to go and how very pleasant it was for us to visit Havana with our friends the McElraths.

Wednesday, we spent exploring the city, which is without doubt one of the strangest places in the world and as thoroughly as foreign as tho' it were in Africa instead of so near us. The homes are queer enough most of them but one-story high and the windows all barred like a prison but the strangest thing is to look in the rooms as you pass by and see in them the carriages, stand perhaps just by the dinner table, they dive right in, take out the horses and leave the "volante" standing at one side of the room, none of which are impeded being marble or stone. In the center of the parlor is a large font around which are placed in a hollow square, rocking chairs of all sizes. Here the ladies are rocking themselves using their tongues and fans with great dexterity until evening when in the lovely dresses and Spanish reels, they drive in their volante, stopping in the squares to listen to the music, which is playing in all quarters of the city.[63]

We received a great deal of attention from the officers of the *Gettysburg*[64] some of whom came for us each day in their boats and devoted their time to showing us the curiosities of the city, which as you may imagine was a great kindness to us being strangers and not speaking the language. We also did a little shopping but as all our money had to be changed to gold, we tried to be careful and resist the many lovely things that met us on all side. You know the stores here are celebrated.

Wednesday night, as the steamer did not leave on account of the storm, we went out to the city to see the place by lamplight and hear the music, but as the night was not pleasant and we missed hearing it we contented ourselves with driving about and going to the circus. We returned to the ship as the Capt. wished to sail early the next morning but on awaking, we found the norther so severe that our steamer would not live in such a sea. The waves were frightful and the wind was increasing, so we made up our minds to another day on shore, which we passed much like the others, visiting the places of interest and seeing at every trip, things new and strange. It was altogether very interesting and will afford us subjects of thought and conversation for some time to come.

Nelly has written you how we spent our Christmas,[65] so I will take up the visit at Saturday, which we spent in rather an unsettled state of mind, not daring to leave the ship and yet uncertain of her going for the storm had left the sea so high that we dared not venture out of the harbor. Therefore, when the Admiral came out to see us and invited us to go out on the *Gettysburg*, we were very much pleased and relieved for Capt. Clap admitted that he might be in Key West the next day or it might be several [days].

We were in Havana at a very interesting time. We were not allowed to leave the city as the insurrectionists were fighting within five miles and we could see the pickets on the surrounding hills. The city was full of soldiers a shipload arriving from Spain while we were there. Christmas was the day fixed upon for entering the city and therefore everyone felt excited and expectant but the rebels were not as successful as they hoped so we left them in about the same state.[66]

I must write to mother. So, with many wishes for a happy New Year and with a heart overflowing with love for my dear father, I am his very loving daughter, Emily

Memphis, Dec. 29th, 1868

My lovely wife:

Yesterday I rec'd two letters dated the 15th and 17th, which as soon as placed in my hands, I could not refrain from pressing to my lips and kissing—kissing often as I have you, my angel. Can you imagine how welcome they were? When I read that you had walked down to Mrs. Hinds,[67] I exclaimed Bravo! And when you said that you felt decidedly improved and that your cold was much better, I was too happy for anything. You have been, as a rule, too silent in regard to your health. I want to know how your lungs are and whether your other complaints are better or not. Your ability to walk rather inclines me to believe that your general condition is better, but fearing that you had not improved. I have been very anxious that you should go to Nassau.

You and Nelly are very kind in remembering Mrs. Rawles on Christmas. Her sadness did not escape me. I can assure you, although I said nothing about it, I do hope R. will reform.

Yesterday, I rec'd an order detailing me on a General Court Martial at Louisville, which convenes Jan, 6th. Several officers are to be tried; among those is the Major of the 2nd Inf. who is now up, I believe, the third time for drunkenness. It seems when whiskey has once gained the mastery over an officer, his fate is as certain as a man on the rapids of Niagara. They plunge regardless of advice or fear from one excess into another until brought before a Court Martial, their career is terminated by being cashiered. This end sooner or later is reached by all, gallant service and firm efficiency may tend to avert their doom, but patience finally gives way, the law is given its say, and after fair trial, they are cast upon the world, often penniless, and with a character ruined for life.

The overcoat came today and with it a most gratifying surprise. The cushion is just lovely, and when I unrolled it in the presence of Gens. Ayres, Porter and Babcock they were unanimous in their praise of its beauty and fine combination of colors. You are a sweet little girl to work these for your husband and while he loves you all he can, he is not unappreciative of these efforts of yours to prove your love to him. I wish I could give you a good hug to which, I fancy, you would submit with good grace, considering my strength.

Porter and Babcock returned from Little Rock this morning and left for New Orleans at 3 p.m. Ayres left at 3 for Little Rock, so I am alone. Col. Christopher, my neighbor in our double house is on the same Court Martial as myself and Mrs. "C" is quite exercised over her approaching separation. We shall probably be absent two weeks. I send you, darling, a piece of Nettie Haines wedding cake. I think you ought to reciprocate by sending me some of Marcus Huus[68] and then we could bury the memory of flirtations we both struck up in the "winter of our discontent made glorious summer" when I took you in my arms in the "back car" Nov. 17th, 1867. This is not all from Shakespeare but you will comprehend the sense.

We have rec'd orders to make estimates for building a six-company post; which we will be ready to occupy about the time your return to me. The Colonel's quarters will be very comfortable four rooms all on the same *floor*. In addition, there is a bathroom, dining room, kitchen and servants room. Won't Mistress Upton have a snug little house?[69]

My love, how I miss your kiss every time I go out for the day and when I return. Could you only welcome me I would be happy, but as I enter my quarters, a bright fire and a lamp only show me how desolate my house is. Vi, who is getting to be a beauty gives me a short greeting and then goes to gnawing a bone or stretches herself before the fire. I kiss you a thousand times over,

Your devoted husband, Emory

4 Emory to Memphis

Emory

Memphis, New Year's 1869

My dear wife:

My heart this morning is with you at Key West and from its innermost depths wishes you a Happy New Year.

The day has not dawned very brightly upon us. For days we have had rain, fog, and mud, the kind of weather I was afraid to have you encounter, but we have the satisfaction that it can only endure for two or at most, three months. In the meantime, we shall have long intervals of sunshine. *This* year my "hearts life" is to join me, and were it policy, I would make out a list [of] months, weeks, and days which must elapse before that happy moment; but I fear that so doing it, would only delay the time.

I more than yearn, my dear darling to see and pet you. I need your sweet influence. I want someone to say "dear" to, but she will come soon and then how full of joy will be our cup. Emily, I do love so that I am not reconciled to simply say so on paper. I want to impress it upon you by a thousand visible proofs. Wouldn't I kiss you? Wouldn't I press you closely to me if I could but have you with me at this instant? You should lay your head upon my shoulder and sit on my lap as quiet as a mouse and as long as it pleased you.[1]

In a short time, Capt. Poole and myself will start out to pay our New Year's calls. The circle of our acquaintances is not long, but we shall enjoy them very much. With you, I suppose Key West will generally tire out. Would you be surprised to see E. Upton walk in tonight? The officers and the ladies of the garrison have invited themselves to the commandant's quarters, where they propose to have a festival—hardly festive for I haven't even a cracker to offer them a good time. I regret that my love is not here to do the honors, but will do the best I can under the circumstances.

Please give my love to Nelly. Write me long letters, they always interest me and give me in your absence the only real pleasure I can receive.

With a heart full of love, your affectionate Emory

Memphis, January 2, 186[9][2]

My dear Emily:

I have been scarcely good for anything today, tired and sleepy from the effects of yesterday's dissipation. Shortly after finishing my letter to you I started out with Capt. Parkinson[3] and Lt. Madden[4] to make our New Year's calls, and being poor, instead of "riding in chaises," by places we walked.[5] The streets were in a terrible condition, mud about six inches deep and smooth enough to reflect your face. One of our calls was upon Mrs. Bainbridge, formerly Miss Easterly of Auburn.[6] She is a very fine-looking woman and is considered stylish in Memphis. Before leaving the house, she took us to see her baby, a prenupt [sic] production in her past—considering she was married a short time after the Willowbrook wedding.

In the morning, Capt. Poole and Mrs. Pettit proposed that the officers and ladies of the garrison should assemble at my quarters on the evening and have a Happy New Year. It being incumbent on a Commanding Officer to provide the happiness of his post, I could not object to the program, so the post string band was sent for and shall I blush to say it—there was dancing in your house. The refreshments were of a recherché[7] order—4 dozen sandwiches, cider, almonds and raisins & coffee. I felt like apologizing for the quality of the sandwiches but they disappeared before I could frame the necessary excuse. There were present Col. and Mrs. Christopher, Capt. & Mrs. Estes, Lt. & Mrs. Conway,[8] Maj. & Mrs. Hugo,[9] Mr. & Mrs. Morris,[10] Mrs. Fitch,[11] Miss Choat[12] and her fiancé, Capt. Parkinson,[13] Capt. Poole, Lts. Huston,[14] Madden[15] and Kyle.[16] While the musicians were at supper, we had a game of Blind Man's Bluff, which all enjoyed hugely. Dancing then was resumed and lasted till 1 A.M. General Granger[17] and Mrs. Sherman of New York firm of Duncan Sherman & Co.[18] were present. The latter will stop at Key West and darling, lest he should represent that I wore too beaming a countenance, I will tell my love that nearly every moment my thoughts are with her who should have been the hostess. I send you Wilson's[19] speech made in Chicago. It may interest you. I am anxious for letters. Your mother seems anxious that you should try Nassau and I hope ere thus you are on your way. I am afraid that your large airy room is the cause of your frequent colds. Act with judgment and do what you and Nelly consider best. Two months at Nassau might do wonders.[20]

Your fond husband, Emory

Emily

Key West, Fla. Jan. 3rd 1869

My dearest Evy,

I cannot let the first Sunday of the New Year pass without sending you a letter even tho' it is a short one. Nelly and I have not written to you as often as our hearts prompted, for without letters home and to my husband, our hands are very full and Mother writes us. She sends our letters to you and Andrew. We received your letters just after Christmas and were very glad to get them and hear all about yourself, dear Andrew and the baby. Nelly and I, much to our surprise, spent Christmas at Havana. It happened in this way. Several days before Christmas, Major and Mrs. McElrath[21] and several other officers came over from Fort Jefferson, Dry Tortugas to go to Havana and we went with them expecting to stay only one day. Instead of that, a violent "Norther" kept us in the harbor for four or five days so we had a good chance of seeing this strangest of all old places and I assure you we improved the time.

The old town, you know, was walled and outside of it is the new city, both of which we explored quite thoroughly, finding at every step, something to amuse and interest us. The quiet houses of the people only one story high with an immense front door through which they take their volante, which is left standing in the hall of the dining room while the horses are taken into the court beyond. Then [came] the pretty women with their Spanish veils, riding in the evening in their volantes, with their servants in such gay liveries [postilion]. Indeed everything was as strange and foreign as tho' we were thousands of miles from home.

Our visit was a great success. We dined on Christmas aboard the *Gettysburg*, one of the gun boats stationed at Havana, which we enjoyed very much as the officers were all very pleasant and we had known them at Key West. In the evening we were invited aboard the Flag Ship where they had a little entertainment. Admiral Hoff we found a charming old gentleman. He was very polite to me and called on me the next day on the *"Alliance"* and offered to send us back to Key West on the gunboat. Upton had been making him a visit a month or two before, on his way to Memphis. We had a very pleasant time coming back to Key West on the *Gettysburg*. The officers gave us their rooms and did all in their power to make the voyage pleasant. I only wish Emory could have been with us, for we all enjoyed ourselves very much and a great many funny things happened. I was most able to endure the fatigue and excitement of going about than during any of my time and was astonished to see how well I bore the exposure for I came home very well tho' for the last few days, I have not been quite as well. As I have a little cold, and am tired a little from the gayety of last week when the officers of the *Gettysburg* were here and we had two parties besides their being here most of the time.

Did they write you from home of the arrival of my bust? I am glad it is good. It was Emory's vanity not mine. I think it was the most satisfactory present I could bring mother and now I am so glad your darling baby looks in some way like her aunt Emily. I think it is sweet of you to say so. I would give anything to see her as well as yourself my darling sister and shall not be able to stay away from home when you get to Willowbrook. You, my dear sister knows better than anyone else the trial it is to me to be separated from my dear husband so many, many months especially when the cause is ill health. I have at felt at time as if I could not bear it and it takes all my courage to be contented and patient.

Emory writes me what a nice command he has, the post of Memphis with four companies and he is as busy as possible making up for lost time as the men have suffered much neglect during his absence. He has a nice house, six rooms, some of which he had already furnished. The others he will leave for my return. Do you wonder [why] I feel ready to fly when I think of him alone and know how much I could do for his comfort were I with him. But I am really much better than when I came down here and hope to return to him in the spring much better. I find it takes about all my time to write to Emory and my other correspondents suffer. My great trial is the mail, which come so irregularly and seldom on time. I did not hear from Emory or from home for three weeks. Good night my dear sister with love to Andrew and yourself and a kiss for my dear niece.

Believe me, your loving sister, Emily

Emory

Memphis Sunday Jan. 3, 1869

My darling Emily:

The duties of the day are all done, so with nothing to disturb me I have arrayed myself in mother's dressing-gown and my wife's slippers and have seated myself for a chat with my dear absent wife.

The day has been perfectly beautiful, more like April than January. After inspection I went to Calvary Church and attended communion and then at the Altar of God, as you once did for me, I offered up my prayers for you, my darling wife. I hoped at the same time you were receiving the communion at Key West. I feel now more and more that each time the sacrament is partaken that my sense of duty to God and my neighbor grows stronger and stronger and I hope ere long to have that clear faith which possesses true Christians.

This evening we had a dress parade, which was largely attended, but the assemblage was very promiscuous. People love to look at soldiers and had we only a band, the first people in the city would be glad to attend. Mrs. Norris desired that I should remember her to you. She is a very sweet woman and is always glad to welcome officers and their ladies to her home. Her husband is cashier of the 1st National Bank and both are nice people. Mrs. Pettit, Mrs. Christopher & and Mrs. Estes are also anxious to be commended to you. The fact is very clear; I have talked so much about you that they all are very anxious to see you. Evy,[22] I suppose is busy making her preparations to come east. With the uncertainty of Alexander's being ordered in, I believe she will repeat the step. I hope she is acting on his suggestion for I am sure I would not like to be abandoned in such a place.[23]

Tomorrow Col. Christopher and myself start for Louisville to be gone possibly a month. Your letters please send as before to Memphis.

I am exceedingly anxious to hear from you, your last being Dec. 17th. You have doubtless the same feeling toward me but you have the consolation that you know I must be well. I shall be prepared at any time to learn that you have gone to Nassau and I shall be rejoiced there at. I want to hear that you are improving. Your mother too is anxious to have you go to Nassau.

With a heart full of love, your affectionate, Emory.

Memphis January 4th 1869[24]

My dear Pet:

I am soon to leave for Louisville and have time to write but a few words before I go. This morning I rec'd a letter from your father stating that he had telegraphed to you to go to Nassau if you thought best. I instigated the telegram about the same time I wrote you & Nelly so strongly to go and I hope now you are on your way. I am only sorry that it will make our mail communications less frequent but I trust the benefit to your health will more than counterbalance all such considerations.

My darling you do not know how much I pity you for having to go so far away from me when you are not well, but if your health is restored, think of the pure unalloyed happiness that is still in store for us. You have not yet tasted the happiness of married life. You have been in so much pain that your thoughts instead of going out to others have been turned within yourself and you have quietly suffered. But this we will hope may not continue. Nassau will do wonders for you and soon your abundant spirits will make a whole household happy. Let this be our last separation and to this end avail yourself of every opportunity you now have.

With ever increasing love for my dear wife, her affectionate
Emory

Louisville, Jan 6th 1869

My darling Emily:

Yesterday I received your telegram of [the] same date, which was forwarded to me from Memphis. I was delighted to hear from you, to know that you were improving and that you would go to Nassau. This letter, my love, I direct to you at Nassau and now my hopes and spirits are again at high tide. Key West did not do for you what we had anticipated and the fears of a separation next winter were so great that I could not remain quiet till I knew you were at the spot where Molly and Gen. McMahon received so great benefit. I begin to feel now that you will be restored to health, but I have been very discouraged by the frequent colds you caught at Key West. I think your large room had much to do with it, and while I am about it, I think the whole house was bad, the wind penetrating and passing through it from all directions.

Now from Nassau I want you to write me minute reports. You will be out of these damaging northers. You will have society, and I doubt not both you and Nelly will enjoy yourselves more than at Key West. Dressing will not harm you. I think it does a lady always good to dress and see herself looking well. If the effort be too much then remain quietly in your room.

My honey, I feel that the time is coming when I shall have you with me and all my calculations of happiness are based upon it.

I arrived yesterday in this city and shall be here about a month. Had you been at Memphis, you might have lost me for a month, so you may deduct that from the time you have to remain away from me. Col Christopher and myself are comfortably located in a good boarding house, room lights & fuel for $10 per week. The board is better from our days experience than that of the Louisville Hotel.[25] Tomorrow we commence our trial and as you are not with me, I care not how long this lasts, but if you will keep it to yourself, I will tell you that I do love you awfully. Je vous aimes du tant mon amour. Vous ete si joli, si charmant. Je ne puis pas vous aime assez, ma petite, ma chere femme.

[*Translation: I love you so much my love. You are so pretty, so charming. I cannot love you enough, my dear, dear wife.*]

My love to Nelly. Write me long or short letters as suits you best. Your slightest favors are thoughtfully received. Please present my kindest regards to Dr. & Mrs. Kirkwood and thanks for their kind offices to you. I love you darling and can hardly wait for the time when I shall again take you in my arms.

Your affectionate husband, Emory

Louisville Jan 15th 1869

[*no salutation*]

Tis two months tonight my darling Emily since our last kiss, since with a sweet wave of her hand I last saw my Emily. But there is great comfort in knowing that I shall possess her and that if time will but pass like the last two months, she will soon be with me again.

I have just come, my precious one, from the theater[26] and even then, I have learned the solemn duties a husband owes his wife. The last scene was tragic, and showed how a true woman, churched, broken hearted, could die of grief—forgiving in her last breath the husband who had forsaken her. It secured to me that no husband could witness the play without forming a good resolution, and how sure I was, darling, that never in my life would I give her, who has surrendered to me herself, almost her very soul, one word that would cause pain, one look that would cause grief. I have darling wife, to let thoughts of you to engross my mind, and tonight as Col. Christopher, who invited me to go to the theater, asked me to point out my style of beauty, I told him I could not for there was not even an approximation to it. It was in Nassau, and in the person of my wife. Well Emily, you are mine and soon, how happy your loving hands will make me.

Today the court adjourned over till Monday. I can't tell when we shall get through, as our last case may be tedious, but I am very anxious to get back to Memphis. Then my days are so divided up that they pass like the wind, while here, they sometimes drag. Most of the members of the court are married and I heartily sympathize with them in their desire to return to their families.

It is almost twelve o'clock and I love darling, each night to fall asleep thinking of you. Sometimes you come to me in my dreams, but only to tell me how much I lose in your absence,

With many caresses my little pet.

Love, devoted husband, Emory

Emily

Key West, January 17th, 1869

My dearest Mother,

It is now several weeks since I have had a letter from you but Tuesday when the *Maryland* comes I shall expect to see your dear writing and find one of your good letters. Our letters telling you of our determination to remain here were quickly followed by others throwing a change of plans. Tho' I did not like to think of Nassau where I first started, yet I now am perfectly willing to go there, indeed am very glad for we have waited in vain for a change and improvement in the climate of Key West, which one and all day is different this winter from that of times past.

I do not feel as tho' I improved fast enough for the changes [in the weather] are so sudden. The climate is damp and the Northers so frequent that I often lose one week all I have gained in weeks before, which is quite discouraging. At Nassau I think I shall not have as many disadvantages to struggle against and doubt not with what I have gained here. I shall make rapid improvement. A change always seems to do me good. Aside from this I am tired of Key West and feel relieved that the next three months will be at some other place where new scenes and people will interest me for time passes rather slowly down here and I feel often very impatient to get home to Emory.

I suppose Lily has by this time returned to Albany and you are once more alone. I send you back Mr. Marsh's letter, which I was very glad to see. I wrote to Mrs. Marsh last week. I am very glad that you were able to send Mrs. Marsh something for her school. I was so anxious to do a little at least to help her.

Have you heard of Mrs. Wood's arrival in Europe and where she is at present? Nelly has written father all we are doing so I shall not send you a longer letter tonight. I am feeling better than at the beginning of the week and shall take great care of myself till I start [for Nassau]. Nelly joins me in love to all at home, not forgetting Aunty who I hope is well this winter.

Your loving child, Emily

Emory

Louisville, Sunday, Jan 17th [1869]

My dear Emily:

Last evening, I received five letters from you of Dec. 31st, Jan. 2nd, 3rd, 4th, & 5th and after reading them I must confess I felt very blue, for I had counted upon your being now in Nassau. It seemed that time had gone back to Nov. 15th when I heard that you would not arrive in Nassau till Feb. 8th, for I had anticipated for you so much benefit during Jan. Feb. & March that I thought you might with safety leave Nassau the 28th or 29th of March and join me early in April.

But I shall not allow myself to be despondent over it, for you may have gone to Nassau by the Coast Survey Steamer[27] and even if not, your health may have improved as rapidly at Key West as I would have at Nassau. A time table of the Nassau Steamers sent me from New York informs me that the steamer for Nassau leaves New York

Jan. 28-Feb 25 & March 25th and from Havana Jan 9th, Feb 6th, March 6th. I shall not count upon definite information as to your departure till the steamer of March 6th. If it is not prudent to come by the steamer March 29th then by all means stay in Nassau till June 1st and go to Willowbrook where I will meet you.

From the tone of your letters, I believe you will act with the best judgment—that is, you will follow Dr. Kirkwood's advice whatever it may be. I had hoped the mail communication with Nassau might be oftener [sic] than once a month and I think by sending my letters to the American Consul at Havana, I can at least give you a mail by the Havana steamer on the return trip. You ought not to be at all anxious about me; you know that I must be well; that it would be scarcely possible for anything to befall me, and that I am as happy as any husband can be who loves his wife and she, absent from him in ill health. I don't now call you sick, my anxiety being in regard to your progress. I shall write to you as often at Nassau as heretofore, but you need not write to me oftener than every three or four days, unless, as with me, you find it a pleasure and a quick way of passing the time. But one word, my darling can express my desire to see you. I am famished, I am hungry for your love.

Time in Louisville does not pass with me as at Memphis. There I have responsibility; there my hours are divided in various duties, and fully occupied. Today I attended morning service at Christ Church and after it dined with Gen's & Mrs. Swords[28] at the Louisville Hotel. After dinner attended afternoon service at same church, after which walked home with Gen. Crawford, 2nd Inf[29] and took tea with him returned to my room a few minutes ago, re-read your letters and am devoting the rest of the day to my pet.

Had I her with me, I should not have to look to other means to pass the time, but absent like Mrs. Christopher the two husbands have to wrack their brains how they may spend the day. You will feel the absence of my letters as since Jan 5th, I have directed all to Nassau save a short one apprising you of the fact. You will find a big mail awaiting you, which I trust you will enjoy, but like me, I suspect you would prefer the letters drop in one after another, rather than all in a lump. I think, my darling you will find it very pleasant at Nassau.

I am a little anxious to know why you and Nelly speak so decidedly against Dr. Storrow.[30] Did he show ignorance in his profession, or was he not as honorable as society demands? His letter had nothing to do with my telegram, which was based upon your statements that you were constantly catching cold.

The overcoat arrived safely and is a great comfort—right for Memphis climate. The Court Martial I hope will adjourn this week for I want to go home. I shall send this letter to Nassau but shall write two or three and send them care of Capt. Dukehart[31] to Key West.

My love to Nelly. I am not so blue and feel all right. I wish I could caress you and call you my pet.

Your affectionate husband, Emory

Louisville, January 18, 1869[32]

My little Pet,

The uncertainty of your movements makes me anxious to get to you as many letters as possible, so for the next eight or ten days, I shall send every other letter to you care of Capt. Dukehart. If you go over to Havana on his steamer, he will deliver them to you, but if he finds you gone, then he will mail them to you at Havana. If this plan succeeds you will get these letters before the January mail from New York, so I will repeat what I sent in my letter of yesterday that I received the day before, of your letters of Dec. 31st, Jan 2nd, 3rd, and 4th. Others will follow them, but I am sorry you will not receive more from me till you arrive in Nassau. I believe darling, that you are really growing stronger and give myself hope but it does not do to anticipate too much for the disappointment is not so pleasant. One thing I feel certain of, that with my consent, you will never again pass so long a time away from me. But you ought to see how philosophical or stoical I am in bearing as compared with Cols. Swain[33] or Christopher who are separated from their families but for ten, or three weeks.

I dined Sunday with Gen. and Mrs. Swords and upon showing her your photograph she asked me if you did not endure your pain with great patience. I told her most assuredly yes! No incidents occur here to make a letter interesting. Every day is the same. The weather is not cold but the streets are in a sloppy condition.

The Court tomorrow arraigns the Collins case.[34] He is charged with having drawn mileage for servants where he had none with him on his journey. A week, I think, will finish the case, and will heartily rejoice, for I want to return to my duties at Memphis. I received yesterday a long letter from your mother. She says your father has appropriated you $2,000 for furnishing your house. I think he has done enough for his worthless son in-law, who like his brother officers, should be made to live on his pay and take good care of his wife at that.

I kiss you fondly, my pet and wish you every possible happiness.

Your devoted husband, Emory

Louisville, January 19, 1869[35]

[no salutation]

I wonder, my darling wife if writing so often will have the effect of making you think my love too cheap? At any rate, this being the 19th, I will write, if for nothing else but to remind you that I remember its significance and especially the fact that in another short month we shall have been married one year. All that one being can be for one other; you have been for me my wife, my [illegible] self.

Last night Col Christopher and I strolled around to the Minstrels and some of the comedians were so good that I can't refrain from repeating them as you always appreciate a joke. One darkey says to another, "Sam, how long does a beautiful young widow wear mourning for her husband?" "Brother Bones, I gives dat up." "For a second, Sam." The audience did not comprehend it for a moment and then roared. Another, "Why is a cat the most musical of animals?" "Because she is chock full of fiddle strings." I have now at least the authority for using the expression "Soured on me." "Gus, says Sam, I lost my sweetheart the other day, Miss Lemon." "Miss Lemon, how did you lose her?" "She soured on me."[36] The performance closed with some dissolving views, which were wonderful. One was the Custom House at Venice. How vividly, my Pet did it carry me back to the time when we looked upon it from our apartments in the Hotel Barberi, St. Marcs, the Doges Palace, the gondolas, all passed before me in an instant.[37] Then I could fold you in my arms, but now alas, I cannot.

Maria wrote me a letter in French, which I received today, and I answered using two sheets of this notepaper. I shall have the means now of keeping up my French and am very glad of it. My love to Nelly, and darling what shall I say for you? You are the joy of my life, my beloved Emily.

Ever fondly your, Emory

Louisville, KY, 19 January 1869[38]

My dear sister,

I received your letter from 11 January today and I eagerly welcome your tacit proposal to conduct our future correspondence in French.[39] It is the only means that I can increase my knowledge of this language. Military officers should know, at least, two or three foreign languages—the French language in particular because it is the language of the courts and a great deal of military literature is in French. I have often regretted that Emily can't speak with me. But in spite of that, we can write to each other always in French and we will gain from it a very precise knowledge of the grammar and of the spelling.

Your letter has been forwarded to me from Memphis to Louisville where I arrived a few days ago. At present, I am a member of a court martial, a very disagreeable duty since an officer has been charged. We must declare his innocence or guilt. The accusation is very serious and once established will terminate his commission.

It is beautiful weather here, like April. But don't think that we haven't had bad weather. The snow and the mud have made the roads very difficult, very disagreeable to cross, but today the sun shines and everyone is happy. After the last news from Emilie, she is feeling better, but I'm not happy about her progress. After personal observation, I fear that the climate of Key West is too humid for her illness. This is why, on January 4, I sent her the following telegram: "Whether or not your health is making progress go to Nassau. Don't delay." I hoped that she would go by steamer from Havana on the 9th of January but she has not had the time to make the preparations for such a voyage, so she is still in Key West. But she and her sister will leave from Key West the last day of the month and will take the steamer to Havana from 6th of February for Nassau. On their arrival, I don't know if they will stop at the hotel[40] or at the home of Dr. Kirkwood,[41] a friend of their family. It is regrettable that there is no communication with Nassau except once a month, but aside from this objection, there are advantages that weigh well in her favor, good climate, etc.[42] If her health is better she can join me in Memphis the first days of April but on the other hand, I wrote her to stay in Nassau until she is as well as she can be, and it is possible that she will not leave there before the first of June. And then she will return to her home at Willowbrook where I will hasten to meet her.

I love her and I am sad in her absence. If you see Mrs. Parsons, nee Haines[43] would you tell her that I received the invitation to attend her wedding a few days after the date and that I want now to offer to her my congratulations and wish her a happy life. The news of our siblings was welcome. God will protect them. Would you, my dear sister, give my respectful regards to Miss Haines and [*illegible*].

Your loving brother, Emory

Louisville, KY Jan 21st [1869]

[*no salutation*]

Now my lovely Emily that you are not to receive a mail from me but once a month, I feel I have an excuse to write you almost, if not, every day. For as you have done sometimes at Key West, you may when you get lonely, take my letters out to some quiet place and then sift from them some crumb of comfort. My great fear was just as I became engaged how can I write Emily Martin as often as lovers are known to write, but as time passed on I soon discovered that love was the living spring whose clear pure waters supply the murmuring brook. My pen could not hesitate but was skillful in a thousand ways to paint my love for that dear girl who has since become the [*illegible*], the comfort, the very essence of my being.

Do I find it difficult my angel, to write you daily? As well might you ask the Sun if he ever got tired of shining? My love for you like his rays radiates into all space, but its splendor you cannot perceive save through the narrow crevice of a monthly mail. Never mind, my darling pet. You shall soon have a nearer view and then won't I make you happy? How many times will I take you in my arms and commence those kisses which love to dwell on every feature of your lovely face. I am going to be good to you, very good. I am going to give you a rest; and anticipate your every want. You shall lie on my bosom and as you hear the beating of my heart, you shall say it knows no thought—save duty to its God and love for the dear sweet girl who has given it her whole confidence.

My dear, sometimes I vary the time of writing you, and this letter is the commencement of the day. I usually write you in the evening, but I love to write you at any time. Nothing at all is transpiring. We are going on with the Collin's case and hope to finish it this week. I shall try to get one or two letters to you though the American Consul at Havana. You must let me know every opportunity there is of reaching you.

My love to Nelly. Your ever fond, affectionate husband, Emory

Louisville KY Jan 22nd 1869

My darling wife:

I am engaged now-a-days in providing for the comfort of my pet when she shall join me and to this end am economizing as much as possible. Yesterday, I bought her a nice four seated, light-bar coach so that when she comes to Memphis, she will have at her disposal a good carriage for herself and friends. It is not exactly new, but is not soiled to an extent that damages it, and I got it at a great bargain. To pay for it will require my January & part of my February pay, but I can spare it easily. I think I have done very well in a pecuniary way since leaving you.

As Army people, our parlor is well enough furnished and so is our bedroom. Our dining room furniture will not be very expensive, and then there is the spare room. I don't think I shall do much more till you arrive except I would like you to tell me what kind of dishes you desire, so that should you write me by the March steamer that you will join me in April, I may be able to get our mess in working order before I go to meet you in New Orleans, so that when you alight from the 3 O'clock train you may sit down to a good dinner. Say whether you want Chinaware or Ironstone China. It is economy to buy the best. The two carpets we still need you will have to select for I want them to suit you.

My health is excellent. Our court is drawing to a close and I shall expect to get away from here Saturday or Monday at latest. My stay has been very pleasant and when I am again ordered on Court martial at Louisville if you are with me I shall take you along. I send this letter to the Capt. of the Steamer *Eagle*,[44] hoping it may reach you sooner than via N. Y. To you then, has doubtless been a big break in your mail, because I sent all my letters to Nassau after Jan 4th so don't think, my pet I have ceased to love you, for you will find some very tender words awaiting you. Write me, my precious wife a good long letter by the time you arrive at Nassau and enter minutely the condition of your health.

With ever tender and increasing love if that be possible and an affectionate embrace, your fondly devoted husband Emory.

Louisville, Saturday Jan 23rd/69

My dear Emily:

I received yesterday your two letters of Jan 6th & 8th and was glad indeed to learn you were getting better. From the tenor of all your letters I infer you are getting heartily tired of Key West, and will be delighted when you get to Nassau where your surroundings will be more in accordance with your tastes. Your disgust with R[45] is no stronger than mine and my opinion is that he will be brought up with a second time before he knows it. By his drinking, he has made enemies at his post who will not hesitate to prefer charges the moment he gives them the occasion. I am disgusted with drunkards and having remonstrated with R to the best of my ability, if he now falls, I would not feel like lifting my finger to save him.

I enclose you a letter from Julia Benjamin.[46] I see she signs herself Julia *K*, instead of Julia F. Benjamin. I wonder if you were in advance of the fashion in dropping your Mrs., dear little girl. Your reminder of a remembrance to Betty Blair came yesterday, just after I had made raise to pay for your carriage, but the thing is eminently proper to do, and Monday I will send a draft to Ball and Black[47] and let them select. I don't believe I could find anything pretty in Memphis or Louisville. Everything I have done thus far has been on my pay & by 1st of March I shall be just out of debt. My settlement with the Appleton's[48] takes place the 1st of Feb. I do hope there will be enough to pay Torbert;[49] but fear it will have to run on for another six months. But this gives me new uneasiness for had I been a businessman, he would have accepted five hundred as soon as a thousand dollars for his reviews, and now he must wait for the book to pay him.

The Court will probably adjourn today and I shall be glad of it. Have had a very pleasant time, but cannot be happy without you. Memphis has greater attractions—more to do etc.

My dear pet I do hope the 1st steamer from Nassau will bring encouraging reports. You do wrong not to tell me more minutely how you are. I am left entirely in the dark whether you suffer most from your cough or other troubles; this ought not to be.

With a heart full of love, your affectionate husband, Emory

Memphis, Sunday Jan 24th 1869

My dear Pet:

Bless your heart. I have just received your two letters of Jan 10th & 11th and am glad you are recovering from your last sick spell. You take our separation no harder than do I, for to my own mind, I simply exist, my ingenuity being directed solely to devising means to pass the time.

I returned with Col. Christopher at 3 P. M. today from Louisville; Col C. to go directly home to his wife and a repast specially prepared for him, I to turn my face from my quarters and go to the hotel for my dinner. When I came back, Vi did all she could to supply your place, overwhelmed me with caresses, and capered around the room delirious with delight. The faithful Reuben was also on hand with a warm welcome and all the officers seemed pleased at my return. The house is as pleasant as ever and I know you could not but be happy were you with me to enjoy it. Not knowing anything of your present condition, I am in a great quandary how to act or to advise you about your future course. *You* have said nothing to me about a visit to Willowbrook next summer, yet I know you will want to go, now taking this and your health into consideration what shall we do? If you come to me in April you will go north the latter part of June; if you stay at Nassau till June, you will return here early in August.

I am revising my Tactics, and when completed, which will be about June, shall ask to be ordered to Washington to lay the changes before the Secy. of War. I shall then try to get an order placing me on special Duty—say for two or three months to superintend the printing, and ask authority to make Willowbrook my Hd. Quarters. If you come in April we shall have to commence and break up housekeeping, the expenses of which will necessarily be great. If you go directly home and we pass the summer there together when we get ready to return, my finances will be in a splendid condition and we shall set out in life in earnest. Your father has done so much for you that my self-respect will soon be involved if I allow him to do more.

But my darling, money shall have nothing to do with the question of our separation. If Dr. Kirkwood shall be conscientiously of the opinion that you will not be the better for remaining at Nassau till June, then by all means take the steps to join me early in April, which is said to be a delightful month. I only mentioned the subject of housekeeping as it might tend to reconcile you to the decision of Dr. K should he say you ought to stay in Nassau till June. You must know, my darling, that I am as anxious as a husband can be to have you with me. A bird in the hand is worth two in the bush. When in Europe, although I said scarcely anything about it, I yet felt morally certain that we would not be together in Memphis this winter & if you do not join me in April, who knows when we shall settle down in life.

Your carriage and horse I bought for you will be down from Louisville this week. The horse is not pretty, has a white face, two white feet, and is a dark chestnut, but he beautiful under the saddle and although ugly, you may have him for the same reasons that you do your husband, because you think him good.[50]

This is perhaps the last letter you will receive by the steamer of Jan. 28th, but I shall try one or two via N. O. I am sorry you have been disappointed at Key West in not getting letters from me but it will be made up at Nassau. I enclose a letter from Mrs. Benjamin. I have heard you whistle also and therefore send you a scrap from a newspaper. My health, my love, is perfect. I look as rugged as a bear. My best. Love to Nelly.

Your ever-devoted husband, Emory

Emily

Key West, January 24th, 1869

My dearest Mother,

I think before leaving Key West it is best for me to write about the things I wish sent to me at Memphis as the mail after we reach Nassau seems so uncertain.

Emory writes me that tho' the house he is living in this winter is very comfortable yet as Memphis is to be a six-company post and they are to have new quarters, he will be living in his new house when I join him. Our quarters will be very comfortable; four rooms all on the *same* floor, in addition, there is a bathroom, dining room, kitchen and servants rooms. This you see will be quite a large house and as Emory's being in command, will entail upon me considerable entertaining. I think I shall require all the silver, linen, etc., I have at home. I do not know when I shall need anything more than I will now and I am therefore going to ask you, dear mother, to pack and send my things to Memphis so that I shall find them on my arrival the middle of April and will be able to commence housekeeping as soon as I get there. I send you a list of things I can think of that are at home.

Emory had quite a party on New Year's night; fifteen guests. I do not know how he entertained them.

I am delighted with all that I hear of the post at Memphis and dream and plan a great deal for next spring. I shall enjoy my own house so much and I have some hope of taking a very valuable servant with me from here who will make my cares very light.

I am feeling much better this week and am getting over the cold I took about New Years. I feel assured two months at Nassau will do me a great deal of good and I am anxious to get there.

We were very much shocked to hear of Mrs. Walker's[51] death. How sad for her poor little children. So many people have died since we have been down here it is frightful. We heard from Evy this week. She seemed well and happy. I am very anxious to hear from you dear mother and trust we shall get a letter before we leave for Nassau.

With love to all, I am ever your affect. child, Emily

Emory

Memphis, January 25th 1869

My dear wife:

I must try to get one more letter to you by the Steamer of Jan. 28th, as you will have to wait a long time for another mail this month. I have been very faithful to you having written you nearly every day, but this you know, never tires me as it is a labor of love.

Memphis is the same as when I left and the post move on in the same old way. I shall pitch into matters en guerre and lose myself if possible. The days I begin to count and while they pass rapidly my heart goes out in sympathy to you my dear who have more time than

I to think of your absent mate. But it is hardly possible that you should think oftener of me than I do of you for all day is but a succession of thoughts. Reuben and Vi are my only company, & Vi has become so demonstrative that I have forgiven her all her former coldness. Just this instant she has time to kiss me.

I was sorry to hear that Nap was sick. What has become of him and did he grow ugly as he grew older?

Maria writes me that she has received charming letters from you. I like to have you write her often in New York. She finds little genuine sympathy; in fact, she begins to believe the world to be heartless.

You cannot imagine darling pet how anxiously I shall await the first Nassau steamer. Will it or will it not tell me you are to come to me soon? With me there could be no time to either of us so great as your absence, and my love you may come whenever Dr. Kirkwood gives the word. You must present my warmest regards to them for their kind care of you. It will be delightful for you at their house and I wish we might reciprocate it someday.

With many kisses, your fondly loving husband, Emory

Memphis Jan 26th 1869

My dear dear wife:

This letter I shall try to send to you via Havana so that you shall receive it there. I rather think you will get all of your back mail there, at least if Dr. Kirkwood should think to send it to you. I have been very sorry that you have not received any of my letters at Key West, but you know I had good reasons for sending them to Nassau, and they will afford you a treat when you get there.

Your letters from Havana I shall await with great interest. Perhaps they will tell me when my bird will commence her flight to me. Be assured, my pet, I have not the heart to say no to any project—looking to an early reunion, unless it shall undoubtedly appear to you and your medical advisor that you should stay away longer. It seems to me that my heart is drying up, a lease with you absent I have no happiness and I look forward to our meeting as the commencement of a new existence. How everything with us will change there. I shall again be responsible for the happiness of another whose love will infuse new life and new energy. To make her thoroughly happy will be a sufficient object; and then she will give me that peace and contentment which in this life can only satisfy the soul.

You need not fear my going to China,[52] unless with such a magnificent offer that it would be folly to decline, and then I most assuredly would take my wife. This winter's separation is enough to satisfy us both for a long time to come. I am quite sure I will not let you go next winter and if it be necessary, I will sooner apply for duty for a year or two in New Mexico. I must now go to my office for an hour and will then finish my letter.

The weather here now is perfectly charming—almost like May at Willowbrook. I rise early to take my breakfast and always breath the fresh morning air. I hope, my darling, the time may come when you will enjoy with me long walks. You shall have a carriage to ride in but there are many times when it is more pleasant to walk. [*Here Upton's letter ends.*]

Memphis, Jan. 27th, 1869

My darling Pet:
This is the last letter I shall expect to get to you by the Str. *Eagle*, and I shall send it to Havana, care of Capt. Greene.[53] I received yesterday your letter of the 17th, and perceive that there has been a break in your letters, some of which I have not received. Yet I am satisfied as long as any of them tell me you are getting better. Poor thing, you have had to wait long and hopelessly for letter from me, but when they come you will find a host [of them]. You ought to give them into the hands of the

P. M.[54] with instructions to deliver one to you daily. In this way you might beguile the weary hours away.

I am beginning my love, to look for you the first of April, and shall almost expect definite information to that effect by the return mail from Nassau. But do not make up your mind too positively, so that in case you should receive unexpected benefit at Nassau, you may be able to remain there till June.

We are having the most delightful weather imaginable, warm, sunny, and equable. I have said a dozen times could I have anticipated this kind of winter, I would have kept you with me. But love, we will make up for lost affection when we get together. I begin to think you a model wife, for we have never had a disagreeable word and I now so often learn of jars[55] in other families. To quarrel is decidedly vulgar and I thank my stars that our tempers are so equable that we have more in prospect.

Last evening Mrs. Hugo, wife of the Adjutant[56] gave a small party, which was very pleasant. The last thing I did up in my room after I put on my uniform was to walk to the mantel piece and kiss your photograph, which hangs on the little bracket you gave me. My lips no sooner touched it than it fell right over toward me as if pleading mutely for you to come to my arms. Do not, my darling, remain away longer than is manifestly for your good. I am just infatuated with your bust. I am sure now from the photograph of it that the present was appreciated. I only regret that I should have been in doubt about it when in Florence, but my darling you know there was a concurrence of circumstances to make me very blue at that time. I keep the photograph over the mantel piece in the parlor and look at it very often. I wish you would collect all the likenesses of yourself you ever had taken and give them to me, so that they might confront me everywhere.

This morning I wrote letters to Admiral Hoff[57] & Capt. Moore[58] for their kindnesses to you & Nelly. They will receive them the 31st and perhaps this appreciation of their kindnesses may have the effect of dispatching the *Gettysburg* ostensibly to Key West to coal, but really to carry you back to Havana.

Now my darling, about our mails—I have written the Consul at Havana to see if I cannot sometimes get letters to you by enclosing them to his care. He may call to see you on the *Eagle* and will let you know. I think I might send all my letters up to the 10th of each month to him and after that time, via New York. You may be able, in like manner, to send some letters to Havana to connect with the Baltimore boat.

The china sets seem very reasonable, but the bank has been compelled to suspend payment for a few days, but will be all right by the end of Feb. The carriage takes all my January & half of my Feb. pay. I think I have done splendidly since my return to duty, and that once established in housekeeping that we can live easily on our pay. There is not much danger of Army reduction. The country is not quiet enough for that yet.

Comstock's cards have come and have been duly acknowledged. Give my love to Nelly and both write me from Nassau. You must have received letters explaining why I wanted you to go to Nassau. In the first place I was not satisfied with your improvement and in the next place I knew that your situation taking R's habits into account was anything but pleasant. I expect you will have disagreeable revelations to make concerning his conduct.

Now darling, write me a long letter at Havana. Your health to be the main item, and after you get to Nassau, a note if you cannot write longer.

Please present my regards to Dr. and Mrs. Kirkwood.

Your loving husband, Emory

5 Nassau

Emory

Memphis Feb 2nd 1869

My dear wife:
The pleasantest part of the day again finds me indulging in the pleasure of writing to my Pet; who is now I suppose at Havana, or is on her way there, en route to Nassau. Today came your two letters of Jan 21st and 22nd from which I was glad to learn that you were better than you were a few days before. I do hope Nassau will benefit you but for obvious reasons, I do not allow my anticipations to rise too high for I would not again be disappointed. My breast is a battleground between hope and fear. Hope like the good old Army of the Potomac has been after defeated but with heroic constancy renews as often the combat. My great strength however is past and bitter though it was, I have at last been taught to say "Thy will be done." It will be much less trying when you are with me, and when I can do for you all these things a lively affection may dictate.

But is it to be in April or June? It does not seem that I can wait till June yet it may be better for us. You will need whenever you come, good servants and I hope you will secure the one you mentioned. Reuben will do to take care of me, build the fires, do the errands and take care of the horses.

We will want another for cook and now my dear; I hope you will pardon me if I talk finances a little. We don't know what we may yet have to do for your health, and I have written your father that if necessary I will try to get a personnel order to go to New Mexico for a couple of years for your benefit. Whatever we may do it ought to be a husband's pride to take care of his wife, and the more so, now that her parents have done so much for her. Since you were married, your good father has given you $5,000 and proposed in a month or two to send you $2000 more—in all $7,000 on account greater than two years of my full pay. Could you of this amount, lay by $2000 with interest at ten percent, you would secure annually $200; an amount almost sufficient to hire two servants. My yearly pay is but $2450 and as we shall have to come to that figure, the sooner we commence, the better.[1]

I hope this expose will not startle you, but I have thought that the sooner made, the better as you thereby might avoid anything like extravagance. You may not be able to appreciate it but, I can tell you that all husbands worth having prefer a wife to be dependent upon them, rather than independent of them. The latter condition has ruined the happiness and usefulness of many an officer, and while I think under no circumstances could my usefulness be destroyed, I am sure you would study my happiness by ultimately looking to me for everything.

Now my darling, what do you think of my letter? But I will turn to other

[*Here the subsequent page of Upton's letter does not track the narrative, and the following transcription may be part of another letter.*]

Right where, by a turn of the head, I can look at it, stands the portrait of your bust. I never tire gazing upon it and the only criticism I have to make is that he [the photographer] did not cut it off quite short enough, yet should I see it, I might yield to the artist.

Today, I received a box of books from the American Bible Society. I suppose your mother had it sent and I hardly know whether to open it before you come or not. I suppose I ought [to] as in doing good, one cannot commence too soon. My great objection to your absence is the unsettled existence in which I live. Some evenings, indeed many, I have to pass out[2] instead [of] remaining with a beautiful wife and being domestic. The lady by whom I sit every day at dinner, Mrs. Smith,[3] is a devoted wife and her husband a young gentleman naturally worldly, is as domestic as possible. They often invite me to pass the evening with them, but as yet I have only spent one.

Mrs. Morris[4] has left town her husband being quite indisposed for whose health they have gone on a short trip. They are nice people and we miss them very much.

The court martial at Paducah in which are so many of my officers, has yet adjourned. I shall be glad to see them back. The drills go on as usual and I am laboring faithfully to present a good command. I am now revising the tactics and hope to have the revision completed before your arrival so that we can go north at the proper time. Good night, my love. Had I you here I would kiss you a thousand times. You shall never go away from me again.

Your ever-affectionate husband, Emory

Memphis, Feb. 4th, 1869

My darling wife:

Won't you just come and sit in my lap for a little while and let me kiss you as much as I would like, and tell you how much I love you? I know your inclination would lead you there but unfortunately the distance prevents. But my pet, if everything now goes well it is only *Month* after *next* that I shall see you. It is now Feb. and March is the only full month to intervene unless Dr. Kirkwood comes in with an emphatic *no!* The danger of this keeps me unsettled; yet I allow myself to hope that you will come to a certainty by the March Steamer. You cannot imagine what an unsatisfactory life I lead in your absence. Tonight, for instance, Dodge[5] invites me to go to the theater, and I accept that the evening may pass quickly, but do not have my apprehensions that I am becoming worldly, on the contrary, when you return, I shall only appreciate [all] the more, the bliss of passing quiet evenings with you at home. I suppose we shall always have someone from Willowbrook to brighten our household, and you may tell Nelly she will always find a welcome home with us.

What are her plans? Will she stay with us till we can go on to Willowbrook or will she speed away as fast as the cars can take her? I imagine she will want to go home after so long a separation but I trust she will establish us before her departure for Memphis.

A disgraceful affair took place in the city last night. A Catholic Priest gave a ball to raise funds for building a church.[6] He had music and a bar at which liquor was sold. The receipts of which went to him. Low people and gamblers attended and one of the latter having taken a chamber maid for a partner on a dance, was requested to relinquish her to another; an altercation ensued, the gambler fired at and wounded the other claimant, whose friends took up the quarrel and killed the gambler on the spot. Last year the same priest gave a ball and concluded a speech saying, "Let's all take a drink."

Such are the practices indulged in Romish priesthood and justified under the name of religion. I have attended several churches and when you return [I] will take you to them and let you take your choice. Having had strong ideas on that point, you may make your selection and I will accompany you [to] whatever denomination it may be.

I enclose [a] letter from Betty Blair. I don't know what was sent her, but am sure it was tasty. Maria and Sara have written me of receiving your letters. I am very glad you write them for I know they appreciate it. I wrote to your mother that she might select a couple carpets for you in New York. The market here is rather indifferently supplied and

I know she will suit you. Little as there is in the house, nearly everything will have to be changed before you come. The carpet in this room will have to be laid down in the dining room while the one in the sleeping room will have to be transferred to the spare room. How queerly it will seem to see you flourishing around mornings and I doubt not I shall fall into indolent habits in regard to dressing. When I can have you to bother Vi now takes up some of my time. In the morning she is crazy to see me and goes out with me to attend reveille.

Col. Dodge will remain in Memphis about two months, and soon take rooms elsewhere. He is good company but worldly. The only objection I have to entertaining friends at present is that I don't have the quiet time I desire to communicate with my love. To write a letter to you gives me more happiness than any other deed of the day, and when I do it, I always want to be alone. After two or three rainy days, we again have a cloudless sky. How I want you my dear, dear pet to come here and enjoy it.

Your ever-loving husband, Emory

Today I suppose you are in Havana.

Memphis, Feb. 5th 1869

My dear Emily:

It is the afternoon and I have just taken a knap [sic] on the lounge, from which I have risen gappy[7] and stretchy [sic]. Vi too, after her dinner has regaled herself with sleep, and I hear stretching and gapping at an unusual rate in the next room. I think there is something in the air, for I feel unusually sleepy. I am commencing now a big mail and shall try before the next steamer sails to write you almost daily. It will be, my precious one, but trash, nevertheless, you will have something like thirty days to digest it and you may find some crumbs to comfort. I wonder you don't tire of reading how much I love you, but my pen flies off in that direction every time I give it a chance it is so rational for me to tell you so. And my dear, when you join me you will not find that I have written idle words. I just ache to take you again in my arms, and let you know how dear you are to me. That I am living now unhappily is entirely owing to you. You taught me how sweet and pure is a lovely woman's society; how her gentle ways can win and soothe a man and now I miss your presence. I miss your fond kisses, never mind darling you will soon resume them. April will soon be here. This morning for the first time I drew out our horses and carriage. The turnout is indeed very creditable for an officer, and you would not be ashamed to be with any of your New York friends to drive them with you. We went out to the Mississippi depot where you will doubtless arrive and I thought of the time when I should drive you to *your first* home.[8]

The ladies of the garrison are quite anxious to see you. Mrs. Tremain you will like very much. She is, all things considered "entre nous," the most dignified and cultivated lady at the Post. Mrs. Christopher, our neighbor, is a warm-hearted impulsive person. Mrs. Estes has a sweet face. Mrs. Conway has, some say, the prettiest face of all, but she has not much intelligence to back it. Mrs. Hugo is a good straight, out and out Presbyterian, but of limited attainments. Two nights ago, Col. Dodge and I dined at Dr. Tremain's and had a pleasant evening.

I had intended to try one or two letters to you via Havana, but the uncertainty is such that I will only try one or two for I do not like to have you lose one of my epistles.

Today you are in Havana and I doubt not, will over exert yourself in shopping and sight-seeing. You know you have never given me reason to believe in your prudence, but you have said you would take care of yourself and I trust you will. Your letters from Havana I shall look for with deep interest, for I want to know how you are when you leave for Nassau.

By the Journal[9], I see that the 5th Artillery is ordered North. Rawles' Company to Fort Adams, Newport, R. I.[10] You see that you only left in time to avoid being turned out of doors, and are you not glad? I wonder what the Rawles' will do to establish themselves in new quarters. R has not saved anything, and I should think they would be in straitened circumstances. Their expenses since you have been there ought to have been reduced but that will do very little. I desire to see what your fingers will do for the appearance of our house. I want to have it as near ready as possible and I shall start my mess the first of April if I hear that you will join me at that time.

Please give my tender love to Nelly. Tell her she is a devoted sister to you and to me and that she shall never want for friends, and tell Mrs. Upton, while you are about it, that I love her too, and consider her the best little creation I have ever met. J'aime ais bien la baiser mais le temps viendra et alors. [*Translation: I would like a kiss, but the time will come.*]

Adieu my darling, with and from your affectionate husband, Emory

Memphis Tenn., Feb 6th 1869

My loved Emily:

It is just sunset and at this moment I suppose you are steaming out of the Harbor of Havana on your way to Nassau. Again, on the briny deep and going away from the man whose whole existence is wrapped up in yours, who lives only for you. I have thought a great deal of you today and shall offer prayers for your safe arrival at Nassau. How I wish my dear, I might be with you to support you and to know how great is my devotion. I would gladly take the sea, sail and all. Your letters from Havana, I shall receive very soon and I hope they will convey the intelligence that you will join me in April but I shall not feel decided on that point till the Nassau Steamer from Havana of March 6th.

Weather could not be more delightful than we had since January 1st and I can't believe it will be dangerous for you to come here in April. The Str. from New York March 25th will get you to Havana April 1st. You will have to wait there [until] the arrival of the Baltimore Str. which sails April 1st reaching Havana April 5th leaving Havana April 6th in the evening. You will arrive in New Orleans about the same time on the 9th. So, if you telegraph me in the morning of your departure from Havana, I shall be able easily to meet my Pet in New Orleans, for it is only a twenty-two-hour ride from here there. I shall take a seven days leave and this will enable you to come up river in a steamboat if you desire it. Col. Dodge will take up his quarters with me while he remains in Memphis, which will be about two months. So, I shall have company but such company when compared with a lovely little wife. Today I drove out your carriage having invited Col. & Mrs. Christopher. The horses drive elegantly and I know you will like Max. Did I tell you your mother sent me a box of bibles for distribution to the soldiers? What a good mother she is! Give my love to Nelly and think of me often as you speed through the waters tonight. May God be with and ever bless my darling wife.

    Your devoted husband, Emory

                      Memphis, Tenn. Sunday Feb. 7th 1869

My darling Wife:

My thoughts have been with you a great deal today, for I know that you are on the sea on your way to Nassau where I suppose you will arrive sometime tomorrow. It has rained very hard today, but there was no wind, so I hope your trip will be as pleasant as possible. I can imagine you and Nelly, quite forlorn, yet no doubt your naval friends placed you under the charge of somebody and that you are not wanting for friends.

    Today was communion Sunday, which I attended at Calvary Church and how much I wished you might have been with me. I did not however forget to offer up my prayers for you and to commend you to the kind care of "Him who doeth all things well." May He bless and keep you. There were very few people in attendance on account of the rain and I have observed that the congregation depends entirely on the weather. This is not right and is my great fault with the Episcopal Church. Its religion is one of convenience in which form too often is substituted for substance. Thus therefore, if you desire to attend a Presbyterian Church then I will accompany you. At Nassau, I suppose you will have to attend the Church of England, to which you became accustomed while abroad and this calls up Mr. Kingsford[11] and his associate at Belaggio.[12] Kingsford was a very sweet man and I enjoyed his stories very much. I shall write to Dr. de Cosson about inauguration day. I wish you could avail yourself again of his wisdom for I think him, all in all, the best advisor you ever had.

But woman is an enigma. It seems so strange she should be the exception to the female creation that she also should be born to suffer from the cradle to the grave, while man is totally exempt from pain. To see you suffer is to me a cause of pain. I could not love you were it otherwise, and as so much of happiness depends on health, do I beg of you be prudent while at Nassau and strive to get all the benefit you can. Nelly, I am sure is a good nurse and has quite supplied my place in that particular, but I think you will be soon contented with me, and when you return you will find I have forgotten nothing of my previous lessons. My heart fairly aches to see you and separation has become wearisome.

I am now going on with the revision of the Tactics,[13] which progresses favorably. I shall have it all ready to apply to go to Washington at the proper time and yet sometimes I think it a matter of doubt but properly for you to go home for every considerable reason. Were it not for Evy's return, I certainly think it would be better for you to remain at Memphis. But sufficient unto the day is the evil thereof.[14] I shall look with pleasure for letters from your mother after her Washington visit. The wedding must have been a distinguished affair. Maria wrote me after your mother's visit to New York and is as much in love with her as ever. Sara is now in Battle Creek enjoying herself and is most free from care or anxiety. I must confess, I would like to see her and Maria suitably married for so long as they are single, I feel a certain responsibility on that account. Married life is only true life for woman while a man can live single without so much inconvenience. I really pity Col. Dodge who sees little chance for years of having his wife join him. Her mother is playing Mrs. Tremain's & Quackenbush's character with a vengeance and will not allow her only daughter to leave her. Isn't it a hard case?

Steamers pass up and down the river at all times and just now one arrived serenading the town with its calliope. Our band makes little progress, but the subject is being agitated. It all turns on the ability to secure a leader.

Now my pet, I must draw to a close. Write me long letters from Nassau giving me a good description of everything new. I suppose it is full of Rebels, but you can turn up your nose at them and tell them that Reconstruction is a success, Clayton's Militia and all.[15]

Good night. I kiss you fondly. Your devoted husband, Emory

Memphis, Monday Feb. 8th 1869

My dear Emily:

I was quite agreeably surprised this morning to receive your letter of Jan 28th dated at Havana. It quite relieved me, for I did not know how you could make the close connection with the Nassau Steamer and I was afraid you could not; being with Nelly along, find a good stopping place while at Havana and feel perfectly protected. But your naval friends seem to have anticipated every want and deserve especial praise for their politeness. I hope we will be able someday to reciprocate their kindness.

Your remarks about Rawles and Storrow[16] rather puzzle me. I wrote to Rawles sometime after my arrival here. I believe before I received any of your letters regarding his drunkenness. Just before I left, in front of the officer of the steamship company, you may remember I called Rawles aside, where he gave me his pledge that he would not drink any whiskey or intoxicating liquor excepting in the officer's quarters of his garrison, or onboard the naval vessels. My aim was to get him away from the same shops downtown where he was spending most of his time and which could only terminate sooner or later in making him a confirmed drunkard. I found when I came here that Davies,[17] another classmate had become a disgraceful sot and had lost his commission as [a] consequence. I took hold of this fact to write Rawles as a last effort to reclaim him from his downward tendency, fearing that he had not observed his pledge. It so happened that this letter was received by him about the time of his particularly bad treatment of his wife and family and he may have attributed its origin to your letters to me, which was not the case. All the time I was at Key West he was *full*[18] and his harsh treatment of his children was its consequence. Every day he was becoming more and more brutalized and in my letter I told him that love his wife as he might, drink would make him cruel to her. He is now ordered north and returning to civilized society; I hope will have a tendency to reform him, but a man who has been under the dominion of alcohol has as little chance of reform as a fallen woman. As to [Dr.] Storrow, your letters gave me no encouragement as to your cough and as I know you were going over to Tortugas and would in all probability undergo an examination by him, I wrote him to let me know how you were, and particularly in regard to the climate of Key West in which I had lost all confidence.

Before he received my letter, you had visited Tortugas and he had examined your lungs, whereupon he wrote me his first letter stating his opinion that Key West was not at all suitable for you and urging your removal. Before receiving this letter, I sent you the telegram to go to Nassau. After receiving my letter, he wrote another telling me about your case, and reiterated his opinion about Key West. I never met him, but for a few hours at Tortugas, and as he was an Asst. Surg. of the Army, I had necessarily to depend some little on his advice but his manner was such that I did not have great confidence in him. Why you should loathe him I am unable to divine unless he was impertinent and would have behaved unprofessionally toward you. If the latter you should not have failed to let me know it. At any rate, I have but little confidence in doctors either as physicians or men. They often betray the secrets they can only acquire professionally and it does not do to trust oneself to them unless equally confident of their ability and then have—curiosity often, and not the desire to benefit the patient, prompts them to make examinations, as good old Dr. de Cosson frequently told me. Cases of necessity may and do frequently arise when these examinations cannot be dispensed with but as a rule they should not be granted except upon the advice of true physicians. On this subject, I think your mother's ideas much nearer correct than Evy's.

Tomorrow night, the last before Lent, a masked ball is to be given by the Chickasaw Club[19] to which Col. Dodge and I am invited, but have not fully decided to attend. If we do not go, then Mrs. Christopher will give a nice little entertainment. So, one more evening is provided for. With me, my darling, it is but a problem how to pass the time till you return, and this again brings me to the subject. You wrote me that your cough at Havana is better, now if when you go to Nassau it should improve *very* rapidly and so continue up to the last of March. I think you ought to stay till June but should you go along deriving no more benefit than when at Key West, then you might just as well be here as there. I believe I can trust you to do what is best for your health and to ensure our happiness. It is only in case of doubt as to deriving greater benefit at Nassau that should decide you to come in March. My doubt—I hope the March steamer will dispel, until I know, it is foolish to fix up our quarters, which can be done on very short notice. I shall look for you two months from today in New Orleans. I want to take you in my arms and realize that you are a wife indeed. You may be sure my precious one, I shall never let you go again.

Your fond husband, Emory

Memphis, Tuesday Feb 9th 1869

My dear Pet:

To what sorry uses my dear, is put the place one year ago, I anticipated you would fill. The house, which you were to enliven and make happy, whose graces and hospitality you were to dispense, has alas become a den, a den of bachelors and married bachelors. The Firm consists of Upton and Co. Dodge and Ayres being the Co. The wives of these poor men are scattered from Dan to Beersheba[20]. The wife of the head of the firm is a British subject at Nassau. Mrs. Dodge is in New York, Mrs. Ayres at Portland Maine. They bear their troubles with equanimity, but Dodge is a demoralizer. He is already urging upon us to break up and go to Salt Lake where wives are so numerous that a husband can never be left solitary. I must avow that this is the sole advantage I have ever seen in Mormonism, but I cannot be a convert so long as I have a darling with all her love besides. Yes, my pet, the happy moments you have already given me are sufficient to live upon for a long time to come and those in store for me give me the brightest and most hopeful anticipations.

Just think, our first anniversary will be soon at hand and we must pass it a thousand miles from each other, but it shall not be so with others. Those we will spend, God willing, together. Your absence I have taken much harder that I thought I would, and this dose will be sufficient for my lifetime. I want you to come back and soften my time, to resume your sway over me, and increase my usefulness. I want again to experience my darling Pet's love and tenderness. I want her to stimulate again into life the better part of my nature now dormant. I want to pet and caress my love till my heart's content.

My love to Nelly, your ever-devoted husband Emory

Memphis, Feb 10th 1869

My little wife:

Yesterday I was invited to spend the evening at the hotel[21] at the Smith's, Ayres & Dodge being with me, and I had to beg very hard just now to break away that I might come down home and commune quietly with my love. I will not neglect her who is dearer to me than all the world beside, no matter what may be the inducement.

Last night the masked ball took place which being the first one I ever attended amused me very much. The costumes were very grotesque, and everybody so disguised that recognition was impossible. Among the ladies, many were personated, one an Irish Apple-woman who attached herself to Mr. Smith made him promenade a long while, dance the quadrille, and upon unmasking, proved to be one of his gentleman friends. The masks were removed about 1 A.M. just before supper. On these occasions and whenever I see several ladies together, I always analyze their faces and compare them with my darling's. Your face, my Pet grows upon me every day, reflecting in its parts of outline, the depth and nobleness of your nature. Should you try hard I am sure you would not find it difficult to make me fall in love with you.

This morning some of your letters came. Jan. 23–4&5 from Key West and Jan. 30th from Havana. They delighted me and I almost begin to think I may stop doubting as to whether you will join me in April.

I commend heartily, your enjoyment of Nancy's services, her wages being extraordinarily low. She is the right person to have, one who will be more strongly attached to you than to place, and whom you can carry about everywhere. Reuben is very reliable, so I think we carried on very nicely.

It is quite late and as I did not get to bed late—three o'clock this morning, I will defer till tomorrow the answering in detail your good letters. I thank you for these and kiss you tenderly. How happy you shall be when you again join your ever loving and devoted husband, Emory

Memphis Feb 11th 1869

My dear Love:

I have just returned from tea; Ayres has gone back to New Orleans and Dodge is out, so I am going to sit down and spend the evening with my precious little wife.

My dear Emily—how good my darling it will sound to pronounce that name for almost ever since I left you I have only seen it on paper. There is no one with whom I am so familiar as to permit me to speak of you as Emily. The other day, fully a week ago, when Ayres was here en route to Arkansas, I managed to bring your name into the conversation, a bright smile immediately overspread his brow and he spoke up feelingly "Why that's my wife's name too." It struck a tender chord and how many sweet memories may it not have awakened in him?

Today he told me his Army experience. When he married as a lieutenant, his pay was but sixty-nine dollars per month. Orders and change of station came oftener than his purse could provide for, and as his wife was the daughter of an old Army officer, she had no dowry so she had to remain absent from him many times from a month to eighteen months each, the majority of his time he has spent away from his wife, to whom he is thoroughly devoted. Now they have to be separated because, having five children, the wife has to say where they can be educated. Of the effect of being absent from a wife you may judge from his case. Today he told me he was a wanderer, that he had no other desire but to see the time pass. For him there is nothing in the present; restless and uncertain, he has nothing to do but peer into the future to see what it has in store for him.

Dodge's case is worse. Now my darling how differently do we set out on the journey of life? We have a rank and pay sufficient to always live comfortably, and we know that time cannot but better our condition and bring with it promotion and honor. Poor Ayres, deprived of his just reward, finds himself at forty-three with the same rank that I have. I look to you, now that in time of peace, there is nothing to engage my ambition as the loved being in whom centers all of my future happiness. With you to bear me company, and in comparative health we will always cling to the present as ensuring what is uncertain in the future. I shall have you to pet, to caress and tenderly love, which you by a thousand and one charms will be the blessing of my existence.[22]

I suspect you are in Nassau far away from me, but in taking up my pen to write you, I have mastered the lapse of our other twenty-four hours. The less-than-two-months will soon pass away, and you will find your head in the arms, which will ever remain your pillow. Oh, my darling you know not what affectionate embraces await you, what loving kisses I have for your sweet lips and lovely face.

Molly has written me that they have received letters from you and Nelly at Havana and the officer there was something worse than *Northers* at Key West which, must be she thinks that "Rawles drinks." Astute Molly! She wasn't far wrong. You surprised me with your accounts of mosquitos and hot weather, although here today it was uncomfortably warm and the streets dusty.

The naval officers have been extremely good to you and Nelly and have proven themselves friends in time of need. I hope they will be at Havana to assist you on your return. Nelly's [dog] must be a perfect nuisance, but Vi is the loveliest, dear, little creature you ever saw. She keeps herself in my mind all the time. She cannot run out of doors for fear of being stolen. The dining room has been assigned her for quarters. Reuben issues her rations to her there and the dear neat little thing has covered the floor all over with grasses. There she litters up every room, regardless of common decency, and acts as if she had done a good thing. Sometimes she shows an ardent desire to learn, goes to the étagère; seizes a Webster's dictionary or other book; devours the contents, leaving all the papers out after she has done with them. She even shows appreciation of your handiwork, two or three times she has taken my nice slippers and as she could not discover how they were made, she has tried to tear them to pieces, till now instead of seeing my dressing gown on the arm chair awaiting my evening return, with the slippers on the floor nearby, you will find the slippers on top of the writing desk or bureau and the dressing gown in the hall. Oh, she is so lovely that I want you to come and see her right away before I let her go.

My, or rather, your horses are very nice and you will enjoy your carriage very much.

Lent is now at hand but does not seem to change Memphis very much. I send you two of your mother's letters. I would not be surprised if she did yet send us to China, where you will be Mrs. Mandarin Upton en lieu de Madame le General. How would you like it? You must write me whether you want me to have everything in absolute readiness for you to go to housekeeping or whether would like me to let you exercise your own taste in some of the purchases. Your mother writes me that she will send two carpets, table linen and furniture from New York so there will be but little left for you to do. If Nancy can do the cooking, I will not start our mess till you come, but everything can be made ready so that you can come from the cars directly to the house. One thing I have made up my mind to that is I am going to have a bureau to myself. Until I came here, I did not know. I grant how much you had imposed upon me, but I forgive you.

We will be friends and I will promise to kiss and hug you as much as if nothing had happened.

Good night my pet. Decency requires that my letter should not exceed in length those written during our engagement.

I love you Emily, dearly. Your fond husband, Emory

Memphis, Feb 12th 1869

My dear Wife:

For the past week I have received letters from you almost daily, and this evening I received two more of Feb 2nd and 3rd. I was very sorry to hear that you were suffering so severely from neuralgia, which you bear like a true heroine as you are. How you can write letters when in such agony is more than I can imagine, for I am sure I could not lift a pen much less think. The time must come, I sincerely trust, when you will be relieved from pain and enjoy good health and to this end for your sake I would be happy to see it with you after the manner of other married women, when we might hope that Nature, devoting herself in a new channel, would produce a complete change in your constitution and enable your lungs and other troubles to heal. This is the cure Dr. de Cosson was so sanguine of but it has not yet been vouchsafed to you.[23]

The day has been uncomfortably warm and I have thought of putting awnings over our parlor windows. I speak often of the weather that you may know what to expect when you arrive here. This month and January have been unprecedentedly mild but the winter everywhere has been so. It is gratifying to know that your cough still improves and I devoutly trust it will receive a fresh impetus at Nassau. You are now there and I suppose counting the days till the next steamer arrives. Your present to me for our first anniversary could not have been more acceptable and is just what I want. A present is doubly appreciated when it meets a requirement and I think I shall make it a rule never to make you one without having heard you express a desire for the article.

The day has passed without incident and is gladly numbered with its predecessors. One less intervenes between us and May. They all pass quickly so that I may take you again in my arms and call you my Pet. Good night Darling.

Your ever fond, Emory

Memphis Feb 13th 1869

My dear Pet:

Dodge has just said "I suppose you are going to write to your wife again?" and I can assure him he was never nearer right in his life. Tonight, I received another letter from my dear wife dated Feb 1st. It must have come by the *Maryland* and was postmarked Baltimore.[24] It pains me to learn that you are suffering so acutely from neuralgia, but I always console myself that by the time I receive your letters, the attack is over. You must have had a most trying time the first Sunday in Havana to be confined as you were to your bed all day.

The Nassau mail you must have received on board the *Eagle*, as I wrote Dr. Kirkwood to forward it to you. This I did because there might be things in it you would like to answer immediately and the opportunity would be given you by sending them to Havana. It is little my darling, at the great distance we are from each other, that I can do for you and what little I can do is seized upon with avidity.

Just a year ago now I was spending my time at home before taking my departure to Willowbrook to get final possession of my treasure and what a treasure she has been to me. I know my dear that you love me truly and unselfishly and have much comfort there is in that thought alone your desire to return to me is not stronger than mine to see you and may God speed the day.

I enclose [for] you Rawles' letter. I touched him in a render spot and hardly think he liked it. Well, he may go his way but I pity his poor wife.

I must write Nelly some but I suppose you read her parts of my letters. Throop[25] seems to be doing well in Albany. I guess he and Nelly will get together yet.

With much love, your devoted husband, Emory

Memphis, Sunday Feb 14th 1869

My dearest Emily:

It is ever a pleasant conclusion to a day to sit down and hold sweet converse with the being one loves and that privilege is mine tonight.

The day's duties are done and my darling Emily is the sole occupant of my thoughts. It seems to me a little strange that go where I may, do what I will, active or passive, in excitement or quietude, my love is in my thoughts till although invisible, I *feel* you are present. But as my senses contrived this sentiment, I am not comfortless, for I know that the reality will soon be mine, and that again I shall have you all to myself, to care for and protect and one way or other.

Tonight came up to my mind the stormy time we had on the *Cuba*, and especially the night I made a bed down for you and Nelly at the head of the *Cuba* stairs. I thought I would get out of your way and stay in the Captain's room but when I went back, I now recall in what a remarkable way you kept me by you. A little alarmed yet would not say so, and then, for dear little thing in order to feel the comfort of my presence you first insisted that I should sit down, then you vacated half of the mattress, made me lie down, then gave me pillows and thus carried your point. But my pet, if ever again afraid, tell your husband, so for at such times, above all others, would it be his joy and pride to prove his devotion and extend his protection.

Have I ever told you how I spend a Sunday? I rise at 6:45 the same as weekdays, take my breakfast at 7:30, inspection at 9 after which in office till 10—Church 11 (all churches have service at 11) Dinner at 2, parade 6. Tea at 7 & perhaps Church. This morning I attended

Calvary. A curate was in the congregation and behaved with perfect propriety till after the benediction when he shouted out "Knowledge is good; wisdom is better, the Lord's Prayer is mine." As we passed out after church, he came up to me in the aisle and said "Present my compliments to Gen'l Upton." I said gently "That will do" he roared out "Obey orders! Present my compliments to Gen Upton. I'm an intimate friend of Gen. Sykes,[26] I never missed a roll call in my life." He then went ahead and as he left the vestibule, he said, "Gen Grant is not President of the United States, he is [a] Military Governor." Of course, nothing could be done under the circumstances.

This evening I went for the first time in my life, to hear a Swedenborgian[27] and found in general terms, that I agreed very well with him. They reject the Trinity, make Christ God, believe in spiritual resurrection and many other things. Through God's mercy, I think my desire to submit to him and to do his will grows stronger every day.

I see by the papers that the *Cuba* on her last arrival at Baltimore was seized for smuggling cigars from Havana but was released in time for her regular trip. Before this time, ought to have your letter of Feb. 6th from Havana but now I may get letters from the *Eagle* first.

Our weather was so warm last week that two or three days we needed no fire and I changed my underclothing two times as Canton[28] flannel was too heavy.

Do you know my dear that I am more contented here than I have been for a long time? Had I you with me, I should have but one complaint and that is time passes too rapidly. How pleasant it would be to drive out every evening in your carriage and especially since the horses drive so nicely. Thanks to rank you can have better than a mule to drive if you are an Army officer's wife.

It is now after eleven. In one short hour, February will be more than half over and, in a few days, I can say *Next Month*. Be prudent and gain all the strength you can for I do not want you to disappoint me.

Good night my love. May the blessed lord have you in his Father's keeping.

Your affectionate husband, Emory

Memphis, Feb. 15th 1869

My precious Emily:

I could not let a single day pass to without writing to you without feeling conscious that I had neglected a duty, but while I confess this, it is not duty that seats me at the close of day to write you, but to gratify a longing desire I have to talk with you and to tell you over and over again, and never to tire of it, that I love you. These last three words are to me a source of true happiness doubled by the knowledge that in return, my ever good and sweet Emily loves me. Well darling, you shall not be disappointed in any dream you have had of love. The word is a Talisman to you, ever ready to shield you from the cold blasts of the world, and to surround you with all the comforts, kindness and sympathy can bestow. Notwithstanding, the days speed by so swiftly, I feel your absence every moment and want more and more to enjoy your *presence.*

What a comfort it will be during another winter to look up at any time in the evening and find my cherished Pet sitting peacefully and happily beside me. No word need be spoken, twill be enough that you are there, and then how many times I shall creep up noiselessly and plant a kiss on your lovely neck or sweet lips. I am sure I shall be prodigal with kisses. And then again, my dear I shall feel again your soft hand. How many times when you have slipped it into mine at Church when lonely or peaceful I have felt poorest, grateful and happy that it was mine and that I was its protector. How I want it again, the poor pen cannot describe.

Today absolutely nothing has transpired but tomorrow I look forward to hearing from you both at Havana & Nassau. Write me encouraging letters and if possible, make me joyful by telling me you *will* be here without fail in April.

You must remember me to Dr. & Mrs. Kirkwood.

Your fond husband, Emory

Memphis Feb 20th 1869

My darling Pet:

Don't you get tired of my daily scribbles, containing so little of real interest; and so much of trash? I feel my dear, in high feathers[29] tonight for I have received a letter from the Appleton's, showing that the book, our nest egg, has done splendidly enabling me to pay off Torbert and leave a large sum besides—Sixteen hundred and ninety-five ($1695.00) in six months is pretty good for Tactics. Our European experiences[30], the bust and everything paid for leaving still on hand $1200.00. Then to cap the climax, your good father, notwithstanding, I wrote him you would not require it, will send you in May $2,000.00. His letter, which I enclose, will speak for itself. They send you also two carpets, China set, table linens & with this left my dear, we are *rich* and we will never have to tap your parents again. I am bound, my dear, while we are single to lay aside enough to supply any future wants. The book will do this of itself and by the time you are *thirty*, I hope to see your every wish gratified. Lily may beat you in the long run, but I intend that the sight of her brownstone front shall not make you *miserable*.

When you return to me, you must be as free from anxiety as possible and have little to do. Good servants you must and shall have and from your disposition, servants once in your employ, will scarcely ever want to leave you. Reuben is as faithful as ever and I like him fully as well as the boy John who was with me so long a time.

You soon will have to be up one flight of stairs but you must not move up and down too often. The kitchen, which is yet to be built, will be outside the house, just in [the] rear of the dining room, a descent of four or five steps heading to it. I shall write you a good, long letter tomorrow so will close tonight by wishing I had you in my arms and could kiss your dear face all over and over again. I love you Pet so much I cannot tell.

Your ever-fond husband, Emory

Memphis, Feb 21st, 1869

My dear Love:

As today's mail may be the last to connect with the steamer of the 25th, I deviate from my usual custom and write my Sunday letter before going to Church. I shall be glad to see the 25th lapse further at least till the return mail from Nassau. I can think that the next steamer from New York will bear from Nassau to Havana a freight more precious to me than all else in the world. Time only seems to increase my yearnings for you, and could I only feel sure that you would come to me in April I would want nothing else to complete my happiness. That you will come, I fully believe after some time, my belief is especially strong that you would stay still two months longer, could you feel the assurance of a permanent cure. I was so glad to learn that the pain in your face did not proceed from neuralgia, that your cough was improving, and that your other troubles were less aggravating.

The weather here, as I have told you in nearly every letter has been perfectly charming. April, I am sure will be settled warm and pleasant. I saw a Dr. White the other evening who told me he knew of no better region for persons afflicted with lung troubles than Memphis and instanced his own case. Yet, my dear Emily, as much as I want to see [you] don't let me induce you to leave too soon. With ordinary health, we have thirty years of married life before us, so act today the wiser part—secure health even at a great present sacrifice, and happiness then, cannot not but follow. It is only in case you are receiving wonderful strength and benefit that I would advise you to tarry at Nassau, but your being with your husband and relieved from anxiety might do you equal good. So, my love, I am all at sea and leave you to do just what Dr. Kirkwood, Nelly & yourself in counsel assembled may decide.

I am dying to take your dear self in my arms. How I wish I might take the place of this letter as it goes on board the *Eagle*. I imagine somebody would be glad, which I infer, of course from her letters. Benjamin seems very happy. I enclose a letter from him. It is splendid for them to go to Fortress Monroe instead of Alaska, and by the time he is ordered away, it is more than probable his battery will have left Alaska.

Yesterday Molly sent me a photograph of the bust, front, and profile view. I think it splendid and was almost provoked when I kissed it affectionately, that its lips would speak to me.

I think, my dear, we shall be prepared to love each other very devotedly when we get together. Separation has whetted our appetites for affection and for my part, I know you will have all the petting and caressing that you desire. You will have time to write me a letter at Nassau before departure of the Str. Give Dr. K an appointment to examine your case and so that he may write me when he thinks you can leave with safety. Stay till June if necessary, but if you came to me in April, I shall be too happy for anything.

I embrace you tenderly, your devoted husband, Emory.

PS Benjamin's letter I have mislaid. I sent Ball & Black $60.00 for Betty Blair's present. Benjamin speaks of his as being very beautiful. I kiss you my darling Emily, my precious wife.

Memphis Feb 23rd 1869

My dear Pet:

My success in sending you letters through Capt. Greene of the *Eagle*, emboldens me to take the same steps with the *Moro Castle*.[31]

Last night my love, I did not write you because there was no use, as the letter could not go out via New York and now that I shall have a chance via New Orleans, I seat myself almost with double pleasure to assure you over and over again how dear you are to me. The time will now be soon at hand when I shall take my dear little wife again into my arms, where she shall sit on my lap and let me tell her how I love her and caress her as much as I desire. I shall soon be able to say next month instead of April, and each time I utter it a thrill of joy will run through me as I think of our approaching happiness.

Nelly's letter to your father, which was sent to me, gave me more encouragement than did yours. It shows that whatever may be your improvement, *Nassau will not do it all*, because she said upon your arrival, you coughed hardly at all. I therefore take courage and hope the return mail will certainly fix the date of your return early in April.

The weather has suddenly turned cold, probably the last effort of winter. I am glad to have it come in its season so that you may not be subjected to any sudden changes of temperature when you join me. I imagine myself now receiving the dispatch from Havana and hastening to pack up my bags to meet you in New Orleans. I shall take a seven-day leave so that we can have a regular spree in the Crescent City if we desire. Our parents seem to have set us the example in their late travels to New York, Washington and elsewhere, and in whose paths can we more worthily travel?

Dodge is still with me. My society is as extensive as I desire, and if I do not remain at home evenings, which I am much inclined to do, I have but to remain at the Overton after tea, and I call upon any of pleasant people there passing the winter—Mr. and Mrs. Smith,[32] Mr. and Mrs. Curtis,[33] Col. & Mrs. Wolford[34] and daughter, Miss Morris[35] & several others—all northern people are charming society, so I get on very comfortably.

In beautiful weather, I drive out every day, and always invite some of the officers and ladies of the garrison or some of my friends at the hotel. When you come back, my dear, I am going to make you ride out a great deal, and it will always be pleasant to you, if we don't prefer to ride alone, to invite some of your lady friends. I wonder, darling, how I am going to look going uptown with a market basket on my arm to fulfill your order for breakfast & dinner? Just think what a new field for ambition and usefulness you are going to open to me. I am placing my house in order before you come, and my command are beginning to understand that my quarters are *private,* not to be rushed into on any frivolous pretext.

We will never be interrupted at meals as were the R. My office hour is from nine to ten A. M. All business has to be transacted within that time, or, unless of great importance, go over till the next day.

We are going to, my dear, take genuine comfort together. My ambition shall sleep till the next war. Our pay is sufficient so that we can live well, there will be nothing to harass and we shall pass our days in peace and quietude. Our evenings will be delightful as keep each other company, read aloud, to be interrupted sometimes by the silent proximity of my lips to your sweet face. I am just going to make you a happy wife. I am [*Here wording in the original letter is missing.*]

My love to Nelly and kind remembrances to Dr. and Mrs. Kirkwood. From Nelly's letter I am delighted to learn of your having Julian Davies to escort you clear from Nassau to New Orleans. It will be splendid, and relieve you from all anxiety. Now my velvet Pet, accept my dearest love, with affectionate kisses.

Your dearest husband, Emory

Emily

Nassau, February 25, 1869

My dearest Molly,
On my arrival here, I found two letters from you, for which I am very much obliged, as well as for the advice they contained. I am happy to say the Doctor's advice and my wishes coincide exactly. So, I shall

carry out my first plan and leave here on the March steamer making a slow journey down to Memphis where I hope to be the latter part of April. Were it not advisable for me to leave here as soon as that, I fear I should not be much benefited by another month, for I should be so anxious to get away. I do not think my stock of patience would last another four weeks for I am so anxious to go to Emory and settle down in our place where I could feel at rest. I have not remained six weeks in one place without having to pack my trunks and change for over a year.

I am very much obliged to you for having my bust photographed. I think it excellent and Emory writes me he is delighted with it. All your friends here look with perfect amazement at your picture remembering you as you looked while at Nassau. Mrs. Kirkwood, Nelly and I take a great deal of comfort together. I think she really enjoys having us here very much and it has enlivened her a great deal. She has grown much older looking since you saw her. I think she needs a change from this climate. She and the Doctor expect to go to Europe this spring or summer.

The house is delightful and larger than when you were here. The garden is filled with the most lovely roses and other flowers and everything is looking as fresh and pretty as possible. Dr. and Mrs. Kirkwood are good and kind to us as they can be and will not hear of our going to a hotel, so we have concluded to stay and make ourselves as agreeable as possible. I am sure Nelly does her part toward amusing the Doctor for she plays billiards and backgammon to his full satisfaction.

In the morning we usually read or go up to the hotel and in the afternoon, we often take a drive. I enjoy going down to hear the band play very much. None of the officers you know are here now. Tho' the regiment is part of the second East India, there are some pleasant people at the hotel but not many. The hotel is badly kept this year and is much complained of. The climate here I find full as delightful as you told me, and the moonlight nights are perfectly glorious. I cannot bear to shut my blinds tonight, it looks so bright and silvery everywhere.

Well, I must say good night with much love, your truly affect. sister, Emily

Emory

Memphis Feb 25th 1869

My darling Wife:
At last all doubt as to the date of your joining me is set at rest. Last night, the *N. Y. Herald* announced that the 25th Infantry was to change station with the 32nd, the Head Quarters of which are at *Tucson, Arizona*. It quotes Gen. Order No. 6, which has not been received but doubtless issued. I do not however believe the Order will be carried out for the reason that Congress is evidently determined to reduce the Army to at least thirty regiments of infantry. No officers will be thrown out of commission, but promotions will be at a dead lock till the number of officers is reduced to the wants of these regiments. I don't care much personally for my eye is securely placed on a brigadier-ship, which in any event, will come about as soon as I could expect a Colonelcy. Great changes undoubtedly will be made soon, so darling this morning I telegraphed you care of Capt. Adams, Str. *Moro Castle*, to leave Nassau the last of March so as to join me and be ready for any orders.

I think my dear; your suspicion in regard to the mole on your right shoulder will prove correct. You certainly will travel, and some way or other, believe that through life we shall have all the money that is essential to happiness. Wouldn't it be strange if you were to meet Evy in Arizona? Almost a romance, although I would prefer New Mexico or California. To go to Arizona even will benefit you and I hope my darling will not be sad when she hears that we are likely to be ordered so far away. To go there and remain five years would best prepare us to appreciate West Point.[36]

I will not write you any more my love tonight as I will finish the letter tomorrow. I am delighted however to think that four weeks from today, the Str. will leave New York to take my precious Pet to Havana and to me.

Feb. 26th

Gen'l Order No. 6[37] has arrived, my darling, from which it appears that the officers only of the 25th & 32nd regiments change stations, the men remaining at their present posts. I am not at all sorry about the order. I have got a blessed good little wife to bear me company and to care for her wants alone will give me occupation and make me happy. We shall be, my love, a society within ourselves and therefore the [*illegible*].

Ames'[38] regiment goes to Texas. Our stay in Arizona will not be long. The reduction of the Army will necessitate changes of station within a year or two and we shall soon see ourselves in civilization again. Should you & Evy both be in Arizona, Nelly would certainly go out and spend a year. My present plan is to remain in command here till a field officer comes to relieve me for Arizona, then apply for a three month's delay which we will pass, my love, at Willowbrook. By this arrangement we would leave about June 1st and would not go to housekeeping at all—as directly opposite us is a boarding house where we could take our meals and have yours sent to you in case of bad weather. This letter will surprise you, won't it? But I believe it all for the best. You will be kept in a warm dry climate for two or three years just what you want and will come back to your friends a hale, hearty woman.[39]

Bring *Nancy* with you by all means as she will be a great comfort to you. Reuben says he will go too, and there we will be independent.

I am almost counting the hours till you join me my precious one and rejoice that this is our last separation. With love to Nelly and a heart full of affection for my pet.

Your devoted husband, Emory

Memphis, Feb. 27th 1869

My dear darling:

Even that endearing title little expresses the love I bear my Pet, yet I must be content with such expressions till you are returned to me and can drink from that pure fountain of love which now bursts forth at every mention of your name. I begin to feel, my darling that my love for you has undergone a great change since we were married; that it has become more tender, more nervously sensitive to your every wish and thought. I feel too that every day it responds more closely, more nearly to these gentle abiding affections, which only our Emily can know, and as my heart approaches yours in purity, I feel a better, nobler man. Thanks to my dear Emily she has opened to me a life of unselfishness and now I want no greater boon than to have to make her happy. To think that soon I must go too far off, distant Arizona but that then I shall from day to day experience the sweet pleasure of your society, be the recipient of your gentle, loving acts of kindness, makes a thrill of joy run through me, and robs the trip of every hardship.

I am in fact, glad that we are ordered there for your sake. It will do everything for your health and another satisfaction we shall, in the order of this military life, encounter the worst hardships the Army can offer. But I think they are very few & so must Evy. We have, my lovely one, a great advantage over many Army ladies in this that we can never be at a less than three company post. So, you must have more or less society. I shall move our bed down to the room directly in [the] rear of our parlor so that Petters [sic]⁴⁰ won't have to climb any stairs.

I told you I thought we better take our meals across the street rather than go to housekeeping.

No details yet in regard to the execution of Order No. 6, but I suppose the first detail of lieutenants for Arizona will start soon. Two weeks I must yet wait for my darling, but I am not anxious as I feel you are improving. Some one of Col. Dodge's acquaintances just returned to N. Y. from Nassau gave a most deplorable description of the place. I hope with the Kirkwoods you have a better accommodation.

Now my love let me kiss every line of your dear face and accept the love of your fond, Emory

Memphis, Feb 28th 1869

My loved Emily:
One more opportunity presents itself of getting a letter to you via Havana, which I cannot fail to embrace. I love to do anything that will make you smile or gladden your heart. Fortunately, my acts of love will soon be substantial, as tomorrow I can feel that next month I should see my dear thing. I could not again submit to so long and trying a separation. Hereafter, sick or well, I must be with you to comfort and cheer you. Just think, I haven't done a thing to relieve your pain or increase your comfort for nearly four months, but I assure you my Pet, I shall make up at a rapid rate all the time I have lost. I write you this letter just after my breakfast and before inspection. Dodge (poetic license) is snoring on the sofa, not yet risen.

The day is quite cold but perfectly clear and I think a good spell awaits us. The last cold snap gave me a cold, which settled in my right lung, but *my cough* is now better. I wonder my dear, if the locket and charm are still around your neck and if at this moment, I could look upon you probably sleeping sweetly in bed, I should see it shine against your velvety bosom. This morning as I was dressing and gazing up on the photograph in the blue case, which you gave me,

I recalled particularly its charm and locket and I thought of the loving way in which you approached me to have me hang them about your dear neck. All such little evidences of your pure love are not lost upon me. I recall and dwell upon them with intense pleasure.

    I shall be quite anxious to learn what you think of the Arizona trip. I think to go to California is a nice thing, and that we will enjoy returning over the Pacific R.R.

    Please remember me to Dr. & Mrs. Kirkwood. Did you get the ring Feb 19th and if not have you received it since? The Shakespeare is lovely. Good bye my darling till the next steamer which will bear you to my arms. With an affectionate embrace, your loving husband, Emory

Emily Upton. This carte de visite is dated 1869 in pencil and was taken by photographer S. Hall Morris of the Union Picture Gallery, 112 Genesee St., Auburn, New York. If the date is correct, the photo depicts Emily during the late summer and fall of 1869 when she visited her home, Willowbrook, and before she moved back to Nassau for her last rest. Editor's collection.

Photo of Emory probably taken just after receiving his second star for meritorious service during the Valley Campaign of 1864. Library of Congress.

Maj. Gen. James H. Wilson, Upton's last commander and frequent correspondent immediately after the war. Public domain.

Emily, her sister Cornelia (called Nelly), her sister Eliza (called Lylie, Leily, or Lily), and Myles Keogh, friend of the Martin family in Auburn and a casualty of the 1876 Battle of Little Big Horn. Keogh's body was brought to Auburn and buried in the Martin family plot. Princeton University Library.

Maj. Gen. Thomas Ruger. Official West Point photograph. Upton got to know him after the war and urged him to apply for the job of superintendent of the military academy. He did and the two served nearly concurrent terms. Editor's collection.

Upton as commandant of cadets at West Point. Official West Point photograph. Probably taken at the same time Ruger's photograph was done, around mid-1871. Upton served from July 1, 1870, to June 30, 1875; Ruger from July 1871 to June 30, 1876. Editor's collection.

The entire Upton family gathered to honor their parents, Daniel and Electa, on their golden wedding anniversary, September 31, 1871, at the family home in Batavia, New York. The Uptons had thirteen children, eleven of whom lived to adulthood. Emory is in the back row, second from left, next to his brother James. Standing in the center are Maria and Sara. Sara was Upton's provisional "housewife" after Emily's death. She and Maria were recipients of much of Emory's correspondence. Sara became the executor of Upton's estate. Genesee County History Department.

Emily Upton's parents, Enos Thompson Throop Martin and Cornelia Williams Martin. Emily corresponded regularly with her mother during her brief marriage, and her father subsidized the couple as they struggled to set up household in Memphis and Atlanta. Princeton University Library.

6   Ordered to Atlanta

Emily

Nassau, March 1st [1869]

My dearest Mother,

I am sorry you were so worried by our last letters. It does sometimes seem hard to know what to write home. If I do not feel as well and as tho' I had not improved the last month as much as I did at first. I do not think it is best to conceal it in my letters for it only leads you all to expect too much when I return and you are disappointed in the end and yet if I write just how matters are, I am afraid of your being anxious. This time I am, however, going to state things just as they are.

I am much better than when I came up here, I have more appetite and I am more comfortable in every way than when I last wrote. Still, I am very weak and often quite ill, sometimes it is many things sometimes, the other trouble. The last six weeks have been rather trying; so many Northers and I have had several colds, which of course have made me rather miserable. I never was more comfortable in my life than I am here. We have two large drawing rooms pleasantly located and quiet, in fact, the prettiest rooms in the house. There is nothing that I can think of that I do not have. I sometimes think I am rather the pet invalid in the house for all the little delicacies are sent to me by the proprietors.

Nelly is perfectly devoted to me. She dresses me every day from my stockings to my hair and seems to have only one thought to spare me fatigue and make me comfortable. I never saw her better or happier in my life and we have a pleasant, cheerful time together.

The ladies in the hotel are very kind to me. If anyone has flowers first or any luxury sent them, I am sure to be a sharer and sometimes I overwhelmed with their bounty. I think the change of scene and society here has been a great thing for me.

You ask me, dear mother, if I want anyone to come down to me. I really do not—not much as I should enjoy seeing you or my dear father or my husband. I do not think there is any necessity for it. I know I am just as comfortable as I could be in the best of climates, with the best of care. Here at the hotel, I can do just as I please and am not obliged to make an effort as I do when in a private house. I not think I shall leave here until I return home. I would much rather be independent. Dr. Kirkwood comes to see me every day and dear Mrs. Kirkwood turns up here every day too and seems just as fond of us and as sweet as tho' we were her children and sends us all sorts of nice things.

Well my dearest mother, I have given you a full account of matters and I hope you will feel relieved about me for I am as pleasantly situated as well could be and whether I am better or not is in God's hands. I am as prudent as one could be. I have written so much about myself that I have but little space or strength to tell you how much pleasure your letters give me. I was very glad to hear such good news from our little church! You seem to be devoting yourself to the neighborhood this winter. I know your labors will be rewarded.

Thank you, my dear mother, for the lovely book you sent me. I shall prize it very highly and enjoy the lovely ballads very much. The first thing I saw when the book opened was that sweet little poem "I am praying for you." It seemed like my dearest mother's voice to her sick child who needs and values her prayers very much and I took it as such.

I shall do all the good I can with the cards and the books. I have already given away a good many I brought with me. I find sometimes I can do a little good.

[*Here the letter ends.*]

Emory

Memphis March 1st 1869

My darling Emily:
It was not long since that I had to say I shall not see my wife till next year. Now my love, I can say I shall see her next month, and can easily count the days till she shall join me in New Orleans. There I shall take her on my lap, draw her close to me and allow her and Nelly to talk till their tongues weary of what they have done and what has happened to them since our long absence from each other. Happy day when I shall again see you in my arms and call you my wife, pet, darling and every sweet name love may dictate.

Tonight, or perhaps tomorrow morning early you will receive my letters and have a feast. I hope your love will be so full that with patience you can await the coming of the steamer, which is to bear you to the affection of your husband. The telegram will astound you but that will be dissipated when you get further news via Havana & a return of the steamer *Moro Castle*. The ring I am now anxious to hear about, I shall be so sorry if you did not receive it Feb 19th the anniversary of our nuptials.[1] Your mother wrote me a letter half in love, half giving me fits, so I immediately called up the Sergeants and requested all the enlisted men who had no bibles to come to take them and already I have distributed quite a number.[2] She withdraws her china scheme since it might open [*illegible*] of ambition, destructive of your happiness. I have become thoroughly contented with my position, and only want the warm earnest love of my beautiful wife to make me happy.

Hurry up April 10th. I am going to make the days pass with a whirl and you will see one happy man when your husband looks into those beautiful blue eyes of his wife.

My love to Nelly, your devoted, Emory

Memphis, March 2nd 1869

My dear Emily:

Notwithstanding I try to make myself believe the time is not far off when I shall see you, it yet seems to be far away. Still when you get this, I shall be in the excitement and expectation of meeting you, so if you do know that I am pining to see you it will not have a bad effect on you.

No details in regard to our going to Arizona have yet been received, but the order announcing the fact set all to thinking. Its effect on the wives varies with their dispositions. Mrs. Col. C[3] thinks she can't leave her mother, and therefore purposes not to accompany her husband. Mrs. Conway[4] will be as contented with her husband in Arizona as elsewhere, same with Mrs. Hugo.[5] Mrs. E[6] shed a few tears, then dashed them from her eyes and set to work bravely studying Spanish, and preparing herself for the journey. I told Mrs. C that if my wife were to abandon me at such a time I would step over into Indiana and rid myself of her. This I did deliberately that she might know I thought it was the duty of the wife to go with her husband, wherever he might be sent.

I know that my pet once with me again will be made so happy that the thought of separation on any account, would be positively painful to her. But my dear, I am glad we are field officers, and that we shall not have to scrimp the way some of the families do at the post. I see some officers who spend on cigars, drinks, and billiards, the money that should go to dressing their wives and I rejoice that your husband is not of that order.

We shall soon have a new President.[7] Grant's reticence is more puzzling to the politicians than ever, and from indications, I believe he is going to run his own administration.

I have very pleasant dreams of you occasionally, but I only feel the more desolate when I realize they are but dreams. All this however has its end April 10th my love and thence forward we shall be two happy beings.

With much love your devoted, Emory

Emily

Nassau, March 3, 1869

My dearest Father,

I have two letters for which to thank you, as the steamer that brought us here did not remain long enough for us to answer the letter we found awaiting us. Since our mail came this week all my plans have been so much altered that all that I was going to write you of is now of no avail and my mind is just now so absorbed by the contents of my telegraph that nothing else seems worth writing of.

I must confess that I was surprised by Emory's telegraph. "Leave last of March. Regiment goes to California," for, I really thought, despite my knowledge of Army life that we were to remain in Memphis for some time. I will not deny that it was not without a heartache that I relinquished all my bright anticipations of the pleasant home in Memphis that you my dear father and mother as well as my husband had been preparing for my return and the rest there at last after my years wandering. Also, the long sea voyage and an ocean once more between me and my dear ones at home seemed a real misfortune. But the struggle is now over and my mind is made up to whatever may come. It is about time that I should commence my soldier life and take some of the hardships like the rest.

Of course, I am very anxious to know the particulars and shall await with great impatience the return of the steamer from Havana, which will, I hope, bring me letters from Emory better than my telegraph. I am glad it is the regiment, not ourselves alone who are ordered to California for I wish to be with our own men, but I wish I knew where our destination was.

I am very much obliged to you for the detailed account you give of your finances, which interested me very much. I am so glad you have sold your house so advantageously and been able thereby to remove some of the burdens from your mind. I think it is too much for you to give us two thousand dollars more besides all you have done for me during the last year and I am truly obliged to you for this new proof of your thoughtful kindness for my welfare. And we shall try and make the best, possible use of it. The five hundred dollars you sent me here I shall not use, I trust. And I have given it into Nelly's hands to be taken home as I think the three thousand ought and will last us to our journeys end.

I am also, my dear father, very much obliged to you for offering to pay Lily as I have no greenbacks now, all our money being in gold or silver. The truth is when I commence now on paper to make some acknowledgment of your kind thoughtfulness of my comfort, I cannot stop.

The tea [*illegible*] and breakfast set mother says is from you on my wedding day and I thank you most heartily for it. I suppose the things have not been sent to Memphis now that you know our plans, which I suppose is to leave the first of May, but time will show.

I am very glad you and mother had such a delightful visit in Washington and Betty's wedding went off so nicely.[8] I do think Betty's happiness is now insured for life. Nelly has written you a full account of our arrival and life here. I do not think we can do anything but offer Dr. and Mrs. Kirkwood the hospitalities of Willowbrook, which I think they will be glad to accept as they go to the states this spring.

I write you but a short letter but have others to finish.

Your affect. child, Emily

Emory

Memphis March 3rd 1869

My darling Pet:

I have just torn myself away from fourteen or fifteen officers that I might enjoy myself in having a nice quiet chat with you my dear, just before returning. I will admit that I am quite tired and sleepy owing to a little party Mrs. Conway had last evening. It passed off very pleasantly all the ladies of the post being present, which you know includes Mrs. Christopher, Mrs. Estes, Mrs. Hugo & Mrs. Conway. Mrs. Tremain[9] is in mourning, and does not go out. Besides the post ladies were two others, one Mrs. Bainbridge or as you know her Miss Easterly of Auburn with whom I had the pleasure of dancing the Lancer.[10] The widow, Mrs. Pettit[11] is still here and cuts a wide swath. She is a curiosity, not beautiful by any means, yet she is so full of animal life, so full of the d___l [devil] that all the young bachelors are desperate over her and in vain throw themselves on their knees before her, but to no purpose. She has two little girls, has enough money to support herself and has such a jolly good time flying around single that she is not disposed to marry.

One officer I know has offered himself three times, a [*illegible*] attendance at all hours, a crumb once in a while falling from her table to encourage him, while a wealthy old bachelor, ignoring any such idea as love has made up his mind that she would suit him very well, and he too lingers patiently about waiting his chance to put in his claim.

No news yet about going to Arizona. The order, if carried out will be providential for you as I shall expect & return after one or two years with a wife in the full vigor of health and womanhood. Your being absent my dear, necessarily will detain me here till the second squad takes its departure. I am now counting the days; I can't help it. I want to see you so much. Absence does not quench my yearning for you, and nothing but your presence can appease it. Just think, a few more letters only to write you, and then you will sail to meet me. All goes on smoothly at the Post.

My love to Nelly, good night. I am tired and wish I had you here to pet me and drive away fatigue. With many warm kisses, your loving husband, Emory.

Memphis, March 4th 1869

My darling Wife:

I have just told Dodge for variety's sake, I was going to write to my wife and he said "I would." So, I shall.

We are still in "status quo" nothing having been heard of the disposition awaiting us.

There will be two details and in your account. [?] I shall certainly go with the last. If we go via the Isthmus, the first squad will have the advantage but should we wait till June or July, we may have the benefit of Pacific R.R.

I wonder often how I shall find you when we meet at New Orleans. Stronger, I hope than when we parted my darling, but I shall not be disappointed if you are no better than when I left you at Key West. I *want* you with me and I shall just be too happy to do anything for you to relieve any pain or increase your comfort. If you go with me to Arizona, and I make use of the expansion, because so many wives at this post seem doubtful about accompanying their husbands, I am just going to do my prettiest to make you happy and I think I shall succeed.

My dear, you don't know in your absence what strides you have made in my affections. I began to appreciate you at your worth and to realize, sick or well, how great a treasure a husband has in your heart. I want the day to arrive when we shall have our own home. Circumstances keep us from it for the present but when it comes, like the squirrel who has gnawed through the thick crust of a hickory nut; we shall only find the kernel the sweeter.

Dodge is standing over me urging me to go to the tea, but I will have my say out. I will tell my Emily that my heart is brimful of love for her and that one smile from her lovely eyes would make me supremely happy. Good night, my darling, may God watch over and keep you, your fond husband, Emory.

Memphis, March 4th 1869[12]

My dear Emily:

Quite an animated discussion has just been held in my quarters between Dodge & Granger in reference to the route we are to pursue in getting to our new posts in Arizona. The question is shall we go via the Isthmus or Santa Fe. However, they conclude, it signifies nothing, as the route is to be decided at Washington. Gen. Granger however has recommended the Isthmus route. I wish you were here that we might go with the first detail, as it will be so hot both in the Gulf and in making the march from Ft. Yuma to our posts if we wait till June. But "sufficient unto this day is the evil thereof."[13] I am pretty thoroughly convinced that all things will in God's providence turn out for good to us.

The news has quite upset their nice plans for our comfort at Willowbrook but they take a cheerful view of it. Granger says that people never take cold in Arizona, so that would be especially nice for you. Were you in good health, we might get out of this arrangement by going to West Point but I do not want to go there until you are strong for I know you look to West Point as an Army heaven. If you are willing to go with me, I care not if they send me to a desert for wherever we are I think with your disposition I can make you happy and I know you will do so by me.

Grant's inauguration was very short and to the point. The best cabinet appointment is that of A. T. Stewart to the Treasury Department.[14] Give us economy and honesty in the administration of the revenue laws and we shall be all right.

Throop writes me occasionally and seems to be getting on well. Evie and Lily went to Washington and stopped at the Sands during the inauguration. I shall soon receive a mail that is in eight or ten days. Just think, I haven't heard from you since Feb 8th. You may imagine my anxiety and desire to hear from you but I feel sure you are improving. The days I have now get reduced to a certainty and my only thought is to meet you at New Orleans.

My love to Nelly. Ever your affectionate husband, Emory

Memphis, March 4, 1869[15]

My dear Maria,

Your letter dated 23 February gave me much pleasure and I thank you for it. It is today that saw the inauguration of the administration of General Grant as President of the US, an important day in our history. I think that from the present we will start to enter into a period of prosperity without example in our time and that in the four years that he will continue in office. We will see peace in our country solidly established and everyone happy.

There is nothing new here since my last letter but we have received orders sending us to the Arizona Territory. The officers of the 25th infantry regiment must change postings with those of the 32nd who now occupy the territory.[16] The details of the execution of the orders haven't arrived, but it's probable that one corps of officers will leave soon, and that the others will stay until the first corps of officers of the 32nd have arrived here. The order pleases me because the climate of Arizona[17] will be good for Emily and believe me, her health is always the first consideration. Seeing that she can't join me before April 10, I must stay here until the time of departure for the Second Corps, which could be as far off as June 11.

I will wait for Emily by the steamer leaving New York for Nassau the 25th of March and I will welcome her at New Orleans the 8th or 10th of April. As our stay will be so short, instead of setting up housekeeping we will take our meals at the hotel opposite. Our carriage, horses, and furniture—must all be sold at a reduced price, but we would have to do this for any change of posting.

Not a word have I received from my dear wife since the 8th of February, but on that day, she was better than before. I am sure that the climate in Nassau will be better for her than that of Key West, which was too humid. A steamer will leave from Havana the 6th of this month via Nassau, New York and, I hope will bring many letters by the 16th. Once my wife is living with me again, there is no reason for us to separate in the future.

Her sister Evy, who is now in Arizona, will visit Willowbrook in the spring and it is possible that they will meet each other before we leave. I hope to have the time.

I hope to have the time to take en route, Battle Creek,[18] Batavia, and Willowbrook, paying a short visit at each place, but there is such uncertainty that I can't calculate. I was glad to hear that John had bought a house in Decatur [Michigan]. We can visit him in the future with little trouble and there are other advantages for him—enlarging his business, reputation, etc.

In the last six months as of February first my pay has provided me $1695.[19] Very good, I think, isn't it? I am worried of finally hearing from Willowbrook and about what they think of our movements. Because of Evy it is probable that they will be at ease about it. Colonel Dodge is still staying at my house, but he will look for apartments before Emily's arrival. You can't understand how much I long to see my Emily, a feeling equally felt by her.

Please present my compliments to Miss Haines and the young ones. I am certain that I will see you before my departure for Arizona where it is unlikely that I will remain more than two years.

With a heart full of love for you, I am always your devoted brother.
Emory

Emily

Nassau, March 5th, 1869

My dearest Mother,
I must not let another day pass without commencing my letter to you. I was very glad to receive your letters of Feb'y 18th and 19th and thank you very much for writing me on the 19th. It was rather sad, dear mother, to spend this first anniversary so far from my husband but I was very much pleased to find that the day had not been forgotten for in the morning, Dr. Kirkwood presented me with a token of Emory's thoughtful love, a beautiful amethyst ring like yours, which he had sent down some time before to be presented on that day.

Nelly also gave me a carved bread trencher and knife, also a butter dish and knife to match. You also wrote me that my dear father and yourself have sent me a substantial token of your remembrance of the occasion. What can I say to thank you suitably for all these things—carpets, linen, china, etc. I am delighted and truly grateful to you both. All winter I have found my great desire has been to make and buy things for my house. I have been so interested and delighted with the accounts, which Emory has sent me of all he was doing to make our home comfortable and pleasant. My riding horse was well as our pretty carriage and horses, I have thought of with great pleasure, but I will not say anything of my disappointment for I have made up my mind not to utter a word of complaint however, I feel for it will be no less a disappointment to Emory to find all his works and hopes in vain. And I am so thankful that I am not too sick to go with him and that he has not to seek a new home and friends himself. Still, my heart sinks at the thought of an ocean between my home and the dear ones, but I suppose there is some good in it, if I can find it out.

I am very glad you got the carpets alike; they will be so much more useful and I hope I can take them with me. However, I am all in the dark till Emory's letters come telling me the particulars of the move. As to the china, I had just written to Emory about getting a set and he was only waiting to recover from the purchase of the carriage before getting it. What a dear sweet mother you are to buy my table linen as a present, you know I only want you to choose it for me. I think you and father are doing too much for us, but I assure you we appreciate your kindness.

I am so glad Mrs. Rankin has been to see you. I know you enjoyed her visit. What a delightful time you and father must have had in Washington. Betty's wedding seems to have been a time of real rejoicing where all the quarrels were made up. What a blessed thing! Where is she now? I am glad you met so many interesting people in Washington. I wish I could write you a longer letter for I have much more to say, but my head troubles me so much the last few days that I cannot write the letters I would.

I am very much interested in all you tell me of the mission work. I just marvel at your success; it is so complete. If you think best you might take the money I sent you for Mr. Brown,[20] as the other mission seems so flourishing.

Nelly and I will send you some more. Dr. and Mrs. Kirkwood are untiring in their kindness. They really are glad to have us here. Several times the last few days, Mrs. Kirkwood has exclaimed, "What shall I do when you are gone, girls? You will leave me before I know it." We are with her all the time, walking, driving, sewing together.

With fondest love to all at home, your loving child, Emily.

Sunday, March 8th

I must add one line more as I have the chance to say that I am much better than when I came and find my improvement is continuous. Only three weeks from tomorrow and we shall start towards Memphis. I am so delighted. Still, our home is *very* pleasant.

Emory

Memphis March 8th 1869

[*no salutation*]

To sit down tonight my dear love, my precious Emily, is to mark off the lapse of another twenty-four hours. Twenty-four hours nearer meeting than when I wrote you last night. I know now, my Cherie, to borrow use of your pet names, you are looking forward with the same impatience as myself to be again clasped in each other's arms. Will it not be bliss itself to see each other again and may God grant that no more separations may occur.

Today has been quiet and monotonous and anticipating your arrival and the time we will require to talk to each other.

I have been trying to complete the revision of my Tactics, but so numerous have been my interruptions so unexpected demands for my time that I made little progress.

The last evidence of your love, the Shakespeare lies before me on the table and I might just before commencing my letters, in culling some of its treasure. I thought how much I would give could I throw myself on the lounge, draw a chair close to me, and then holding your soft white hand, hear you repeat Gray's Elegy or any other beautiful piece with which your memory is stored. Sweet girl. My loved wife. I cannot tell you how much or in how many ways I miss you.

Still on orders. You understand that the order for our transfer is published but it has not been sent to us. The Army has been reduced to twenty-*five* regiments but no officers mustered out. As vacancies occur, consolidations are to be made and when twenty-five regiments only exist, then promotions will again be resumed. This check makes little difference to us Pet for as I have told you, *we* shall be brigadiers as soon in one case as in the other until we get orders.[21]

I am going to hold onto the carriage and horses that you may have some benefit from them. Today I suppose the *Moro Castle* left Nassau bearing your letters. What a treat in store for you about the 16th. I can only, at the outside, write you twelve more letters and am I not glad that then your dear voice will give place to epistles? Today, a month, I shall get your telegram. Send it so I may receive it the day you sail in time to leave for N. O. Good night, my pet, I kiss you fondly

Your devoted, Emory

Memphis March 9th 1869

My dear Emily:

We have had very cool disagreeable weather since the first of March and now we are paying for our good weather by heavy falls of rain. It is the transition period between winter and summer and long before you reach us we shall have settled, delightful weather.

I caught cold about two weeks ago and it has persecuted me ever since refusing to relinquish its hold either on my lungs or in my head. I am however, a stout looking invalid so am not alarmed.

I received a letter from Gen. Whipple, A. A. G. at Louisville[22] saying he expects daily to receive the order specifying who shall go to Arizona in the first detachment. I am sure we shall not go to the last and now that the reduction of the Army leaves about twenty supernumerary Lieutenant Colonels, I shall have no hesitancy in requesting a delay till fall.

The rain has fallen for two days and I presume will continue for some time giving us quite a flood.

Mrs. Liscum, wife of Cap. Liscum[23] stationed at Columbus, Ky is quite enthusiastic over a prospect of going to the Pacific and is resolved to stick to the Capt. through thick and thin. She is here on a visit for two or three days and I shall escort her home so as to see the Captain's Company.

The *Moro Castle* is well on her way to *New* York with the great treat is to await me. I will guess ten letters and how eagerly they will be perused.

The 6th Infantry passed through here today en route to New Mexico. I have seen none of the officers so don't know how they like their orders. One officer of the 32nd on leave has already been ordered to report to this regiment.[24]

I am quite anxious to get your accounts of Nassau. Give my love [to] Nelly and let me know how she likes the idea of going to Arizona.

With much love, your devoted husband, Emory

Memphis March 10th 1869

[no salutation]

How often do I wonder what my darling is doing, yet knowing little of the attractions of Nassau, I can form no idea. Soon however, I shall see you in your daily duties, and how amiable I am going to be in your house. Writing, reading, or whatever I may be doing, you interrupt me whenever you please, may sit in my lap, or present your sweet face to be kissed as often as you please. I am going to love you and make up for all lost time. In you darling, centers all my future, and anticipating the bliss you can afford me, I am willing to suppress all ambition.

Discontent and unhappiness can only be suspended by the pursuit of ambitious projects, but the object attained, they shall remain, and move into equally futile undertakings. In peace with God, true happiness does not exist outside the family circle, and I bless them daily for having given me a companion so suited to my temperament and so lovely in her every act.

The day has passed without anything to mark its flight. Just before setting down to write this, I played four games of "Croquet" with Mrs. Pettit, against Capts. Poole and Parkinson. The games stood two and two but night set in to prevent the rubber.

I received a letter for Nelly, which I send on.

Like a straw telling which way the wind blows, it is a pleasant forerunner of your coming. I get plenty of letters, two and three every mail, but for a month the backhand has not appeared on their superscriptions. [?]

Dodge is still with me and is a fun companion. I entertain him, Willowbrook fashion, which means that each goes his own way, talk when we please, and remain silent when we please.

Now Pet, imagine me creeping up to you and impressing kisses on your lovely neck. With a heart full of love your ever fond, Emory.

Memphis, March 28, 1869[25]

My dear Maria,

I am very happy this evening because next Sunday I will embrace my wife in New Orleans. She will leave Nassau tomorrow and by a happy coincidence, she will find in Havana a steamer that left from Baltimore the same day that the steamer via Nassau left New York, on which she will take her passage for New Orleans. I will go there Friday and expect her Sunday.

Have you learned that our destination has changed? Instead of our regiment going to Arizona, we will go to Atlanta.[26] It is a place with a good climate where it isn't possible that my dear wife will not do well and I hope that a three to four-year stay will be sufficient to re-establish her health. I am not sure that I will be given the command of the garrison in Atlanta, but that matters very little to me, as long as I can stay in Georgia. It is a hot and even climate that I am looking for. Under the current conditions of my dear Emily's, I will keep myself near, alert to a change of plans, but under the circumstances, my first concerns are for her. Whether or not we set up a household is now the question, but I hope that it is one that will be resolved in my orders to follow. With little expense, I can take my carriage, horses and all my household goods to Atlanta and if we stay there, we will be comfortable in very little time.[27]

I hope that your health is good. My mother in law wants you to visit her at her home en route from New York to Batavia. She told me that she loves you and that you think alike and understand each other. Be sure to visit her. She will welcome you eagerly. I love her very much—almost as much as my wife.

Your affectionate brother, Emory

7 Return to Nassau

Emily

Havana, April 2, 1869

My dearest mother,

I suppose with this [letter] you have received via Memphis our telegraph stating our safe arrival here and plans for the next move. The first news we heard yesterday morning was that we were lying just at the side of the *Liberty*,[1] the Baltimore steamer, which had come in the night before, and there sure enough, this fine, large vessel was just in time for us. General Morris Miller[2] sent me word through Capt. Balch (of the *Contoocook*)[3] that my servant was on board so then I thought I was indeed favored. Capt. Bartlett[4] and Lt. Green[5] soon appeared and gave us a hearty welcome, sent our trunks on board the *Liberty*, much to the horror of the officials who however, did not dare to resist a man of wars boat. Capt. Van Slice[6] invited us to breakfast with Capt. Balch. Capt. Bartlett and Mr. Green as well. He gave us a beautiful breakfast, which we all enjoyed very much.

Soon after we started for shore stopping on our way at the *Liberty* where I found Nancy[7] delighted to see me. We thought, as the steamer did not sail for nearly two days, we should be more comfortable at Mrs. Almy's,[8] so we went there and found our rooms awaiting us. Mr. McIlvane had engaged them before he left. Mr. Green got our trunks for us and in the afternoon, Capt. B took us out for a little shopping, which we accomplished.

Last evening, Capt. Balch, Capt. Bartlett and Mr. Green spent with us and Capt. B has also been here this morning. Yesterday when we were passing the *Contoocook*, Admiral Hoff[9] came out to see us. He was pleasant as ever. I think we shall go aboard the *Liberty* this afternoon so as to be ready for a start. I am very glad General Miller's family is to be our "companions de voyage."

I have not had time this morning to answer my letters from home. This will do from New Orleans. I am glad that we are going to Atlanta instead of Arizona and feel as happy as possible in anticipating the summer now. Emory seems crazy to have me once more and I am wild to get to him. We telegraphed him yesterday and he will meet us in New Orleans Tuesday, I trust. I do not know whether I am going to Memphis or Atlanta. I don't care much. Our voyage from Nassau was delightful and Capt. Van Slice was so good to us that I was sorry to leave the *Columbia*.[10]

I am feeling quite well. The admiral and all my friends here were amazed at the improvement the last eight weeks had made in my appearance. I must take care and not get cold when I meet my husband for I want him to see me looking as he never saw me before. Good bye, dear mother, your loving Emily.

McPherson Barracks, April 29, 1869

My dearest Mother,

Your last letter was very welcome and I have wanted before this to answer it. But I have not been feeling very energetic these last few days and so put it off. I have had a cold but am now feeling much better and think, as the weather seems more settled I shall feel well soon.

Atlanta, I like better each day and I think we shall be very happy here. Emory is busy all the time and comes in a dozen times a day saying how glad he is to be fully occupied once more. I find I have all the society I want for there are many officers and their wives here that I find all the time I can spare taken up with making and receiving calls. You know I have met four regiments here.

This afternoon we went to a wedding in town. Col. Smyth and Miss Poole. It went off very nicely and we met some very pleasant people there.

This had been one of the most perfect days, warm and delightful. I was surprised to see the porches in town covered with roses and the gardens full of flowers. The woods are covered with the most beautiful wild flowers and I see quantities carried about. Everyone is very good to me and I have strawberries, flowers and pretty things given me constantly. I have seven vases of flowers in my parlor now.

I suppose by this time you have returned from your visit from Albany and Nelly and Lily are each with you. How dearly I should like to be there too and I trust I shall in a few months. I dearly wish that you and father could come down here this spring. You would enjoy seeing this most interesting place exceedingly and it would make us so very happy. I hope Emory will be able to get ordered North about July. I think before that General Ruger will take command. I suppose you will not feel as if you could leave home till you see Jack safely admitted to West Point. Emory has just written you about the books. I am very glad you are to present them. I have enjoyed distributing the bible. I have myself given away 108, one hundred and eight writing the men's names in most of them a higher appreciation of the book as it makes it a more personal thing. I have been very much interested to find with what interest the men desire their bibles and testaments and with what testimonials and pleasure they answer when I ask them if they would like a bible. I shall write to Mr. Smith soon and give him account of the distribution. I shall find plenty to do here for the field is very extensive.

I am very sorry Mr. Brown is to go so soon, how you will miss him. I shall be very glad to join you in any project you may devise for an offering. I will write you more fully on the subject in a few days. Now I will say goodbye, with dearest love to father and all the family, I am your loving child, Emily

McPherson Barracks, May 4, 1869[11]

Mr. T. Ralston Smith[12]

Dear Sir,

Your letter of March 18th reached me in New Orleans a month ago and I should have replied to it before this late day, but that I have been prevented by illness. In my letter of February, I promised to commit a box of bibles sent to Key West to the care of some reliable person. I accordingly wrote to the express agent to retain the box till called for and also to the lady I mentioned asking her to undertake the duty of distributing the bibles to the destitute of Key West. Before however, the letter could be received, notice was sent to me that in my absence, the box had been forwarded to Gen. Upton at Memphis. On my arrival in New Orleans, Gen. Upton gave me your letter and informed me that the box of bibles had reached Memphis in safety and been forwarded to Atlanta GA (where we had just been ordered). At McPherson Barracks, I found the box safely stowed away in our quarters. Upon deliberation I concluded to retain the bibles for several reasons. First because we had in our barracks more men than had ever been together since the close of the war. The 25th, 18th, 16th, and 2nd regiments of Infantry assembled here for consolidation. Such an opportunity for distributing the scriptures I knew would not soon occur again.

Secondly, I found that Gen. Upton after supplying the want of his men at Memphis had upon being ordered to Atlanta committed the rest of the bibles and testaments to the care of his pastor Rev.

Dr. White, Calvary Church who he knew would make the [best] possible use of them so that I really needed a new supply. The express also had been about $20 already and I knew by the time the box was returned to Key West, this would be almost doubled. I trust therefore that the society will not think I have taken a liberty in appropriating their grant of bibles to other than the specified object. To me there seemed a providence in these bibles being sent here at this time and in such an unexpected manner.

As the 2nd Infantry was to leave in a week or ten days, I commenced at once the work of distribution making it a rule not to give a bible unless it was asked for. As a general thing, I have gone to the soldiers myself and have been exceedingly gratified to see with what pleasure and eagerness they replied when I asked them if they would like a bible. I cannot remember a single instance where I found a soldier who had a bible or who refused to accept one. As soon as I could find means to let the soldier know that I had bibles for them, I had several lists of names sent me from companies of the 2nd Infantry who wished for bibles and the day before the regiment left I found plenty of occupation in supplying the demand and writing the men's names in their bibles and testaments. (I find they value them more when I do this) and it also enables me to retain a list of books I give away.

In the course of this distribution many pleasant and interesting incidents occur, which I have not space for here to relate except these two cases. One morning I called my husband's orderly in and upon finding he had no bible or testament but was anxious to possess one. I gave him a bible with which he went to his quarters much pleased but returned in about half an hour saying that his 1st Sergeant had been trying to take his bible from him, but he had promised to come to me for another to take its place.

Since I commenced this letter I have given testament to the orderly for the day who was at one time one of the worst soldiers but has been reformed more by kindness than punishment and looking out of the window, I see him standing at his post reading it all unmindful of the hot sun. God grant that through his word a light from above may lighten his dark understanding.

I have already distributed one hundred and ten bibles and hope soon to be able to report more work accomplished. Hoping soon to hear of your approval in this matter

E. M. Upton

McPherson Barracks, May 17th 1869

My dearest mother,

I had such a severe headache yesterday that I was not able to write you the letter that I planned to before I go down town this morning. I will write you a short letter at least.

I am anxious to hear of the results of your visit to New York in regard to Ned's[13] hearing and hope that today's mail will bring me a letter. I had a note from Molly on Saturday in which she says that father had hurt his leg by a fall with Lainder.[14] I hope he has recovered from his injuries by this time. I know he would find it hard to be laid up in the spring. How pleasant it must be to have Lily home. Just think in about five weeks I shall be home myself. How much I shall enjoy it and I think Emory will bring me as he has promised to attend the Army meeting in New York on the fifth of July and the Secretary gives six days leave for this purpose.

I hope you received my letter enclosing one to Dr. Smith. I have given away forty-four bibles and testaments this week. You remember sending me some tracts in the trunk. I put a little tract in each bible and gave them to the two companies that left us last week. Yesterday afternoon two Methodist ministers came up to see Emory about having preaching for the soldiers. He has given them a building for the purpose and next Sunday at three, we hold the first meeting. I hope this will succeed and be the means of good to the men. I hope Mr. Zabriskie will have the chaplaincy of this post tho' I fear the companies now here will not continue long together, the people don't like to see so many soldiers in one place. Ever since we came here we have been to the little Episcopal Church.[15] It was repaired and in part supported by General Meade and his officers, so that it has become the army church here and it is the only one where officers are not liable to meet with disrespect.[16] The hard feeling here in Atlanta does not in any way diminish I am sorry to say.

I often wish dear mother, that you could see how pleasantly situated I am here and how comfortable everything is about me. I enjoy housekeeping very much. I know just how much I have to spend and all I can save after living comfortably is so much clear gain and at my disposition. So far, I have done very well for these first months of course, [we] have had unusual expenses. I send you a small contribution for the object you spoke of which I think a very pleasant idea. I wish it were more. Next month when I get my expenses regulated, I shall be able to have more.

I was very glad to get Evy's letter, I see they have given up expecting us. I hope they will remain at McDowell till they come East. Where is Uncle Throop now? And when does he return to Willowbrook? I suppose it begins to look lovely at home now. Molly sent me some violets in a letter, which were sweeter to me than any flowers here. I have them before me now. In the trunk, I found some mats with ribbon run through them, were they made up for the Society?

Emory is reading Dr. Nevius' book on China.[17] I have not seen him so much interested in a book for a long time. Every moment he can spare, he takes it up. The care of this large post and the revision of his book keep Emory at work constantly.

Who preaches in our church now? Mr. Brown's going will leave a burden on your shoulders again. But I must close my letter with a great deal of love.

I am dear mother, your loving Emily.

McPherson Barracks, June 1st, 1869

My dearest mother,

My first thought this morning is of you so although I cannot give you my best wishes in person for many returns of this anniversary, yet I can at least write you a letter as I did last year at Florence. I am sorry we could not have all met at Willowbrook on your wedding day as we had planned before Evy decided not to come home. This must be our gala day of the year and in the future, I hope we shall be more fortunate in meeting.

I suppose father and Nelly are in Salem by this time so you are once more a small family as I think Lily and Gren[ville] went back last week. I hope you are not having the warm weather we are undergoing at present. I have suffered more the last ten days from heat than in ages before. In our coolest room the thermometer has stood for several days over ninety and the coolest hour in the night it is eighty-three. So, I do not do anything but keep quiet and cool as possible.

General Terry[18] came on Sunday and General Ruger[19] takes the command here tomorrow. General Terry brings his mother and two sisters with him, which will add somewhat to our society. He has also pleasant officers on his staff.

I suppose you are still busy with the house and as you wrote me you had much to do. Now that I have allowed my thoughts to dwell on home, I am growing very impatient to be with you. I hope to find out this week if possible whether we are to remain here, so that if we do not return I can have my things in a moveable state. Nancy, I have decided to bring with me. She will be a real comfort to Nelly. I was very glad to get the letters from Evy and Andrew that father forwarded to me. How much happiness their dear little girl gives them. I suppose Jack is all engaged about West Point just now. Emory wrote to Prof. Kendrick,[20] Church[21] and Col. Hunt[22] about Jack this week so they will be prepared to do all they can.

Hoping my dear mother to have another of your good letters soon I am, your loving child, Emily

McPherson Barracks, June 7, 1869

My dearest father,
Before this I suppose you have returned from Salem with Grandmother and Nelly so this letter will reach you at Willowbrook. I hope your leg does not trouble you now, tho' I know that such a bruise is long in healing. I am disgusted because two more companies left this morning to join Major Van Voast[23] at Warrenton.[24] He took two companies with him about a month ago but as they apprehended some trouble they have increased his force to four companies. That part of the state is in rather a bad condition. Still I should be sorry to see violence used for these people are still so bitter that any act of control by the troops is magnified into the worst oppression. But General Terry so far seems determined to show them that the armed forces are not here for nothing but will be used to keep peace and protect Northerners. One-night last week some disturbance occurred in town where upon he sent for some companies and for two days and nights afterward they patrolled the streets much to the disgust of the citizens. All has been quiet since.

I suppose Jack leaves for West Point today. I hope he will be successful for it would be a great disappointment to him to fail.

Next week I shall commence my preparations for leaving. I do not think there is a shadow of a chance that we will return here for I think before fall, this will be reduced to a four company post and even now Emory has but little to occupy him. General Ruger, I see, intends to remain here himself and is now very nicely settled.

The weather now is delightful and all the more enjoyable after the hot weather which is passed. How lovely it must be at home now all so fresh and green.

The carriage is at the door so I must close my letter and go downtown.

With love to all, I am, your very affect. child, Emily.

McPherson Barracks, June 12, 1869

My dear mother,
Your letter to Emory has just come and is a reminder to me that I have not written you this week, so before I am interrupted this morning, I will write you a short letter at least.

I received this week the report of the Arizona Ute mission and was very much interested in it. I think the map is splendid and seems to bring the object of the Association so much nearer and clearer to view. Who got the map up for you? I think your labors in this matter have been wonderfully blessed and prospered. I have been thinking of Jack much this week and my prayer Sunday at the communion was for him. Now we must trust in the Lord—be of good courage knowing that He is able to keep that which we have committed unto Him.

Emory has sent Mr. Zabriskie's application to Washington with a strong recommendation and we think it will be successful but I hear a week or two ago that the application made last fall for a chaplain was refused because the camp was within reach of churches.

I do not know when we shall leave here as Emory has received no answer to his application to be ordered to Washington as yet. If I find that he will be detained then I shall take Nancy and come home without him, as I am anxious to be at Willowbrook. The accounts we have of father's leg make us feel disturbed. I had no idea it troubled him so much. When is Uncle to return? I suppose Grandma is settled in her old room by this time. I was so sorry to hear the sad news your letter contained of little Nelly's[25] death. It will be a great grief to the family as she was such a comfort to Uncle Bradley's[26] old age.

I am glad you were pleased with the cake baskets. I hope Nelly will send me the account of the way the day was spent. I was very glad to see that the headquarters of the 21st Infantry there at McDowell[27] it will be so pleasant for Evy to meet Mrs. Stoneman[28]

I am pretty well but not as strong or free from coughing, as my impatient spirit would wish.

[*Here Emory finished the letter.*]

Nevertheless my courage is good and we hope for the time when I shall be well. I do not recollect what I have written in the first of this letter, but believe me, ever my dear mother, your affectionate,
Emily
PS Emory sent in his application to be ordered to Washington several days ago, we hope for our answer this week and to be home by the 26th or [2]7th.

Willowbrook, October 25th, 1869[29]

My dear George,[30]
I suppose you think I have forgotten all about your letter received several weeks ago but I have not and have only waited for time and strength to reply to it.

We expect Throop[31] tonight and shall enjoy a visit from him very much. I think he will remain a week. Today father received a picture of

Midge[32] at Prescott where Evy and Andrew went for the purpose. It is a real cunning picture. A dear little earnest face with big eyes. We were all very much pleased to see it and father wants to look at it all the time so you will have to wait till you come home to see it. I expect they will be very glad to see you for they will he quite lonely at home when mother and I are all gone.

A week from tonight we shall be on our way to New York. Emory will get to New York the same morning we do so I shall soon see him. You must think of us on the 4th of November at three, sailing out of New York harbor. I hope we shall have comfortable voyage.

Dr. Kirkwood went down tonight to New York. Catherine Thompson is still very sick.[33] I would not be surprised if she died too for she does not seem to improve in the least. I am glad you had such a pleasant time at West Roxbury. It must have been quite a pleasant change for you. I hope, my dear George, that you will write Nelly and me this winter for we shall want to know all about your doings good and bad. Mother has not been very well lately but her back is better tonight. Well, I have come to the end of my paper, so goodbye for the present.

Your loving sister, Emily.

Willowbrook, October 25th 1869

My dearest Evy,

Your sweet and comforting letter came to me more than two weeks ago and I thank you very much for it. As you suggested in each of our pleasant gardens we can point to the stone that causes many a pleasant hope and clear desire, but still the causes of thankfulness are so numerous that our murmurs are hushed before they find utterance and I, for one, feel that I have much to feel thankful for the opportunity afforded me of a chance to regain my health and strength this winter at Nassau, even though it be accompanied with separation from my husband and dear ones. Still when I see people about me dying for want of care and means to do, as it is necessary, I feel that I should not say a word.

I hope that you will pray for me this winter that I may have health and strength for I feel that my life-work is not yet commenced and I see so much work for me to do that I cannot yet accomplish. All your letters interest me so much and I shall miss them very much this winter while I am gone. One of the pleasant things I have to look forward to in this spring is find you and dear little Midge at Willowbrook on my return. How I long to see you I cannot tell, but I think of you very often.

This is my last week at home. I was just thinking how great the change would be this day, this week. Now I am sitting by a large coal fire, having had two mustard plasters this morning. Within two weeks, I shall be sailing into Nassau under a tropical sun. A week from tomorrow morning I shall meet Emory in New York and then we shall go together for five weeks, which will be a great comfort to us both.

I shall write you more from Nassau and till then, with fondest love for yourself and dear Andrew, I am your loving sister, Emily.

Nassau, November 14th 1869

My dearest mother,

I must at least write you a short letter tho' I shall leave all the full accounts to Nelly and Emory.

Our voyage was made far more comfortably than I had dared to hope and notwithstanding the rolling of the steamer, most of the time I seemed to increase my strength instead of losing ground. I also found that the sea air gave me more appetite. We landed several miles off and came in to Nassau in a schooner. The sail was delightful, late in the afternoon when the air was so fresh and warm.

Mrs. K's house was almost as well prepared for our arrival as tho' we had not been absent and we soon had our tea and I was safely in bed before I really began to know how tired I was. I have not yet quite got used to the very hot weather, which makes us all feel very indolent and exhausted. Indeed, I find it impossible to do the slightest unnecessary thing, but we shall soon be acclimated, I suppose and then you will have letters not quite so stupid.

Most of our old friends here have called upon us, tho' I have not seen them and seem glad to welcome us back.

Monday evening before we arrived, I asked Emory to offer a prayer of thanksgiving for all our mercies. So, Emory, Nelly and I had a little meeting. This morning Emory had prayers for Mrs. Kirkwood and we used the books you gave her. I hope it will be the beginning of good things.

You will take this miserable letter for what it is. I find it almost impossible to write just now. I am improving as much as I could hope in so short a time and have no doubt my next letter will be just as good then.

With love to Lily and Gren,[34] I am your loving child, Emily

Nassau, December 3rd 1869

My dearest mother,

As this is a cool day, I am going to improve the opportunity by writing one letter at least. We have been here a whole month now and have spent it very happily and as the first few weeks are always the longest, I have no doubt that Nelly and I shall be very contented and happy here this winter.

Having Emory here this month has been a great comfort to me and I shall feel perfectly satisfied to part with him when the steamer comes for I am strongest and better able to amuse and occupy myself than when I first came down and I know that if our time is occupied, then I can be contented.

Yesterday I came down for breakfast for the first time and did more than the months before so my improvement seems to continue tho' of course, I have days of prostration and pain sometimes. Emory declared this morning that I had gained ten pounds; I was so heavy to carry upstairs. Dr. and Mrs. Kirkwood seem to take a good deal of comfort with us and are as kind and good as possible. They seem to pine for Willowbrook for they have lost their good appetites and are not as energetic as they move. They think they lived on the "fat of the land" while with us. We three, on the contrary, take most kindly to the fare here and are all gaining flesh and becoming very lazy and idle.

Poor young Mallory's[35] death cast a real gloom over us all. It seemed so sudden and dreadful that he should die of yellow fever, when he had just come, but I suppose he would never have recovered his health if he had not had the fever for his lungs were much affected.

We are waiting for the steamer with great impatience to hear of dear Lily and it is a relief to feel that the *Columbia* has started and is now on its way with our letters. A month does seem a long time to be shut out from the world and so much can happen in that time.

Your peaches, dear mother, we have enjoyed very much, they are delicious and fully appreciated by us. The apples kept most well up to the last and Mrs. Kirkwood took a great deal of comfort sending them and the pears to her friends, some of whom, the pears were a new first, never before tried.

December 8th 1869

I will continue my letter dear mother from where I left off last week, tho' as far as our own life is concerned we have no events to record.

Time slips by so rapidly and with so little variety. We are very sorry not to have received letters from you, as we were very anxious to hear all the particulars of the arrival of little Helen. No one told us when she was born. We suppose you must have been written Mrs. Williams[36] and the letters are with her lost baggage as she says you sent a package by her. I am delighted that Lily has a dear little girl and am wild to see her. As Lily has been so well ever since you have been with her, I doubt not your visit in Albany has been a pleasant one and a change for you, which will be beneficial. Throop writes with great satisfaction and pleasure and his enjoyment of your visit and says you were having such comfort together. This dear little baby is going to be a sunbeam for this winter I believe, everyone seems to give her a hearty welcome. I wish I could see you or father with your own grandchild in your arms. I know you will love it as well as your own children. I hope dear Lily continues to do as well as when we last heard. She seems to have been wonderfully well throughout.

I must acknowledge it is with a sense of relief that I see Emory safely through his month without yellow fever. There have been several cases since we came which have made me a little nervous for him, but we have kept him from all damp places and made him take quinine, which is a great prevention.

I saw Mrs. Williams yesterday. She seemed surprised to see me looking so well and I think took comfort from it for her son. I hope he will improve tho' he looks dreadfully ill now. I think we shall find Mrs. Williams a very pleasant person. She said you did her a great deal of good by your visit. I hope Emory will be able to meet you in Albany and have a peep at the baby before he goes back. He will tell you all about us, which is much more satisfactory than letters. I must write a note so goodbye my dearest mother with a heart full of love from, your loving child, Emily

Nassau, December 28th 1869[37]

My dearest Evy,

I was sorry not to write you by the last steamer, but I found my strength not sufficient to do all I had planned so you must take the will for the deed. You have no idea how impatient we become for the mail. It is very trying not to hear one word from home for four weeks. I think this however will be the hardest month, for I miss Emory so much and after I once have letters from him, I can comfort myself with them when I am lonely. It was a great source of pleasure and comfort to me to have my husband bring me here and remain with me till I was settled and had more strength and I feel very grateful for it. Still, it was very hard for me to part with him for six months at the least. You know, even with the strength of mind and body that health gives, how woefully hard it is to part from your husband and make up your mind to a long separation and it is harder still when one feels so weak and helpless. The struggle takes some life out of the soul. I am otherwise very comfortable and happy here and can feel that I am in the best place for me and that I am improving slowly but I hope surely and feel encouraged.

Of course, you were as much pleased with the good news from Lily as we were. It is charming that she has a dear little girl just as I hoped; I feel wild to see it and can hardly wait till next June. What fun it will be to see little Midge and Helen, only I am afraid I shall be envious of your treasures.

I do hope nothing will detain you in the spring for our hearts are closely set upon your coming. Mother let us have a little picture of Midge, which had one eye scratched out as if she had been in a small fight.

Our Christmas passed very quietly here; it was very hard to realize it. The day was so warm and the garden so full of beautiful flowers that it presented a perfect contrast to our cold Christmas at home, which is so pleasant and invigorating. Now that I am able to work, I am making an afghan for Emory as a present on his wedding day.[38] It will be very handsome and is a pleasant employment for me this winter. Nelly reads to me while I work for three or four hours each day so we make the time pass very pleasantly.

Emory received a letter from Andrew by the last mail, which I suppose he has answered. Give my love and a kiss to dear Andrew and with a heart full of love for yourself, I am your loving sister, Emily

Nassau, January 9th 1870

My dearest Mother,

I received all three of your letters by this mail and had a real treat. You told me so much I wanted to know. The letter written on my birthday must have been too late for the last steamer but I am glad it was not lost for it was very sweet. I was so glad to hear all about your Christmas and of Emory's visit.[39] He enjoyed it very much and wrote me all about home and its dear inmates. I was pleased that he saw Lily and the baby. He thought they were both lovely. I am glad that your stay with dear Lily was so pleasant and that you were able to go down to Albany again after Christmas. I can just see Lily with the baby in her arms. I am very glad that she has gone to Lily.

So, you have at last found a chaplain for Arizona. I trust he is the right man and worth waiting for. Emory sent me a picture of Evy and Midge, which I was very glad to get, tho' I think Evy looks very thin. How lovely little Midge must be as she begins to talk and have many pretty ways. How I long to see both the little darlings.

Emory saw Gen. Comstock[40] in Washington; he says "Comstock told me the staff corps might be included in which case he will do all he can for Alexander's transfer. We will soon set the ball in motion to that end." I so hope he will be successful and Andrew may be ordered Northeast in the spring.

I suppose ere this you have heard from Emory of his safe arrival at Atlanta. He found the garrison much increased. He says Nancy has already made the house look home like. I am glad she is there, tho' I suppose it was a good deal of trouble to take her on.

I do not think I told you how we spent Christmas. Very quietly. About ten, Mrs. Williams came down from the hotel to see us and to bring your Christmas gifts. It was very kind of you dear mother to think of this pleasant surprise to us and I was much pleased with my fan, I used one so much. Nelly read me "The Cricket on the Hearth"[41] so that we should be reminded of the many times you had read this lovely story to us at Christmas. I could just see the group at home in times past, sitting around the table in the parlor while you read it to us and the reading [of] it was the best part of the day. I am very contented here and find my pleasant occupation in my afghan for Emory.

When not reading, Nelly has told you all that is of interest in our quiet life, so I will not make my letter a long one. I am still improving and Dr. Kirkwood who examined my lungs today seemed to be quite satisfied with the improvement of two months. This is by no means an answer to your good letters but I must say farewell, from your loving child, Emily.

Nassau, February 5th, 1870

My dearest mother,

As I have not been feeling quite as well lately, I find it very hard to write and am therefore, going to trust to your love and sympathy for me. I believe that I have thought none the less of my dear father and mother at home because I do not send them long letters. You know from experience that sometimes there are weeks when time seems to stand still as far as improvement goes and then take a new start. We all thought the change of coming to the hotel might give me more appetite and strength.

So, we are trying the experiment, which I hope to write you by the next steamer, has been successful. Besides, we thought it a good plan to give our kind friends a little rest from their kind attention to us. Dr. and Mrs. Kirkwood seemed loath to let us go and say they miss us very much.

All our friends here are most kind and attentive. I feel often touched by their efforts to be so nice to us. Mr. and Mrs. Peabody who are our next [door] neighbors are unwavered [sic] in their attentions and as Mrs. Peabody is situated precisely as I am, we can sympathize most fully.

I have written Emory but seldom this month, tho' I have had a host of good cheerful letters from him. He seems to be very comfortable and happy now that he is once more on duty and says Nancy does everything very nicely. I have finished my afghan and sent it to him for a remembrance of our wedding day. I have worked at it quietly and steadily without hurting myself, but now I am surprised to find it finished and that it is so handsome. I could work at it for hours without being as tired as I am after writing a page and it has been so much of a comfort to me to feel that I was doing something for my husband, that it was really a benefit.

Mrs. Kirkwood has just been here and wanted me to send this photograph to you. I think it is very good of her. I am glad Molly was with Throop a few days before she went to New York. I hope he is well by this time. How busy you must be dear mother. I do sympathize with you and hope that you will not wear yourself out with your numerous duties. I wish I could write more but shall have to say goodbye for the present. With love to dear father, Ned,[42] Violet[43] and Miss Lord.[44] Please thank them for their letters; I am, with sincerest love, your loving child, Emily.

Nassau, February 19th, 1870[45]

My darling mother,
I cannot tell you what a pleasant little surprise it was to receive your letter this morning. It was very sweet and kind of you to remember my

wedding day and send me such a dear letter and I assure you I appreciated every word.

This has been a very happy day to me even tho' I have sorely missed my dear husband, but everyone has been so kind to me that it really makes one feel humble. I will give you an account of the day that you may judge for yourself.

Before I was dressed, Miss Prentice sent me your letter, also one from Emory accompanying a present in memory of the day—a lovely camels hair shawl, just what I need so much. I was delighted Miss Prentice sent me a bouquet of flowers and Mrs. Prentice a card wishing me many happy returns of the day. Mrs. Peabody spent the morning with me as a cold Norther was blowing I did not dare leave my room, which was warm. So, Mrs. Peabody dined with me. During the afternoon, nearly all the ladies in the hotel came to see me. Mrs. Hoskins brought me a pretty little bookmark, Mrs. Kirkwood an exquisite little bouquet; Mrs. Cleveland some roses and Nelly gave me a pair of candlesticks and vases. From the time I opened my eyes till this moment, I have had a succession of kind acts and words of affection and all from people upon whom I have no claim. Then above all, I am feeling so much better. All last month, I was miserable and felt discouraged, the last two weeks, I have improved wonderfully and I feel a great deal happier about myself. I feel with you dear mother, that looking back upon the last two years, I find many very pleasant things to remember and be thankful for and my prayers today have been earnest thanksgivings for all my mercies, not the least of which are the friends always raised up to me and the kindness and affection I receive when I feel I am really so unworthy of it. I can say, "Bless the Lord, oh my soul and forget not all his benefits."

Dearest mother, in all I do and see, my heart turns longingly and lovingly to you and tho' I have been able to write you but seldom lately, you know it not from want of love and inclination. Good night with fondest love of your devoted child, Emily

PS This is an untidy letter, but I feel I must write tho' I could not do it well.

Mrs. Kirkwood

[*Dr. Kirkwood's wife, A. D., wrote to Mrs. Martin toward the end.*]

Nassau, 6th March 1870[46]

My dear Mrs. Martin:

I feel greatly perplexed to know exactly what to write to you for you all are so much distressed at any unfavorable news of dear Mrs. Upton. I only wish that it was in my power to say that she had improved the last month or two and yet there is nothing to occasion any immediate alarm. About the time of the sailing of the last steamer, she was feeling very miserable and very much nauseated and of course could eat but very little since then. The Dr. has made some change in her medicine and that has passed away.

Last week she was very much better, the reason for which Nelly has told you and the weather also has been very fine and she has been able to take several drives. She has every comfort at the hotel and is the pet invalid of the place. There are so many nice people and she very much enjoys their occasional visits.

There is a Mrs. Peabody, a most charming lady and they appear to have formed a great friendship for each other. I think that you are wrong in thinking that she is pining for her husband; she does not appear to in the least. But has made up her mind that he must be at his post and never thinks of anything else.

Nelly says that she is quite equal to taking care of her sister and that she has never been in better health in her life. Her horseback exercise is, I think, a good benefit to her. Should Mrs. Upton get worse and require more care, I hope that they will then return here so that I could be of some assistance to Nelly. But we all hope that she may return to you; but whatever the event may be, we shall always feel that her life has been much more comfortable than it could possibly have been in a cold climate.

I see but little change in Mrs. Upton's general appearance. She may be a little thinner as well as a little weaker, but her spirits are remarkably good and she is still very hopeful and talks of what she will do next summer.

I have not told Mrs. Upton that I received a letter from you neither does she know that I am writing, but I presume that she will write to you. Mrs. Bludell has improved since she has been here, but her son has had a hemorrhage and is quite ill and although I think going slowly, the Dr. thinks him a hopeless case and I think I will write for his father to come down by the next steamer. It is strange that they did not think him more an invalid when he left home.

I have not seen the new arrivals from Albany, but Nelly says that they are very nice people.

I hope, my dear Mrs. Martin you and all of your children will meet at Willowbrook in months. I hear that you have very good accounts from Mrs. Alexander. Remember me very kindly to Mr. Martin, [*illegible*], Eddie, & Violet.[47] And believe me ever your friend, A. D. Kirkwood.

PS I send you one of the Dr.'s photos, which I think better than mine.

[Upon Emily's death, Mrs. Martin received condolences from Emily's caretakers and concerned friends. She chose to have them typeset and printed upon Emily's death preserving them in Emily's letter book. They reveal Emily's last moments in a detailed and excruciating manner.]

Anna P. Peabody

[Anna P. Peabody, mentioned in Mrs. Kirkwood's letter, was a resident at the hotel. She wrote this letter as Emily was dying, revealing Emily at her most vulnerable.]

Nassau, March 26th, 1870[48]

My Dear Mrs. Martin:

I cannot feel myself quite a stranger to you, after having known dear Mrs. Upton and Nellie, and I take the liberty of writing to you now because I fear if Mrs. Upton continues in this critical condition, Nellie will be unable to do so, and I am sure you will want to hear.

It was the night of March 22d that the first alarming attack took place, and on Wednesday, the next day, it seemed impossible that she should survive the day. It was then that she realized her condition, but she rallied in the afternoon, and the next day was able to give Nellie many last directions. Nellie did not leave her a moment but sat fanning her and giving beef tea or stimulants every few moments. She watched her night and day, through three dreadful days of suffering; then Emily seemed to rally a little and Nellie slept for a very short time, while Cassie, my maid, took her place. Nobody can ever know all that dear Nellie has been through. Mrs. Kirkwood and Miss Lindley did everything in their power but nobody could take Nellie's place. The mental strain and anxiety these days is very great; but I am glad that only loving hands have tended her throughout all.

Her attacks of numbness or a sort of paralysis of the left side are very distressing; as she herself expressed it after one of them, she felt as if she had died and come to life again. Everything that mortals can do is done for her, for she is beloved by all. It seems as if she were living in the hope that her husband may come in this steamer and only her will kept the life in her feeble frame. She lies propped up in the bed very still and peaceful, but with a world of thought in her beautiful eyes.

I think she is resigned to everything though now she hopes for her husband. God will comfort her if this hope fails her. She is pleased with the way in which Cassie tends her and I try my best to have Nellie take a little rest and take her meals regularly, without which she will not be able to keep up much longer.

April 1st. The steamer arrived the day before yesterday noon, bringing Gen'l Upton's letter, which Nellie read to her. I think at the last she was fully resigned not to see her husband but Nellie can tell you about her last feelings, for she never left her and that was her last night on earth. A more lovely, sweet and patient spirit never breathed. Everybody loved her. The affection with which she inspired all, even the children of the house was wonderful. It seemed as if nobody could do enough for her and I am sure her example of life and death has left a lasting impression on many hearts. From mine I am sure it can never be effaced. I feel deeply grateful that it was permitted me to know her. We had many happy hours together and she was so bright and cheerful that I hoped, and at one time believed, that she would live to return home in June, when she began to fail, she failed very rapidly.

She has often spoken to me of the tenderness of her father for her and of the religious influence, which her mother had early implanted in her heart. It was her comfort in dying as it had been in living. Her life seemed to me like a beautiful idyll. She told me, early in our acquaintance, that it had been a very happy one, and she would like to write an autobiography. I believe her love for her husband was unalterable. He seemed ever present to her thoughts—and she loved to talk to me of him, sometimes because she felt that I could sympathize— though I feel that this was a sacred confidence. She said once that seeing Mr. Peabody so careful and tender of me made her homesick at times for her own dear husband, whom she gaily assured me was fully equal to mine.

We have persuaded Nellie, somewhat against her will, to remain until the next steamer. She has pains in her chest and is so much exhausted that her system would not be in a state to resist any shock from the change of climate if she went now. Besides, I am going home in the next steamer and I promised Mrs. Upton that I would take care of Nellie after her death. It troubled her at first to think of Nellie's being left here alone and I think my assurance gave her much comfort.

I lent her a volume of hymns and when it was returned, I found that she had marked with her initials this one, which I enclose. She was almost dying when she marked it, but unselfish to the last, she could think even of me.

Oh! Dear Mrs. Martin, may God comfort you and all the mourning circle for this great loss. I feel that she is folded safely in the arms of her Heavenly Father; that all her sufferings are ended and that she has entered into her rest. We would not have it otherwise, now.

I hope sometime that I may meet you to talk to you about her for I feel how inadequately I have expressed what I wished to say, but you will forgive my short-comings for her dear sake and think kindly of one who also mourns for her.

Yours, Affectionately,

Anna P. Peabody

[*Enclosed with the letter was the following hymn, which Emily had marked in Mrs. Peabody's hymn book.*]

> *When the spark of life is waning,*
> *Weep not for me,*
> *When the languished eye is straining*
> *Weep not for me;*
> *When the feeble pulse is ceasing,*
> *Start not at its swift decreasing,*
> *'Tis the fettered soul's releasing,*
> *Weep not for me.*

When the pangs of death assail me,
Weep not for me,
Christ is mine—He cannot fail me,
Weep not for me,
Yes! Though sin and doubt endeavor,
From this love my soul to sever,
Jesus is my strength forever,
Weep not for me.

Mary E. Lindley

[*It is unclear who Mary E. Lindley was. From her wordy, voluminous letter, it appears that she too was in Nassau and, like Emily, was trying to escape the ravages of tuberculosis or another respiratory ailment. It is also possible that she was Dr. Kirkwood's patient and knew Emily in Key West. According to her letter she knew Emily only a month.*]

Royal Victoria Hotel
Nassau, March 27, 1870[49]

My Dear Mrs. Martin:
I am sure that you will long to hear everything any of us can possibly tell you of these days of dear Emily's drawing nearer to the heavenly home of peace and rest.

When I first saw Emily here, a month ago, I was quite shocked to see her so feeble and altered, but the dear child has been so bright and hopeful, that in spite of my knowledge of all she suffered, I actually began to think she might possibly have several more years to live, for those she loved so dearly. About nine or ten days ago, I began to see that she did not seem quite so strong after each ill time as she did before it. A week ago, Friday she was not so well as she had been the day before, and when she was telling me, in the morning what a bad night she had, I expressed a fear that she would not be able to go upstairs, to the entertainment the children of the house were to give us. She smiled as she said—"I am afraid I had better to try to go up." But when the evening came, she felt much better and Dr. Kirkwood said that it would not hurt her to be carried upstairs. So, we had a sofa arranged for her and she enjoyed the tableaux etc. very much indeed. She said the next day that she had not felt any ill effects from being present.

April 1st.—She was brave and patient all the time so much so that I could not but wonder at the courage and hope she manifested. I told her so, one day and told her I would not help wishing to die to get rid of this weary life. She said she thought it wrong to feel so. God gave us life and we ought to prize it and do our best to prolong it, and then she said—"Nelly once talked to me when I was regretting giving so much trouble and she showed me how wrong it was to feel rebellious, and from that time I have felt differently about it. She did me a great deal of good."

The day after that talk of ours, dear Emily was feeling poorly, and was lying quietly while I fanned her. I said to her, "I must tell you that your lecture yesterday did me good and I made up my mind to do my best to live." Her face brightened and with her arch smile, she said—"I had made up my mind to say nothing to you about it lest I might hurt your feelings, so I am very glad to know you are going to be sensible." After a little while she added—"There was a good deal of truth in what you said about my having more to live for than you have:" and then said with a happy smile—"I have such a dear, good husband to get well for." She very often spoke of the great comfort Nelly was to her. Often, after Nelly had given her a dose of something, Emily's eyes would follow her as she went out of the room and she would turn to me and say—"It is perfectly wonderful to see how that girl never forgets anything. She is a splendid nurse and so good to me. She never seems to get tired." At another time she would say—"Nelly seems to know by instinct just what I need—she never bothers me—she lets me do just as I want to. She is a perfect nurse, never thinks of herself for a moment." She said it was such a comfort to her that Nelly never looked at her anxiously, watching her symptoms; and would say—"I think one gets used to one person, and you do not want any other nurses about: too many distract your mind." I wish I could recall all the loving words she spoke, of all her dear family. She frequently spoke of the great pleasure in store for her when *all* would be at home, in Willowbrook, all together and how nice it would be at West Point, "so near Lylie that she can come down any day with her baby." We used to think when she was talking so brightly that it would be a very great trial to her if she should find out that her happy days were to come to an end before all her dreams were realized therefore no one said one word of our fears that she would not have the strength to enjoy so much.

Last Wednesday she became so ill that we saw she could not live to go home. We dreaded the effect on her mind. I did not speak to her until the next morning, when on my going into her room, after breakfast, she greeted me with a sweet smile and said she felt better, adding—"I was almost over the brink, but they pulled me back."
As I did not think she ought to talk, just then, I left the room.

Friday morning, I sat by her for a little time. She said—"Poor Nelly! I am so sorry for her, for I had to distress her very much, last night, telling her everything." I said—"do not be troubled on that account, for she was saying to me, a little while ago, that she felt so much relieved because you had expressed your wishes as to what you wished done with your things." She said, "I am glad then, that she feels so." She said—"I can tell you it is wonderful what an amount of thinking can be done in a short time. You would be astonished if you knew how many things have passed through my mind since I was taken so much worse." She said—"I knew I was dying; Wednesday morning and you have no idea what a strange feeling it was." I asked her how she felt going. She said—"I do not mind it at all, for myself, but those I leave will feel so sorry. I grieve for the grief they will endure." I then said—"Emily, are you sorry we kept it from you that you could not get well? Dr. Kirkwood said if you should be told how ill you were, you would die in a week." She said—"No, I am not sorry, for I did have more courage to struggle for life than I would have had, but I am glad to say that I am quite willing to die. I've suffered a great deal and though I would be willing to suffer longer, if I could get well, I have not had one rebellious feeling since I found out that I must die." She said, at another time—"I am not afraid to die, but I wish I knew something more about heaven." She asked me to get her "The shadow of the rock"—no I mean "The Changed Cross," and she herself found the hymn, "The Border Lands," and pointed to the verse—

> *I cannot see the golden gate,*
> *Unfolding yet, to welcome me,*
> *I cannot yet anticipate*
> *The joy of heaven's jubilee.*

and she said—"That is just as I feel." I reminded her that dying grace was not promised until the dying hour. "Yes, I know that, and it is best to wait for it. Just as I told Nelly, that if it is God's will I should not live, He would make me willing to die, and He has."

I said to her—"How gladly would I take your place and give you my chance for life." She smiled and said—"Well, there is a great deal to be said on both sides, living, as well as dying." The expression on her face set me to thinking and at last it occurred to me that she thought I was growing discontented again. The next morning, I said to her—"I hope you did not think I had gone back to wishing for death, because I said I would willingly take your place, to let you live; I was thinking only of how much more important it seemed that you should live, than that I should." She gave me a sweet smile and said—"I am glad to know that was it. I was a little afraid that you had gone back. For the sake of those that love me, I would like to live, but for myself, I feel that it will be pleasant to be free from suffering." The last clause is not exactly in her words, but it was the idea she conveyed. I cannot recall the very words.

One morning, I happened to be in Mrs. Standart's room when Dr. Kirkwood came in there from Emily's room. I think it was Thursday morning. I remarked to him that Emily seemed to fully realize her situation. He said—"Yes, she knows it perfectly and it is most wonderful to see the calmness and peace she exhibits. It is marvelous! I thought she would lose all courage as soon as she knew it, but she is as brave and resolute as before." I said to her afterwards that I was glad she had been permitted to show Dr. K how a Christian could face death. Who knows, I said, but that your example may be the means of leading him to believe in Christ? She said—"I do hope so, too, with all my heart. I wish he would become a Christian, he is as good and kind as need be but he does not believe." She spoke with gratitude of his devotion to her. "He is just as kind and lovely as he can be to me." After she was taken so much worse, she seemed to wish only until the letters came. "I want to hear, once more, how they all are, and then I will be ready to go." Then she smiled and said—"After that if I should die, I would know everything about them without waiting for the letters."

I was very much grieved because I could not be much with dear Emily, after last Saturday, because my coughing disturbed her when she was so very weak. But I frequently sat in the parlor to answer the knocks at the door. You would have been gratified to see how many came to ask "how is Mrs. Upton, now?" and to offer their services. The love she inspired was surprising and the tears, which were shed, the morning of her death, were eloquent testimony to the affection all had for her. Even the children who had seen her only a few times, were very thoughtful while she was so ill and took great care not to make a noise to disturb her. I hardly ever met one of them in the passages but they would at once ask how Mrs. Upton was and then ask if I thought she had been disturbed by what noise they might have made. Her example of cheerful, uncomplaining endurance will never cease to do all who saw it, great good. For my part, I feel that I can never regret having been sent here to see it even though I may not reap all the benefit, physically, which I had hoped to derive. The lesson in patience will do me good for all time to come. I feel it a great privilege that I have been allowed to be with the darling child during the last month of her life. It must a great comfort to all, dear Mrs. Martin that dear Emily was to the very last, so very much satisfied that everything was ordered for the best. She was sure that the trial in leaving her best beloved ones was less than it would or could have been under any circumstances.

Praying that you may all be comforted from above, I am,

With deep sympathy, Yours, Mary E. Lindley

Joanna M. Boyd

[*The third and last letter was from Joanna M. Boyd, who also knew Emily in the last month of her life. It is succinct and hugely sympathetic.*]

Nassau, April 2nd, 1870[50]

My Dear Mrs. Martin:

Will you pardon what may seem an intrusion on the sacredness of your grief and accept my tribute to the worth and loveliness of your daughter, Mrs. Upton?

Just four weeks ago I came to this island with my husband and children. About a week after my arrival, Miss Martin [Nellie] kindly invited me to her room and there, for the first time, I saw Mrs. Upton. She was lying on the lounge, looking so lovely, yet so frail. Still, she was so cheerful and animated, I could not but think that a residence of a few more months in this genial climate would be the means of her restoration to health. I saw her twice after this, for a few moments at a time, fearing to stay long, lest I might weary her. A little more than a week ago, she was taken very ill and for several days and nights, her death was looked for almost hourly. To the surprise, however, of almost every one, she rallied again and lived until the morning after the arrival of the steamer, to which event she had been eagerly looking forward.

I cannot tell you what a gloom and sadness her death has cast over us all. Everyone in the house seemed to love Mrs. Upton, not only the guests, but the proprietors of the hotel, and those who waited upon her and served her in many little ways. It will be a great comfort to you to know that everything was done to promote her comfort and ease her sufferings.

Your friends, Dr. and Mrs. Kirkwood, have been unwearied in their attentions; indeed, they seem to have loved her as if she had been their own child. For the daughter, Miss Martin, I have the highest esteem; so brave, so self-sacrificing, such a tender nurse, such a loving sister. And you can rejoice that dear Mrs. Upton, when told that death was inevitable, received the announcement calmly, expressed no regret—on the contrary, with loving self-forgetfulness, said she was glad it was so ordered so that her friends at home would be spared the agony of witnessing her dying struggles. She desired only to live until her letters should come, and she found that her husband could not reach her in time to see her while living, felt that this, too, was wisely ordered and cheerfully resigned herself to the will of God. How eager she was to be at rest and yet, how patiently she bore her sufferings. Your daughter, Miss Martin, will have told you all.

I feel that I would like to speak a few words to you, out of my full heart, and tell you that while I weep with you, I can but rejoice that your beloved child is at rest, that she suffers no more, that she has so early reached her home in Heaven.

Pray forgive me if I have said too much, when your heart is so sore. Believe me

Yours, in sympathy, Joanna M. Boyd

Emory

[*In April, Emory managed to put some of his thoughts in writing to his old commander, James Harrison Wilson. The letter also reveals that he knew early in the year that he would be reassigned to West Point as commandant of cadets.*]

Willowbrook, April 26th 1870[51]

My dear Wilson:

I am most gratified for your letter of sympathy.[52] The affliction that has fallen upon me is hard to bear, nor could I support it but for the assurance that my darling is in Heaven. In her life as in her death, she was angelic and to my great comfort, I have been permitted to feel that she has but gone a short time before me. The loss of her death is one we may all ponder. What but her Christian faith could have so sustained her when all human support failed her? With God's help, I shall strive to profit by it, and to be a better man than heretofore. You may imagine that life seemed to me unbearable after this great bereavement, but to permit it to remain so would not be heroic, so I now try to look forward to my new field of usefulness as a blessing sent to me. I shall be able to devote to it all the energy I possess.

Your second letter was more gratifying than I could have hoped for. It shows there is a chance that you may be sent to West Point this year. What, my dear Wilson, could we not do for the dear old Academy if sent there together. I have an idea of many reforms that the two together might institute, which it would be difficult for me to accomplish. I shall see Gen. Belknap[53] when I pass through Washington and shall urge to my utmost; both there and in other quarters, your appointment. Do you know that I want the Superintendent *at West Point*—vigor and independence are what I wish to see in my superior. I can then work with a will.

Excuse me if I do not write you more at length this time. You know what are my feelings. These letters I send you that Mrs. Wilson may read them. Let me hear from you soon.

Your ever-attendant friend, E. Upton

PS Mrs. Alexander sends her kindest regards and asks me to enclose the photograph of her little Arizonian.

Willowbrook, May 11, 1870[54]

My Dear Parents:

Mrs. Martin and I will leave to-morrow morning for New York on our way to Atlanta, where, with God's blessing attending us, we shall arrive Saturday, the 21st I shall remain there about ten days, and then break up, preparatory to establishing myself at West Point. We shall go via Washington, and return via Charleston and the sea to New York.

Nelly arrived last Friday from Nassau, quite worn in body and mind. She passed a most trying month in Nassau, mostly because she had no one to whom she could confide her grief and from whom she could receive heartfelt sympathy. All the accounts she brings of my dear Emily convey consolation. She tells us that Emily passed a most happy winter; that she suffered far less at Nassau than she did at home last summer, and the last ten days of her illness were not of that painful nature we had apprehended. I strive to bow to this affliction, and to acknowledge in it the goodness of God; yet I selfishly long for my darling. I know this feeling to be wrong, since Emily, having finished her labors, has simply been called to her heavenly rest. She was prepared to go; her life was complete, and God has called her to himself. I know that in her death I have been drawn nearer to Christ, and that I can now lay hold of the plan of salvation as I never could before.

Surely the resurrection of the body, the promise of a blessed immortality, rob death of its sting, and if prepared I can now see that, with St. Paul, we all ought to be able to say that "for me to live is Christ, and to die is gain."

Those, my dear parents, who, like you, have nearly run the race of life, ought to look forward with joy and thankfulness to the dawning of eternal life, and I pray that with you we, as a family, may all soon be partakers of the joys prepared for those that love God. With tender love, my dear father and mother, Your affectionate son, Emory.

Atlanta, May 22, 1870[55]

My Dear Sister:

Mrs. Martin and I will leave here a week from tomorrow, so as to take at Charleston the steamer of the 31st, which, with God's blessing, will land us in New York June 3d. Mother bore the journey here very well. She stopped over last Sunday at Westchester, rested a day in Washington, and one in Knoxville. We arrived here in good health Saturday morning.

The feeling of desolation has again come over me, as, in entering my home, I realize that the loved one who made it so happy, my precious Emily, has gone from me forever. But God can help me to bear this sorrow, and, while now life offers no attractions, I know that when again in active duty, employed in instilling in the minds of the nation's future defenders ideas of devotion to duty and discipline, I shall experience consolation in the thought that I am again useful in the world. Here I am in the midst of a thousand evidences of Emily's love for me. It was at this desk my heart flowed out to her daily in the letters, which used to comfort her poor heart. But all is changed. She is hidden from me, and already violets, blooming over her sacred form, offer their daily fragrance unto Heaven. I am not tempted to arraign the goodness of God. 1 can humbly thank him for lending me, even for so short a time, his angelic child, who, under his chastening hand, brought me back to a knowledge of the truth, and with her I can say, "Bless the Lord, O my soul, and forget not all his benefits."

Dr. Kirkwood

[*Fittingly, Dr. Kirkwood wrote to Upton nearly three months after Emily's death.*]

Nassau, June 26, 1870[56]

My Dear General:
I have had no heart to write to you before now, since the death of your dear, good, beautiful wife, as all commonplace condolence would, for such an irreparable loss, be out of place, and incomprehensible to you. I have no doubt that you have regretted extremely that you were not with her during her last days, but as there was no decided, nor indeed apparent change until about ten days before her death, it was impossible for you to have reached here, or to have even communicated with you. About two months before her death, Nelly and I consulted about the expediency of sending for you, but as nothing indicated that Mrs. Upton might not live for three or even six months longer, we considered it not advisable to send for you before the time you had arranged for coming; and when your wife expressed a desire that you should not be sent for, we did not feel ourselves warranted in so doing, especially as I must have told you what I told Nelly, and what I told Mrs. Martin before leaving Willowbrook, that there was no possible chance of Emily's recovering. The sad truth would come all too soon when it could no longer be concealed. Your dear wife did not really

realize thoroughly her state for more than a week or ten days before her death, and I think it was a blessing she did not, as in her case no warning was necessary to prepare her for the end, as her beautiful life had been so perfect and good that little change was necessary to convert her to what she is now an angel. But the main thing in the matter of your absence is in this, that she really suffered less, I believe, in dying, than she would have done if you had been present; for the pain of parting would have been increased tenfold, and she expressed herself very decidedly to that effect the day before she died, when she was suffering very much. As I was sitting by her bedside she said, 'Oh, I am so glad that Upton is not here to witness this, it would add so much to both our pain in parting!' and added several similar expressions, showing her conviction that it was better for both that you were not present, and I am convinced that your presence would have made her last parting from this world more painful and bitter for her, and infinitely more agonizing to you; therefore I think you should consider the matter in the same light as she did, and believe that 'whatever *is,* is best.' Then she had every care that loving and sympathizing friends could give. Every person who had the happiness of knowing your dear wife gave, if he could nothing more, his love and kindest sympathy. Indeed, I never knew any person who received so much general love and esteem, and, I may safely add, or who deserved it more.

Atlanta, March 20, 1870[57]

My dear wife,
This is the last talk I shall have with you by the steamer of March 24th. Your last letters have had a peculiar effect upon me; the very happiness you feel and express has made me so happy myself. I bless God that He has surrounded you with such devoted friends, who minister to your most trivial wants, and especially am I gratified that in the midst of so many pains, you can have so many moments of pleasure and

enjoyment. Nothing less than our angel, my love, could suffer as you have suffered and bear it so patiently, sweetly, unmurmuringly.

It is this that has raised you up (more than anything else) such host of friends. You have conquered *self* and accepted god's will in the midst of all your afflictions, blessing him for all his benefits. You may with certainty expect me to come for you and to care for you on your voyage home. I know you will again gladly accept the devotion of your fond husband and how ardent he will be to supply your every wish. I am writing this letter before church, which is not usually my custom. It is a little singular that we each wrote our last letter on Sunday. Your wishes regarding furniture, china, etc. shall all be fulfilled.

Kiss dear Nelly for me, she is very good to you. My remembrances and thanks please express to Mrs. Peabody[58] and her husband and Dr. and Mrs. Kirkwood.

Well, my love, I must close, with a heart overflowing with love that cannot be said.

Your fond husband, Emory

PS. I am glad you liked the shawl. I adore the afghan.

Epilogue

Emily's passing particularly affected Nelly. She had cared for her off and on for nearly two years. In April, as she closed her affairs in Nassau, Nelly told her mother of her reluctance to write letters, as they would not be interesting "since our darling has left us." She wondered how she could "endure all that must follow." She remained at the hotel with the Kirkwoods for the next two months, unable to bring herself "physically to put up her [Emily's] things." She couldn't "bear to leave the rooms where we had passed through so much together." Nelly shared the rooms with a patient, Mary Lindley, but Nelly felt "obliged to let her go back to her room and stay by herself because every time she coughed it would go through me like a knife." Writing further to her mother, "Nothing can make this trial easy for any of us and my great wish is that we may be unselfish in our grief." Nelly made all the "arrangements" herself, and she "hoped they were successful. Our child is at rest," she wrote, "although we are so stricken and sorrowful." She asked her mother to ask Mrs. Roberts to "make [her] a plain crepe bonnet and send it to [her] with a veil." She left Nassau on the *Morro Castle* on Monday, May 2, and expected to reach New York late Friday, May 6. In a last heartbreaking turn, Nelly wrote her mother in this same April 14 letter that "a vessel arrived from New York the other day bringing some letters from Emory."[1]

Emily's death, and later Emory's, were emblematic of the cultural change in society's relationship with death and the afterlife. As historians Thomas Schlereth and David Stannard have pointed out, the puritan generations viewed death as "a final resolution of their quest for salvation." Those predestined for heaven were rewarded, those who weren't "were damned to hell." The deceased were buried in coffins, and reminders of death such as skull and crossbones and warnings such as 'Memento Mori' and 'Fugit Hora,' were displayed in crowded burial grounds near the departed's church. A nineteenth-century society with its verdant and rolling public cemeteries offered a more beneficent landscape generated by "new ideas about nature, family, and heaven." The cemetery became a "domesticated haven; it no longer held the terror of a dreadful last judgment." One Victorian novel went so far as to portray "heaven's roadways, life-styles, and occupations." Even the "coffin" gave way to the "casket," a term long used to describe a small box in which only prized possessions were kept.[2]

Within days of Emily's death, Upton received his appointment as West Point commandant of cadets, a position he held from July 1, 1870, to June 30, 1875. His colleague and commander from Atlanta, Thomas Ruger, joined him as superintendent of the academy the following year. Upton wrote little about his loss of Emily. We can only guess at the depths of his mourning. Undoubtedly, his appointment at West Point was bittersweet. The young couple had hoped to settle at the academy, perhaps as superintendent and his wife. Now he was there, not as the number one, but as commandant of cadets and alone.

Upon completion of his tour of duty at West Point, and encouraged by general of the army, William Tecumseh Sherman, he embarked on an eighteen-month world tour inspecting and observing the armies of Europe and Asia from July 1875 to March 1877. He visited with dignitaries and professional military men in India, China, Japan, Persia, Prussia, and France. Upon his return, Upton reported to the artillery school at Fort Monroe, where he wrote his official report, titled *Armies of Asia and Europe*, which the government published in 1878.

Upton first met Sherman on a train returning to Nashville from a Fourth of July 1865 jaunt to Mammoth Cave. He and Sherman spoke candidly with each other, and Upton described Sherman as still "bitter toward" Stanton for his treatment of Sherman's peace negotiations with Confederate general Joseph Eggleston Johnston at Bentonville. Sherman left Upton with the idea that he might run for president. Later, Upton petitioned the State of New York for his right to be named a general officer, a move he would have despised a few years earlier. "My standing with Gen. Grant, Sherman and Sheridan," he wrote, dropping the names of high-ranking officers, "I am sure is in the highest degree satisfactory." By 1867, Sherman was critiquing Upton's manuscript of a revised tactical manual that would bear his name well into the 1880s. Upton sent him a copy in November of that year, reminding Sherman, "You will remember that I saw you once on the cars on your way to Nashville . . . [during which you] recalled . . . your operations against Atlanta, your army rarely came into contact with the enemy," much of the hard work being done "by heavy skirmish lines."[3]

Upton originally intended the report to be twice as long as it eventually turned out. When Sherman learned that Upton, in his report, planned to severely criticize Congress, which had underwritten his travels, Sherman counseled him to drop the idea. Instead Upton began a separate manuscript eventually titled *The Military Policy of the United States*, which the government published posthumously in 1904. *Military Policy* indicted the American method of waging war. It condemned the civilian management of war from the Revolution through the Civil War. Urged on by Sherman, Upton argued for a professional army. He also favored a military staff based on the German model he had witnessed on his trip—a suggestion too radical for Sherman. According to one biographer, although Sherman took delight in encouraging young officers to effect change, he did little to transform the military during his fifteen-year tenure as general of the army.[4]

In 1877 and 1878, Upton inserted himself into the debate on Capitol Hill over the Burnside Bill on army reform. Sherman would also lend his weight—up to a point. He complained that the bill was too long. Not trusting politicians, Sherman took a confrontational approach at first, and then when the final votes were to be taken, he abruptly left the country, leaving Upton and other supporters to fend for themselves.[5] The bill ultimately failed. The Democrats feared a more muscular army, particularly in the South, and the Republicans did not want to spend more money on the army, which reform would have required.

Upton became convinced that another revision of his military tactics manual was necessary. At Sherman's prodding, he had seen it through a revision and a rewrite to assimilate the tactics to all three branches of the army: infantry, artillery, and cavalry. At the Presidio in San Francisco, he agonized over the efficacy of his work and the impact it would have on the individual soldier. He wrote to Adjutant General R. C. Drum for permission to make the revisions, especially those "chapters on reviews of divisions and other large bodies of troops." He cited none other than Napoleon, and quoted him as saying that "the tactics of an army should be changed or modified every few years."[6]

But just before his new assignment at the Presidio and during his negotiations with the adjutant general, Upton began to deal with a sinus ailment that had first presented itself during his commandant years at West Point. Upton had been physically cleared in 1866. In that year he appeared before a medical board in New York City, where the examining surgeon who signed his paperwork wrote: "I certify on honor that I have carefully examined Emory Upton . . . agreeably to the General Regulations of the Army, and that in my opinion he is free from all bodily defects and mental infirmity, which would in any way disqualify him from performing the duties of an Officer."[7]

To find relief, he took a three-month leave to Philadelphia to visit Dr. Harrison Allen. It is not known if Upton knew Allen previously or if someone had recommended Allen to him. Upton wrote his friend and academy classmate Henry DuPont in July 1880 that "Dr. Allen told" him that he "could cure [his] ailment" and that he "resolved to take two months for that purpose. There is too much at stake to delay longer."

Epilogue 239

It wasn't until September that Upton traveled to Philadelphia "as originally contemplated."[8]

The procedure "consisted in placing a very fine coiled wire upon any particular spot of the disordered membrane and causing it to glow by electricity for a mere instant at a very high heat." Presumably, the technique would stimulate the rejuvenation or growth of healthy tissue, a process often used by farriers called "firing" to achieve the same results with livestock. Dr. Allen had used the method on others with "great and increasing success," which gave him hope that it would work on Upton. At that time, Allen remained unconcerned about any corollary physical problems such as extraneous tissue surrounding the sinus cavity bone structure that could invade the cranial cavity if uncontrolled. At that point, the mucocele had probably begun to press on the frontal lobe of Upton's brain.[9]

It made him "uncomfortable," and as he told DuPont, "I have not as yet disclosed myself to any of my old friends," yet he urged DuPont to visit at his earliest convenience. Immediately after a treatment, he assured his sister Maria that it was "by no means severe. The actual cautery gives very little pain," he wrote. "It was applied about an hour ago and now I feel no disagreeable effects whatever. The worst of my trouble is keeping one nostril stopped with cotton, which makes me talk through my nose."[10]

At West Point, while commandant, Upton had seen Dr. William Saunders, the post dentist, for relief. Saunders wrote later that he had "heard a distinct throbbing in (Upton's) head, very faint, however, and not beating in unison with the temporal artery on which my hand rested." Upton "expressed surprise" that Dr. Saunders could hear it and revealed that "he had noticed" it "for some time . . . and was puzzled to account for it." Saunders referred him to the post surgeons, who were at a loss to explain it also. Saunders reported that "the pulsation and ticking became more distinct, and the annoyance from it increased to such an extent" that Upton "could not sleep unless greatly fatigued." Only when the ticking and pulsing stopped, could he return to sleep. Saunders "feared an aneurism, but never" mentioned it. He did, however, urge Upton see a specialist. "He consulted several physicians," but Saunders remembered, he did not try "any special treatment before going abroad." Saunders saw him after his return from the world tour and realized that his condition had not improved. Upton supposedly told him, "Cure me of this, and I will give you ten thousand dollars ... Allen understands it, and I will submit to his treatment."[11]

Upton became colonel of the 4th Artillery in December 1880, and soon afterward joined his regiment at the Presidio in San Francisco, California. His posting to San Francisco took him away from the East, where family, West Point, memories, and medical care pulled at him. This was his second posting in the West, the first coming right after the war, when he reported to Denver, Colorado. The West had changed considerably since the war—the railroads, telegraph, and subjugation of American Indians had pushed white settlements into the frontier. The frontier no longer appeared foreboding or mysterious. Increased migration gave birth to new towns, which sprang up with incremental speed.

At first, he enthusiastically threw himself into his new assignment. In the first week of January, he reported that he returned to work on the tactics. His first few weeks on the West Coast were pleasant. Upton found the ever-changing San Francisco Bay weather novel. He wrote of incessant fog and rain soon replaced by "many bright and beautiful days—not surpassed by the loveliest autumn at Fort Monroe." He sent sister Maria "violets and heliotrope picked" in his front yard as evidence of the mild winter. He told her of his housekeeping and setting up his quarters. The members of the regiment welcomed him warmly. Three weeks earlier, they had given a grand reception in the harbor in his honor.[12]

But to his friend Henry DuPont and sister Sara, Upton told a different story. He expressed his displeasure with his new station. His superior, Maj. Gen. Irvin McDowell, his first commander at First Bull Run, commanded the Military Department of the Pacific and the Department of California in July 1876. He established his "quarters at Point San Jose (Fort Mason) and his offices in the Phelan Building in downtown San Francisco." In 1878, Gen. William Sherman, moving to economize army operations, ordered "all the military headquarters to give up their rented facilities and move to the nearest army posts." As a result, McDowell resettled "the combined Military Division of the Pacific and the Department of California" to the Presidio.[13]

Legally the commander of the 4th Artillery Regiment and commandant of the Presidio, the move did not sit well with Upton. He told Sara: "The post is a large one and not at all pleasant to command because it is overshadowed by the presence of Gen. McDowell and staff. The authority proper of a Colonel is absorbed by the Division Commander. This I knew before I came and it will make me all the more delighted when the time comes to go East." He wrote DuPont in February, stating that he had "happily" and physically "settled at [his] new station,"

> but cannot say that I am altogether pleased with it. The mixture of authority about which we talked is disagreeable. I have not had any collision with McD and do not intend to as I hope the regiment may go east this fall. The General, thus far has been very considerate and is disposed to do everything I ask, but I have not yet asked the post be made independent of the depot, etc. which seems to be his special hobby. There is not an expenditure of five dollars at any post in the harbor that he does not personally superintend. He plans the houses or quarters, selects the color they shall be painted and then goes over them repeatedly while they are being constructed.[14]

By March, he began to experience increasingly painful episodes of his malady as Dr. Allen's cauterization decreased in effectiveness. Sunday morning, March 13, Upton's academy classmate and now colleague, Henry C. Hasbrouck, a captain in the 4th Artillery, visited Upton in his office and inquired about Upton's health. Upton, usually sanguine and unemotional, threw down his pen, put his hands to his head, and told Hasbrouck through his tears that "he was ruined." Upton complained to Hasbrouck of sleepless nights in the past few weeks. His catarrhal discharge continued to bother him, and he had grown despondent that it would never be cured. He told of frequent headaches and talked of suicide, condemning it in the "strongest terms" possible. That day Upton also saw the 4th Artillery's adjutant, A. B. Dyer, and explained that he "had been in great trouble for the last four or five days." He asked Dyer not to mention it to anyone.[15]

Walking back to his quarters, Upton recovered his composure but told Hasbrouck that his system of fours, which he had developed for small unit tactics, would not work on a larger scale—company, regiment, and larger. Hasbrouck, whose quarters were next door to Upton's house, kept close watch on Upton—meeting him again after church, taking a long walk in the afternoon, and then spending the evening with him. Hasbrouck became concerned as Upton continually returned to the tactics and his perception that they had failed. Upton wished that the revision would be done by a board rather than placing the burden on him. He feared that "wrong pecuniary motives" would be "imputed to him." After all, he had received handsome royalties on his previous versions of the tactics. Chillingly, Upton told Hasbrouck: "Whatever may happen, I charge you, as my classmate, to see that justice is done to me."

Hasbrouck did not see Upton again till the following evening, Monday, March 14 at around 8 P.M. He noticed Upton was writing a letter as he entered his room. The two talked again about the tactics and about a possible trip to Monterey. He left at 9:30, and an hour later, the lights were still burning as Hasbrouck walked past Upton's quarters, where he observed Upton working at his desk. Earlier, he had told Hasbrouck that he wanted to finish a letter. "That was the last time I saw him alive," Hasbrouck testified.[16]

The next morning, around 6:30, Upton's servant, Ah Sing, went into Upton's room to pick up his boots for cleaning and to make the fire, and

Epilogue 243

noticed nothing out of the ordinary. When Upton did not appear for breakfast, Cheow Yung, Upton's cook, sent Sing to Upton's room, where he discovered Upton's lifeless body on the bed. Sing saw a pistol on Upton's chest and blood on the floor. Yung asked Captain Hasbrouck's servant, Wong Ky Ming, to immediately alert the captain, who went into Upton's room.

There Hasbrouck found Upton's cold and lifeless body. Upton hadn't undressed, but had "simply removed his coat, vest and boots and laid himself down, drawing the coverlet over his legs to the knees." He had put his .45 caliber service revolver in his mouth and pulled the trigger. The pistol came to rest on his chest between his lifeless, powder-burned hands. Two pools of blood formed on the floor next to the bed. "The large bullet crashed through the brain, passing through the head and penetrating the top of a hair pillow, dented the wooden head of the bedstead about 12 inches from the deceased's head." Although the cook and the two servants slept upstairs, no one heard the shot.[17]

Initially two letters were found. There were actually three. Two were addressed to the adjutant general of the United States Army. One fragment exposed Upton's fear of failure with the revision of his tactics, the other resigned his position as colonel of the 4th Artillery. The latter provided a clearer indication that Upton's thought processes were not working. Long-standing military custom stipulated that an officer could resign his commission (perhaps this is what Upton meant), not his assignment as commander of the 4th Artillery. *The Army Navy Journal* said it best: "If he meant to resign from the Army it would naturally be so expressed, but if he merely desired to be relieved on account of ill health, from the burden of command, then the letter would naturally be to that effect. Tendering a resignation as 'commander' is a somewhat unusual military form."[18]

The third letter, to Sara, his sister and longtime confidant closely resembled a suicide note. Upton spoke of the "distress" caused by his revision of the tactics. "It has seemed to me," he wrote "that I must give up my system and lose my military reputation. God only knows how it will end, but I trust he will lead me to sacrifice myself, rather than to perpetuate a method, which might in the future cost a single man his life. I need all your prayers, for I would keep my integrity. I don't feel like writing any more. Only let me feel that I have your love and sympathy." He signed it "with a fervent kiss, your affectionate brother, Emory."

Around the room were books in several languages on tactics, tactical diagrams, letters, and photographs. Ashes in the fireplace indicated that he had burned materials, although Ah Sing testified that he made the fire that morning at 6:30. Upton's dedication to his Emily never wavered. The *New York Times* stated that "He was devotedly attached to her, and ever had her photographs before him in his rooms and about his person wherever he went. Letters of condolence to him from her lady friends speaking in her praise, he had printed and framed as mementos of her."[19]

Upton's first funeral took place Saturday, March 19 at 2 P.M. Batteries of the 4th Artillery (600 strong) and 3,000 cavalry and infantry, including the entire 2nd Brigade of the California National Guard, escorted the body from the Presidio to the Bay area. The entourage traveled to the Washington Street wharf, where dignitaries placed Upton's body aboard the *General McPherson*, which carried it across the bay to Oakland. From there, the entourage began the long trek east, escorted by an honor guard from the 4th Artillery. At the family's request, Secretary of War Robert Lincoln "authorized two officers from the division of the Pacific to accompany the body to New York." One Bay area newspaper reported that "all the ex-confederate soldiers residing San Francisco turned out at the funeral" and sent "letters of condolence to the relatives, which" passed into the "possession of one of the Misses Martin"—an uncorroborated story.[20]

The body came east via rail, first to New York City and then to Auburn, to Willowbrook, where Upton's remains lay in state "in a small room" Saturday night, March 26. According to the *Syracuse Standard*, the body had been "embalmed and arrived in a hermetically sealed metallic casket, heavily silver mounted." Gen. Alexander Shaler petitioned Maj. Gen. Winfield Hancock, commandant of the Department of the East, to allow Upton's body to lie in state in New York City Hall. Shaler argued that the large numbers of Army of the Potomac veterans would welcome paying tribute to Upton. Hancock ignored Shaler's request and did not act on it. Somewhere along the way, Upton reposed in an open casket and, as one reporter described, the body was "clad in full uniform and although death took place over a week ago, the countenance bore a natural appearance."[21]

Tuesday morning, March 29, authorities in Auburn lowered the flags to half-staff, and thousands lined the streets to see the funeral cortege make its way to the Sand Beach Church, where Emily and Emory had recited their marriage vows thirteen years before. Arriving on the 11 A.M. train were General Sherman and his aide, John C. Tidball. They were greeted with muted enthusiasm by the throngs of admirers. The procession, fifteen carriages long, included the Upton and Martin families. From Otsego and Herkimer Counties came survivors of the 121st New York Volunteer Regiment, "Upton's Regulars," his first infantry command. "A beautiful double cross from members" of the 121st "reposed on the casket." Honorary pallbearers were a "who's who" of Upton's career: his cavalry commander in Georgia, James H. Wilson; the adjutant general of the army, Frederick Townsend; colleague and tactics collaborator, Henry DuPont; West Point professor Peter Smith Michie, his biographer in 1885; and Maj. J. P. Sanger, his colleague during his world tour.[22]

Upon the conclusion of a brief ceremony, the funeral procession resumed its journey through packed crowds who had been waiting for more than an hour. Upton's body reached its final resting place in the Martin family plot on a section of the Fort Hill Cemetery known as "Mount Hope." The family laid him to rest "beside the tomb of his wife, whose body had been removed from her resting place on the banks of the Owasco [Lake] and brought to Fort Hill, that the two might be together, even in death." The *Evening Auburnian* reminded readers that Myles Keogh had been interred nearby and praised the village of Auburn, writing how rare to witness "the sympathies of a community so awakened for one who was personally almost unknown . . . as Gen. Upton. That Auburn has taken upon itself to honor the brave and talented dead is to its credit."[23]

Yet another ceremony took place a week later, Sunday, April 3 at 11 A.M. at the Sand Beach Church. The Martin family billed it as a memorial service, attended by several members of the Martin family, the Upton family having departed earlier in the week after the interment ceremonies. The Reverend Charles Anderson presided over the reading of psalms and singing of hymns, and he delivered a long eulogy concluding the last service remembering Emory Upton.

Americans love conspiracy theories, and no sooner had Upton been laid to rest when the intrigues concerning his death began to circulate. Official pronouncements and family explanations aside, local and national newspapers breathlessly reported each more outrageous theory. Upton's sudden death stirred immediate controversy, despite an official inquiry that concluded Upton "committed suicide and that the act was not premeditated, but was caused by temporary unsoundness of mind brought on by an overtaxed brain and by his own disappointment at what he considered to be a failure in the revision of a work upon which he was engaged." McDowell, whose General Orders No. 3 announced Upton's death and early plans for his funeral, attributed his death to "suffering under great mental disturbance caused by an illness of long standing." An early news story from San Francisco stated bluntly, "The general impression . . . seems to be that grief at the loss of his wife prompted the suicide."

Andrew Alexander, representing the family and responding to news reports, wrote to McDowell: "General Upton's family is satisfied that the cause of his death was not anxiety about his tactics, but serious trouble in his head of long-standing originating in malignant catarrh.

Please correct newspaper reports." McDowell promptly replied: "I concur with General Upton's family as to the cause of his death and have anticipated their wishes in my general order announcing it. Please give them my deepest sympathy." A year after his death, Sara Upton wrote to Emily's mother thanking her for remembering the first anniversary of Upton's suicide. She passed on a thought from Colonel Hasbrouck, who "was convinced thoroughly that our dear Emory died as *surely from disease* as anyone who we see go calmly into their last sleep. I have never doubted it," she wrote.[24]

It is not known how the family learned of Upton's death. We do know that the day after his death, sister Sara sent brother John Bean Upton a telegram, which read simply, "Emory died yesterday. Funeral next week. Can you come?" Within hours, newspapers picked up the story, embellishing here, adding there. Ulysses Grant expressed bewilderment to the press: "I am at a total loss to understand what could have induced such a man to commit suicide." General Hancock encouraged rumors when he told a reporter that Upton's tactics had been widely accepted by the army and proved in practice and "the theory of depression of spirits in such connection, was not to be believed." Hancock went on to relate that "some officers in New York," thought Upton had been assassinated, offering no proof. Another opinion expressed in the Big Rapids, Michigan, newspaper, *The Pioneer Magnet*, dismissed Emily's death and the feared failure of the tactics to propose a fanciful theory. The paper theorized that since Upton suffered from "catarrh" and "frequently sought relief from an inhaler, which was used by applying to the mouth, which was very likely kept near his bedside," he may "have reached for it in the dark . . . partially awake or half crazed with pain, and made a mistake grasping his revolver instead."[25]

A variation on the inhaler nonsense postulated that Upton, being the ever-ready military man, slept with his loaded revolver, and in a nightmare, instinctively grabbed it and accidentally shot himself. A corollary theory suggested that Upton had taken the weapon up "in a casual, careless sort of way, and perhaps cocked it, and while looking it over with the muzzle toward his face, it accidently discharged." One last outrageous theory was that an obscure tactical maneuver, banned by a law passed during Grant's second term, had caused Upton to take his life. The notion maintained that the only way Upton could save his tactical manual and as a result, save many combat lives, was to introduce a banned maneuver once used by Napoleon. According to a press report, the "French" method had been included in successive tactical manuals written by Winfield Scott in 1825 up until Upton's in 1873, "when it was forbidden by law." Simply put, Upton wanted to include the method in his revision, but the law prohibited it. Hands down, this remains the most bizarre motive for Upton's death and is unsupported.[26]

Years later, comrade-in-arms John Tidball, who attended Upton's funeral as Sherman's aide, surmised that Upton killed himself "because of his unrequited ambition, an opinion at variance with those of some modern historians," according to Tidball's biographer, Eugene C. Tidball. However, those modern historians, such as Edward Coffman, cite Upton's physical ailments ("headaches") and his desire to attain a higher office or status and failing to meet those requirements, as causes of his suicide. In Upton's own words, he would have liked to be the superintendent at West Point. Russell Weigley, an Upton critic, acknowledged in one monograph on the army that Upton suffered from a "brain ailment," and in another that "Upton was suffering from a brain tumor."[27]

It appears that Upton's "unrequited ambition" played a major part in his decision to take his life and that his mucocele impaired his thought processes. In 1990, doctors John M. Hyson, George E. Sanborn, Joseph W. Whitehorne, and William H. Mosberg wrote an article in *Military Medicine* titled "The Suicide of General Emory Upton: A Case Report." In it, the authors determined that Upton did indeed die from his "catarrh." In fact, he suffered from a benign tumor in his sinus cavity scientifically known as a "frontal sinus mucocele." The growth of the tumor would have impinged on Upton's brain, causing as much damage as a malignant cancerous growth. And unfortunately, doctors performed no autopsy; a procedure that might have put all speculation to rest.[28]

Before embarking on his world tour, Upton wrote out his will on July 3, 1875. A year after his death, the Genesee County Surrogate's office began probate proceedings of the will. Upton named sister Sara his executor (although one news story named brother James as coexecutor). Sara had become a surrogate wife upon Emily's death, moving into his quarters at West Point while he was commandant and had attended to him upon his return from his world excursion. Once the royalties of his *Tactics* reached $1,000, the Upton family became the recipients of the surplus. He instructed Sara to apply available funds "to the education of such of his nephews and nieces and other collateral relatives as desire to take a collegiate course and are deemed most worthy of such aid." When no more relatives were eligible for this largesse, Upton stipulated that Sara could apply the same principles to any "necessitous and worthy" resident of the county desiring a college education. In typical Uptonian fashion, he required they pass a "competitive examination, before three competent examiners, to be designated by the executors, and shall excel all other competitors in such scholarship, moral character, natural aptitude and ability." He set the limit to each winner at $600 per year and required each to repay one fourth of the grant within ten years. During the war, Upton had insisted that all officers under his command in the 121st New York Volunteers take competency tests before promotion. He also included the provision of testing of all officers in his *Military History*, published posthumously.

He disposed of his property in Battle Creek, an eventually lucrative enterprise that became the Whirlpool company, with which the Upton family continues a relationship to this day. Upton left his sword to his brother James to eventually pass down to the "first nephew or other collateral relative of the name Upton who may graduate at West Point and enter the army." He left his commissions and other papers to his parents "to be by them distributed as they may think proper."[29]

Sometime just before his death, probably at the end of 1880 or the beginning of 1881 (the documentation is unclear), Emory had ordered a stained glass window honoring Emily. He contracted with the English firm of Heaton, Butler, and Bayne to create and ship the window to America to be placed in the Sand Beach Church in Auburn where they were married. Upton asked his publisher, D. Appleton, to take charge of the process, which raises the question of whether he may have been contemplating suicide in early 1881. Three days before his death the American agent for HB&B wrote Mrs. Martin asking her for details on the subject and substance of the window. He had originally approached Appleton, who begged off, explaining that because "Upton was in California ... he (Mr. Appleton) had no knowledge" of the particulars.

With Upton's death, the process stalled. That summer, New York architect Robert Pickering of Wm. Hume Architects and HB&B's American agent, forwarded a letter to Mrs. Martin from HB&B stating that the window had been costed out and they were ready to begin production. By October, HB&B finished the window and informed Appleton it was ready to ship it to him. Appleton passed it on to Mrs. Martin; his accompanying letter revealed much. During the year, Mrs. Martin had made a major change to the window's purpose—to include Emory. As Appleton said to her, "I am glad to hear that the window has been made a memorial to both. How little did Gen. Upton think that such would be the case when he ordered it."[30] In 1934 the Sand Beach Church survived a fire, and the restored church emerged with a shortened bell tower and all the original stained glass windows destroyed. The restored building is no longer a church but a commercial space and reception hall for weddings and rentals.

APPENDIX

Emory and Emily Timeline

"EU" indicates Emory Upton; "EM" indicates Emily (Martin) Upton.

1867

Fall 1867	EM and EU engaged
November 21, 1867	EU to Maj. Gen. James H. Wilson regarding Emily (Wilson Papers, LC)

1868

February 19, 1868	EU and EM married
March 7, 1868	honeymoon: sailed from NYC to France on steamer *Napoleon III*
March–August	Brest, Lyon, Marseilles, Sorrento, Florence
April 24, 1868	In Sorrento, Italy
August 3, 1868	EU and EM in France preparing to go to London
August–October 1868	EU and EM at Willowbrook

October 1868	EU and EM to Key West
November 1868	EM and EU in Havana, steamer to New Orleans
November 1868	EM returns to Key West
November 1868	EU to Memphis around November 15
December 1868	EM in Key West; EU in Memphis

1869

January	EM in Nassau, Havana, Tortugas
January 1–4	EU in Memphis
January 4–23	EU in Louisville
January 23–27	EU in Memphis
February 1868	EM in Nassau; EU in Memphis
March 1868	EM in Nassau
March 1–10, 1869	EU in Memphis
March 1869	EU ordered to Atlanta, not Arizona
April 2, 1869	EM in Havana
April 1869	EU and EM meet in New Orleans
April 1869	EU and EM to Atlanta
May–June 1869	EU and EM in Atlanta
June 1869	EU to Army of Potomac reunion, Washington, D.C.
June 30, 1869	EM to Willowbrook
July–October 1869	EM and EU at Willowbrook
November 1869	EM to Nassau; EU and Nelly accompanied her.

December 1869	EU returned to Atlanta from Nassau, never saw EM again.

1870

January–March 1870	EM at Nassau; EU at Atlanta
March 29, 1870	EM died at Nassau; EU at Atlanta

NOTES

Abbreviations

ACP   Appointment, Commission, and Personal Branch, NAB
GCHD   Genesee County History Department, Batavia, N.Y.
HLOM   Holland Land Office Museum, Batavia, N.Y.
LC   Library of Congress
NAB   National Archives Building, Washington, D.C.

Introduction

1. There is no direct documentation or evidence for this, but two modern physicians who were apprised of her symptoms speculated that it was most likely the case.

2. Michie, *Life and Letters of Emory Upton, Colonel of the Fourth Regiment of Artillery, and Brevet Major General, U.S. Army* (hereafter Michie, *Upton*); Ambrose, *Upton and the Army* (hereafter Ambrose, *Upton*); Fitzpatrick, *Emory Upton: Misunderstood Reformer* (hereafter Fitzpatrick, *Upton*).

3. See Upton, *Correspondence of General Emory Upton*, ed. Salvatore Cilella, vol. 1, *1857–1875*, 228–30 (hereafter Upton, *Correspondence*).

4. Anderson, *Auburn*, 45.

5. Winship, "Elizabeth T. Porter Beach," https://kihm6.wordpress.com/2010/05/24/elizabeth-t-porter-beach/. De Tocqueville visited the prison July 9–12, 1831. Beaumont continued his characterization of Throop: "Owasco Lake touches its garden, and on the other side it is surrounded by great high trees. He took us for a walk in his woods. While admiring the beauty of the trees we caught sight of a squirrel. At that the governor began to run as fast as his legs would carry him to get his gun at the house. He soon came back, all out of breath, with his murderous weapon. The small animal had the patience to wait for him, but the big man had the clumsiness to miss him four times in succession." De Tocqueville et al., *Alexis*

de Tocqueville and Gustave de Beaumont; Beaumont to his sister, Auburn, July 14, 1831, p. 69; de Tocqueville to Ernest de Chabrol, Auburn, July 16, 1831, p. 77.

6. Mrs. Martin wrote Emily on her honeymoon, and the two carried on an extensive correspondence—newlywed to mother. Mrs. Martin opened her first letter a month after the wedding, admitting that she had noted "today ... the arrival of the *Napoleon* at Brest." She referred twice to "Gen. Upton." Mrs. Martin to Emily, March 19, 1868.

7. Mrs. Martin to Emily, November 29, 1867.

8. Emory Upton to Emily Upton, February 2, 1869.

9. Grenville Tremain, "Emily's Wedding," from "What Might Have Been Expected; Album, 1837–1870," unpaginated album compiled by sister Cornelia (Nelly) Eliza Martin, New-York Historical Society.

10. George Martin to Emily, November 19, 1867.

11. Diary entry, Emily Upton, November 29, 1867. James Wilson remarked to a *New York Times* reporter in 1918 that Upton "never knew a woman intimately until he was married, three years after the war, never drank liquor, never tasted tobacco, never used a profane word." Richard Barry, "Emory Upton, Military Genius," *New York Times*, June 18, 1918.

12. George Ticknor, quoted originally in Morton Keller, *Affairs of State: Public Life in Late Nineteenth Century America* (Cambridge: Harvard University Press, 1977), 2, and subsequently quoted in McPherson, *Battle Cry of Freedom*, 861.

13. Ibid., 860.

14. Foote, *Civil War*, 1042.

15. For an excellent discussion of the political infighting over army reorganization, see Marszalek, *Sherman*, 430–37. Marszalek referred to Upton as "Sherman's Pet," 463. Biographer Lee Kennett refers to Sherman as Upton's "patron and collaborator." Kennett, *Sherman*, 315. As Edward Coffman has succinctly characterized it, the radicals "were ready to economize with the Army's budget" but "were not as imbued with the anti-military fervor which inflamed some of the Democrats in Congress." Coffman, *Old Army*, 245. Coffman also has two excellent chapters on frontier army life: chapter 5, "'Promotion's Very Slow': Officers, 1865–1898," and chapter 6, "'The Roving Life We Led': Women and Children, 1865–1898," 215–327.

16. Irvin McDowell in his annual report of 1867, as cited in Coffman, *Old Army*, 217.

17. Vogdes, "Journal," 2–17.

18. Coffman, *Old Army*, 288–89.

19. Dozens of early and recent articles, publications of diaries, and letters of army officers' wives were consulted for this book and include the following: Vogdes, "Journal"; Baker, "Daughters of Mars," 20–42, especially 22; Alexander, *Cavalry Wife*; Myres, "Evy Alexander: The Colonel's Lady at McDowell" (hereafter

Myres, "Colonel's Lady"); Barnitz, *Life in Custer's Cavalry*; Grierson, *Colonel's Lady*; Roe, *Army Letters from an Officer's Wife: 1871–1888* (hereafter Roe, *Letters*); Baldwin, *An Army Wife on the Frontier: The Memoirs of Alice Blackwood Baldwin, 1867–1877* (hereafter Baldwin, *Memoirs*); and Summerhayes, *Vanished Arizona*.

Less useful only because it covers a period much earlier in the life of the army on the frontier (almost an entire generation) and before the Civil War is Chapman, *Helen Chapman's Letters*. Similarly, Fanny Dunbar Corbusier, *Recollections of Her Army Life, 1869–1908*, deals with the last quarter of the nineteenth century with some emphasis on the early twentieth century. Since Emily Upton had no real experience with the rough life of the frontier and passed away in Nassau in 1870, this bears slight relevance to her.

20. Sandra L. Myres, "Introduction," in Roe, *Letters*, xiv; Utley, *Frontier Regulars*, 59, as cited in Sandra L. Myres, "Introduction," in Roe, *Letters*, xv. Perhaps one of the best general comprehensive surveys of military wives in the West is Eales, *Army Wives on the American Frontier: Living by the Bugles* (hereafter Eales, *Bugles*). Eales used documents from more than fifty wives to build a nuanced and revealing narrative of women on the frontier. It is much lighter and more readily accessible than others on the subject, but well researched. Eales uses many of the same diarists and correspondents cited by others such as Libbie Custer, Fanny Corbusier, Eveline Alexander, Ada Vogdes, and Jennie Barnitz. Her topics are comprehensive, ranging from abortion to water and weather issues and venereal disease.

21. Williams, "Ladies of the Regiment," 158–64, as cited in Shannon D. Smith, "Women and Dependents," in *A Companion to Custer and the Little Bighorn Campaign*, ed. Brad L. Lookingbill (New York: Wiley-Blackwell, 2015), 176.

22. McInnis, *Women of Empire: Nineteenth-Century Army Officers' Wives in India and the U.S. West*, 9 (hereafter McInnis, *Wives*). McInnis maintains that officers' wives collaborated with their husbands in advancing and maintaining colonial and imperial efforts in British India and the American West. On page 209, she argues that "feminization of formal and informal military practices produced a new social reality, an empowered female identity, and a cohesive community that sustained imperialist ambitions." Much "new" research in the last few decades has produced a plethora of scholarship into male-female relations and especially women's issues on the frontier. See for example, Myres, "Frontier Historians, Women, and the 'New' Military History," 27–37. Myres urges that more work be done on sexuality, domestic violence, substance abuse, military politics, and women's roles on the military frontier. Myres faults men and women historians for perpetuating stereotypes of military wives on the frontier. See also her "Army Women's Narratives," 175–98.

23. Eales, *Bugles*, 145.

24. Quote of Katie Gibson, in Katherine Gibson Fougera, *With Custer's Cavalry* (1942; reprint, Lincoln: University of Nebraska Press, 1986), 74 as cited in Eales, *Bugles*, 146.

25. Emily to her father, March 3, 1869.

26. Emily to her mother, May 3, 1868. This is in stark contrast to Martha Summerhayes, who in April 1874 married Civil War veteran and professional soldier, John Wyer Summerhayes. She was a New Englander and he, a New Yorker. Summerhayes had been ordered to Fort Russell in Cheyenne, Wyoming Territory. Martha had just returned from Europe and was now going west to what she described as "the wildest sort of place." By autumn, Martha began to wonder if she "had made a terrible mistake in marrying into the army." She concluded that "young army wives should stay home with their mothers and fathers and not go into such wild and uncouth places," but conceded that her decision was "irrevocable." Summerhayes, *Vanished Arizona*, 13 and 56. Lieutenant Summerhayes had advanced to the rank of brevet major general during the war, where he participated in most of the major battles in the eastern theater. He was discharged from the volunteers December 1898, and he retired January 6, 1900. Heitman, *Historical Register and Dictionary of the United States Army, from Its Organization September 29, 1789 to March 2, 1903*, vol. 1 of 2, p. 936 (hereafter Heitman, *Register*, 1).

27. Alexander, *Cavalry Wife*, entry of September 27, 1866, p. 90.

28. Eveline Martin married Andrew Alexander. The two became acquainted with Myles Keogh through the service. Eveline, known as Evy, spoke of Keogh as early as 1866: "I am glad you liked my dear friend Keogh. We are both very fond of him and it has been a great gratification that he has been to our home. From his letter to Andrew he seemed to be so happy there. I should be glad indeed if we were in the same regiment." Eveline Martin to her mother, Fort Garland, October 28, 1866. Keogh was reburied in the Throop-Martin family plot at Fort Hill Cemetery, October 25, 1877. See *Army and Navy Journal*, November 3, 1877, p. 196. Andrew Alexander and William Seward's son, also named William, attended, but Emory Upton was on his world tour. For many years it was rumored that Cornelia—"Nelly"—carried an unrequited love of Keogh to her grave. Convis, *Myles W. Keogh*, 169. See also Alexander, *Cavalry Wife*; and Myres, "Colonel's Lady."

29. William H. Seward to his daughter-in-law Janet Seward, September 14, 1868; Janet to William Seward, September 8, 1868; Janet to William, October 6, 1868; William to Janet, October 8, 1868, all in William Seward Digital Archive, University of Rochester, River Campus Libraries, Rochester, N.Y. As much as Seward and others depended on Nassau as a cure-all, ironically, Mary Martin died at age forty-five in 1884 from tuberculosis.

30. Emily to her mother, May 3, 1868.

31. Emily to her mother, March 18, 1868.

32. Emily to her mother, March 17, 1868. De Lancey Floyd-Jones, an 1846 graduate of the military academy, was a decorated veteran from New York. He served in the Mexican War when he was breveted a first lieutenant September 8, 1847, for gallant and meritorious conduct in the Battle of Molino del Rey. During the Civil War he served as a lieutenant colonel and was cited for his service in the Peninsula Campaign on July 4, 1862, and Gettysburg, July 2, 1863. During the Indian wars he was commander of the 19th Infantry. He retired from the army March 20, 1879, and died January 19, 1902. Heitman, *Register*, 1:426.

33. Emily to Lily, April 18, 1868.

34. See Emily's letter to her mother, May 20, 1868. Silas Atherton Holman, a native of Maine, served during the war as surgeon in the 7th Massachusetts Infantry (June 15, 1861). He was also assistant surgeon and then surgeon of the U.S. Volunteers in 1863. He was recognized for his service in his department and in the field during the Richmond Campaign. He was promoted to colonel of volunteers March 13, 1865, mustered out January 10, 1866, and died December 24, 1894. Heitman, *Register*, 1:538.

35. Emily to sister Evy, August 3, 1868.

36. Mrs. Martin to Emily, June 24, 1868.

37. Mrs. Martin to Emily, July 14, 1868. See Alexander, *Cavalry Wife* and Myres, "Colonel's Lady." Eveline's army life and experience were directly opposite her sister Emily's. Eveline followed her husband to Colorado, New Mexico, and Texas, while Emily battled with tuberculosis in exotic locales. Emily did manage to join her husband in Atlanta and Memphis, which was the farthest west she traveled.

38. Emily to her father, March 19, 1868.

39. Emily to her father, March 20, 1868.

40. Emily to sister Nelly, March 28, 1868.

41. Emily to her mother, April 6, 1868.

42. Letter fragment, Emory Upton to Unknown, Emory Upton Papers, The Holland Land Office Museum, Batavia, N.Y. (hereafter HLOM). The Uptons were in Sorrento from April 16 to Saturday, May 17, 1868, according to Emily's letter book.

43. Emily to her mother, May 3, 1868.

44. Emily to her father, April 16, 1868.

45. Emory to his brother John, May 7, 1868, in Upton Papers, Genesee County History Department, Batavia, N.Y. (hereafter GCHD). Also published in Upton, *Correspondence*, 1:248–50.

46. Emily to her mother, August 2, 1868.

47. Emily to her mother, October 30, 1868.

48. "Experience the Civil War Walking Tours of Memphis," https://www.memphistravel.com/memphis-civil-war-walking-tour.

49. Emily to Sister Evy, January 3, 1869.

50. Emily to her father, November 19, 1868.

51. Emily to her mother, October 30, 1868, and to her brother Jack, November 27, 1868.

52. Emily to her mother, January 24, 1869.

53. Emily to her sister Molly (Mary Williams Martin), February 5, 1869.

54. Emory to Emily, February 2, 1869.

55. Emily to her mother, March 5, 1869. Emory's tour of duty at Memphis ended April 26, 1869.

56. Emily to her mother, April 2, 1869.

57. Emily to her mother, May 17, 1869. Emily was referring to Emory's tactics manual.

58. Emily to her mother, May 17, 1869.

59. Emily to her mother, June 1, 1869.

60. Emily to Evy, October 25, 1869.

61. Nelly to her mother, January 8, 1870.

62. Emily to her mother, February 1, 1870. Of the afghan she said, "I have worked at it quietly and steadily without hurting myself, and now I am surprised to find it finished and that it is so handsome. I could work at it for hours without tiring as tired as I am after writing a page and it has been so much of a comfort for me to feel that I was doing something for my husband."

63. Emily to her mother, February 19, 1870.

64. A. D. Kirkwood to Mrs. Martin, March 6, 1870. This was in response to Mrs. Martin's inquiry to Mrs. Kirkwood as to how her daughter was *really* faring. Kirkwood told Mrs. Martin that she had not told Emily she (Mrs. Martin) had written to her, and that she was responding. On March 12, Nelly reported that Emily was doing better than the previous three months, and that the last three days showed steady improvement. "I feel quite encouraged and she does too. She wrote a note to Upton this morning in which she told him that if she did not feel as well in April, she should send for him, but she does not want him to come unless she particularly says so." Nelly to her mother, March 12, 1870.

65. Emily to Evy, December 30, 1869.

Chapter 1

1. Wilson Papers, Library of Congress (hereafter LC). For the ever-serious Upton, the letter strikes a modern reader as naive and childlike. It is notable in its playful attempt at blending marital and martial matters. Perhaps a psycho-historian would unearth something more profound in the letter. A modern cynic might view it "too cute by half." It reveals Upton's childlike happiness in finding a mate, which he thought was for life. Emily Martin became terminally ill almost immediately

after her wedding. They were married February 19, 1868, and she died March 29, 1870. Originally published in Upton, *Correspondence*, 1:245–46.

Emily told her diary, "One year ago tonight, I was visiting this diary for my birthday. It is but one year? I ask myself. For to me it passes many judging by what I have experienced. November 17th—a day never to be forgotten saw the fulfillment of my dearest hopes. On that day, I promised General Upton that I would be to him forever a loving wife. That nothing but death shall ever part us in spirit and when we had kneeled and asked God's blessing on the solemn step we had taken, I felt the peace I had longed for took possession of my heart." Emily's Diary, November 29, 1867.

2. Willowbrook was the home of her father, Enos Thompson Throop Martin, on Lake Owasco, near Auburn, New York. More so than his home in Batavia, Willowbrook became Upton's source of solace after Emily's death.

3. This is probably John Adams Appleton (1817–1881), who with his brothers as partners, continued the firm of D. Appleton and Company Publishers, established by their father, Daniel. They published many nineteenth-century memoirs and books, including Upton's books and William Sherman's memoirs.

4. This is possibly Reverend William E. Boardman of New York City. He was a Presbyterian pastor, American Sabbath School missionary, American Home Missionary Society missionary, secretary of the United States Christian Commission, evangelist, and author. He was also a leader of the non-Methodist phalanx of the Holiness Movement in the United States, Great Britain, Sweden, and Germany, and a proponent of divine healing. Williams, "Boardman, William Edwin," https://onlinelibrary.wiley.com/doi/pdf/10.1002/9780470670606.wbecc1561.

5. All unidentified.

6. Floyd-Jones also delighted Emily's sister Eveline. In May 1866, Eveline reported a visit to Little Rock, Arkansas, where she had a "charming visit." There she met with Fanny Rawles and Major Rawles. "Colonel Floyd-Jones of the Nineteenth [Infantry] has been exceedingly polite. He was down on the boat to see me off today." Alexander, *Cavalry Wife*, 34.

7. Mother Carey's Chickens are a folk name for seabirds of the storm petrel family. Also known as the European Storm Petrel.

8. This may have been Mrs. C. Davenport from Cold Spring, New York, which is directly across the Hudson from West Point. American Bible Society, *Fifty-fifth Annual Report*, 1871, p. 86. Emily and Emory were keen on distributing Bibles and proselytizing to all who would listen. At West Point, Emory told his sister Maria that he took "the bible as the standard of morality, and try to read two chapters in it daily." Upton to Maria, April 12, 1857, Upton Papers, GCHD.

9. Yellow wildflowers were associated with the medieval English rulers of the House of Plantagenet.

10. The Reverend Dr. Eldridge was pastor to the American Chapel in Paris. As the *Christian World* depicted him, he "has exerted himself very actively to build up the interest of the congregation. It is mainly by his personal exertions that a debt of 60,000 francs has been paid off. We trust that Dr. Eldridge may long continue in a sphere in which he is so useful and that his church may flourish more and more, standing, as it does, as an excellent representative of American Protestantism." *The Christian World: Magazine of the American and Foreign Christian Union*, vol. 18, January to December 1867 (New York: American and Foreign Christian Union, 1867), 187, 285, 290.

11. One of the historic hotels of Europe, Hotel de l'Athenee on 15 Rue Scribe, opened in 1867. "Hôtel Plaza Athénée," Historic Hotels of the World: Then and Now, http://www.historichotelsthenandnow.com/plazaatheneeparis.html.

12. John Adams Dix (1798–1879), a longtime public servant, was a Union major general during the war, President Buchanan's secretary of the treasury, governor of New York, U.S. senator, and envoy extraordinary and minister plenipotentiary to France, December 23, 1866–May 23, 1869. He was famous for the Dix-Hill agreement relating to the exchange of Confederate and Union soldiers during the Civil War.

13. Unidentified.

14. Unidentified.

15. The Bois de Boulogne became a public park in 1852 and is located in the sixteenth arrondissement.

16. Unidentified.

17. Possibly the Reverend Robert S. Brown, D. D. "acting as interpreter to the American Embassy" in Japan. Griffis, *Rutgers Graduates in Japan*, 34.

18. The two rivers flow through the center of Lyon and join just to the south end of the town.

19. Unidentified.

20. Unidentified.

21. Today it is known as Chateau Borely, which houses the Musee des Arts, decoratifs, and de la Faeince et de le Mode. Located on the city's south side, it sits directly on the bay overlooking the Mediterranean.

22. The Corniche Road runs along the French and Italian "Riviera."

23. Unidentified.

24. In his *The Innocents Abroad* (chap. 11, pp. 100–101), Mark Twain wrote of the Marseilles Zoological Garden: "In the great Zoological Gardens we found specimens of all the animals the world produces, I think, including a dromedary, a monkey ornamented with tufts of brilliant blue and carmine hair—a very gorgeous monkey he was—a hippopotamus from the Nile, and a sort of tall, long-legged bird with a beak like a powder horn and close-fitting wings like the tails of a dress coat. This fellow stood up with his eyes shut and his shoulders stooped

forward a little, and looked as if he had his hands under his coat tails. Such tranquil stupidity, such supernatural gravity, such self-righteousness, and such ineffable self-complacency as were in the countenance and attitude of that gray-bodied, dark-winged, bald-headed, and preposterously uncomely bird! He was so ungainly, so pimply about the head, so scaly about the legs, yet so serene, so unspeakably satisfied! He was the most comical-looking creature that can be imagined."

25. Dr. James Johnson, noted British physician, wrote in 1830 "For one Hotel de Paris in Italy we find five Hotel de Londres." By 1870, Rome boasted a Hotel de l'Angleterre, Hotel de iles Britanniques, a Hotel Brighton, and a Hotel Victoria. Pemble, *Mediterranean Passion*, 41.

26. Civita Vecchia literally means "old town" or "ancient city." It is located thirty-seven miles from Rome in the Lazio region and on the coast. It acted as an ancient harbor and port for Rome.

27. Unidentified.

28. Emma Conn Crow Cushman was the wife of Edwin Charles "Ned" Cushman Sr. (1838–1909). Edwin graduated from the Naval Academy, which he attended 1852–56. In 1865, President Lincoln appointed him U.S. consul to Italy. *Journal of the Executive Proceedings of the Senate . . . December 5, 1864 to February 6, 1866*, 20.

29. Jack, George, Fred, and Violet were all siblings.

30. See Upton's letter to his brother John from Sorrento, May 7, 1868.

31. Recent research does not support the long-held narrative that Christians were martyred in the Colosseum. Emily is referring to Pius IX.

32. Emily's sister Eliza Williams Martin was known as "Lylie," "Leily," or Lily. She married Grenville Tremain, a promising Albany, New York, lawyer who died a premature death in 1878. Leily died in 1909.

33. A Grand Hotel Excelsior Vittoria opened in 1834 and is now a luxury hotel on the Piazza Torquato Tasso, Sorrento. Richard Wagner and Oscar Wilde were guests.

34. This villa and palazzo near Sorrento is no longer in existence.

35. Molly is Mary Williams Martin (1838–1884), Emily's sister.

36. Probably Fort Wallace, Kansas, which served as a cavalry fort from 1865 to 1882. According to the *New York Times*, the fort was "located on Pond creek, the south branch of the Smoky Hill River and about ten miles northeast of the present terminus of the Union pacific Railway, eastern division. It was called after General Wallace and two years ago was known as 'Pond Creek Station.'" See "Indian Depredations. Attack on Fort Wallace, Kansas—The Indians Repulsed with a Loss of 20 Killed." *New York Times*, June 28, 1867. According to the article, four members of the 7th Cavalry were killed.

37. The doctor made a distinct impression on the newlyweds, and when he became aware of Emily's condition, Dr. de Cosson weighed in with medical advice that the Uptons continued to recall during their brief marriage.

38. There were four prominent Civil War–era Crittendens. Thomas Leonidas Crittenden, son of Kentucky senator John Crittenden, is often confused with his first cousin Thomas Turpin Crittenden of Huntsville, Alabama, who in turn is often confused with *his* first cousin Thomas Theodore Crittenden of Shelbyville, Kentucky. Thomas Theodore, also a Civil War veteran, became governor of Missouri in 1880. Thomas Leonidas rose to the rank of major general; Thomas Turpin to brigadier general. All three, despite their southern births, fought for the Union. Another cousin, Maj. Gen. George Bibb Crittenden, a West Point graduate, joined the Confederacy. Warner, *Generals in Blue*, 100–102; Warner, *Generals in Gray*, 65–66; Heitman, *Register*, 1:338–39; *Centennial History of Missouri*, 544.

39. Unknown.

40. Emily's brother Capt. John Williams "Jack" Martin (1850- 1908). Jack was admitted to West Point, where he started July 1, 1869, but dropped out, February 15, 1871. Later he joined the army in July 1872 as a second lieutenant of the 4th Cavalry and eventually became a captain of cavalry in November 1884. He retired February 25, 1891, and died in Redlands, California. Heitman, *Register*, 1:693.

41. William Seward, secretary of state and neighbor of the Throop-Martin family.

42. Frederick Townsend was an Albany merchant who organized the 3rd Regiment New York State Volunteers as the war began. During his brief two years in combat, he was brevetted lieutenant colonel, colonel, and then brigadier general in the regular army. He fought at Big Bethel, Virginia; Lick Creek, Mississippi; Corinth; Perryville; and Stones River. He was appointed acting assistant provost marshal-general in Albany in 1863. In 1867, on his return from Europe after a leave of absence, he was ordered to California, and as acting inspector general of the department, he inspected the government posts in Arizona. He resigned his commission in 1868. He died at Lake Luzerne, New York, September 12, 1897. "Frederick Townsend," in *National Cyclopedia of American Biography*, 459; Warner, *Generals in Blue*, 394; "Resignation of Gen. Townsend," *New York Times*, November 3, 1880.

43. GCHD. The couple sailed from New York on the French steamer *Napoleon III* for Brest. *New-York Daily Tribune*, March 9, 1868. By April 24 they were in Sorrento, Italy. Michie, *Upton*, 229. During the year, Upton dutifully reported to the adjutant general on the first of every month per "Special Order No. 507, dated A. G. O. Washington, D.C. Nov. 29th, 1867," that he was on leave and his location. He reported from Auburn; New York City; Marseilles, France; Florence, Italy; Bellagio, Italy; Auburn again; and on November 1, from Key West, Florida.

44. Charles-Louis Napoleon Bonaparte, a.k.a. Napoleon III (1808–1873). He was a supporter of the unification of Italy and defended the Papal States from being acquired by Italy.

45. The Papal States were lost to the church in 1870, when the Italian army seized Rome as its capital. At that time the pope and the church retreated to Vatican Hill. It was not until 1929 that Mussolini and the church agreed to the Vatican's limited sovereignty with the Lateran Treaty.

46. The newlyweds were home at Willowbrook by August of 1868 where "they remained until October when Upton took her to Key West hoping the climate" would help her. Upton was ordered to Memphis that month. Fitzpatrick, "Upton," 174.

47. George Bliss Martin, a younger brother (1852–1928), was a businessman and a newspaper owner. He moved to Albany in 1870. As his health deteriorated, he returned to Willowbrook, where he died.

48. A hot wind that may be dusty or rainy, blowing in from North Africa across the Mediterranean to southern Europe.

49. The onetime section of Rome inhabited by emigrant Spaniards and the home of the Spanish ambassador. The site of the famous, steep Spanish Steps from the Piazza, at the base to the Piazza Trinita dei Monti, to the top, where the Church Trinita dei Monti is located.

50. Probably the newly wed daughter and son-in-law of John A. Dix.

51. Probably the National Archaeological Museum founded in 1777. It became a museum in the nineteenth century and today holds important Greek and Roman antiquities, including many excavated materials from Pompeii and Herculaneum.

52. Shelley and Keats are buried in Rome in the Protestant Cemetery (sometimes referred to as the Englishman's Cemetery—in Italian, "Cimitero Acattolico" or "Cimitero dei Protestanti") near the Tiber River in the Testaccio region of Rome.

53. In 1508, Pope Julius II asked Raphael (1483–1520) to finish the decorations of his four rooms that had been started by artists Luca Signorelli (1450–1523) and Piero della Francesca (1415–1492). Raphael was perhaps the most celebrated young artist after Michelangelo and da Vinci.

54. The Apollo of Belvedere is a Roman copy of a Greek work from the fourth century B.C.

55. The Laocoon depicts the Trojan priest with his two sons being crushed to death by snakes as a penalty for warning the Trojans of the danger of the Trojan horse. It is of uncertain date and is possibly of Greek origin. It was found in Rome in 1506 in the Domus Aurea, Nero's opulent and large landscaped palace, built after the great fire of 64 A.D. *Rome and the Vatican*, 97.

56. Named after Appius Claudius Caecus (340–273 B.C.), a Roman censor who conceived the strategic importance of a road from Rome to the south. The road was begun in 312 B.C. and eventually ended in the town of Brindisi in the heel of the Italian boot on the Adriatic Sea.

57. Dr. Holman is identified in the introduction.

Chapter 2

1. Via de' Pandolfini is a few short blocks from Brunelleschi's dome atop the Florence Cathedral (The Duomo).

2. The official title of the painting is "Last Communion of St. Jerome," painted by Domenico Zampieri (1581–1641), known as Domenichino in 1614. Raffaello Sanzio da Urbino (Raphael, 1483–1520) painted the Transfiguration (1516–20). Both reside in the Pinoteca ("painting") galleries of the Vatican Museum. Cropper, "Domenichino."

3. Capitoline Museums, Rome.

4. The Dying Gladiator is a Roman marble copy of a Greek sculpture of the late third century B.C. It was originally thought to represent a dying gladiator wounded from a recent fight in a Roman amphitheater. The sculptor is unknown. Recent scholarship indicates that the subject of the sculpture was probably a Gaul and that the piece was commissioned as early as 230 B.C. Art scholars have retitled it as either the "Dying Gaul" or the "Dying Galatian."

5. The "Capitoline Venus" is a marble sculpture probably from the original by Praxiteles in the fourth century B.C. It is also known as the "modest Venus." Several sculptures have survived showing Venus just emerging from her bath, covering her groin and breasts with her hands.

6. Aside from the Colosseum, the Pantheon remains one of Rome's most treasured buildings. Originally a Roman temple, since the seventh century it has been a Catholic church, "St. Mary and the Martyrs." It was commissioned by Marcus Agrippa during Emperor Augustus's reign (27 B.C.–14 A.D.) and completed under Hadrian around 126 A.D.

7. Emily may be referring either to the Lateran Palace, which was the home of the popes until the late nineteenth century, or the Basilica of St. John Lateran, the cathedral of Rome.

8. "Americans are as plentiful here as ants in an ant hill," Frederic Edwin Church wrote to his friend and patron William Henry Osborn on January 23, 1869. "From the studio building we have represented in Rome—McEntee—Gifford—Thompson—Weir—Hazeltine [sic]—Church, six of them have no studios, but are here to see and travel." Blaugund, "Old Boy Network in Rome," 229.

9. Officially known as the Basilica di Santa Maria Maggiore, it sits outside the Vatican walls, but is the property of the Vatican. It is one of four major Roman Catholic basilicas, which include St. John Lateran, St. Peter's, and St. Paul Outside the Walls. See "Historic Center of Rome," http://whc.unesco.org/en/list/91/.

10. Known to Romans as the Pincian Hill in the northeast quadrant of the historical Rome. During historical Roman times it was known as the "Hill of

Gardens," and was renamed for the Pincii family of the fourth century A.D. Today it sits to the east between the Piazza del Popolo and the Borghese gardens.

11. Col. Timothy Bigelow Lawrence (1826–1869) was appointed consul general to Italy in 1862. He died in Washington on March 21, 1869. "March 21," in *Annual Cyclopedia and Register of Important Events of the Year 1869*, vol. 9 (New York: Appleton, 1870), 503.

12. George Perkins Marsh was appointed by President Taylor as minister resident to Turkey from 1849 to 1853. He served as a special envoy to Greece in 1852, as fish commissioner in Vermont in 1857, and as railroad commissioner from 1857 to 1859. President Lincoln named him envoy extraordinary and minister plenipotentiary to Italy on March 20, 1861, where he served until his death in Vallombrosa, Italy, on July 24, 1882. Marsh oversaw the move of the U.S. legislation from Turin to Florence in 1865 and then from Florence to Rome in 1871. *Biographical Directory of the American Congress*, 1502–3.

13. English poet Samuel Rogers (1793–1855), as a result of several visits to Italy, produced a long poem simply titled "Italy." It was published first in 1822, again in 1828, and last, in a lavish, revised, and enlarged edition with J. M. W. Turner engravings in 1830. The stanzas on Venice run several pages, and the part Emily quoted is the first nine lines from chapter 11. She quoted the verse nearly perfectly:

> There is a glorious City in the Sea.
> The Sea is in the broad, the narrow streets.
> Ebbing and flowing and the salt seaweed
> Clings to the marble of her palaces.
> No track of men, no footsteps to and fro
> Lead to her gates. The path lies o'er the Sea,
> Invisible; and from the land we went
> As to a floating city, steering in
> And gliding up her streets as in a dream
> [From Samuel Rogers, *Italy: A Poem* (London: John Murray, 1823), 59.]

14. Officially, Accademia di Belle Arti di Venezia, the Academy of Fine Arts, in Venice, was founded in 1750. "The Academy of Fine Arts, Venice, 1750–2010: Historical Background," https://web.archive.org/web/20140606205051/http://www.accademiavenezia.it/accademia.php?id=1&type=eng.

15. During the Second Italian War of Independence, the Battle of Solferino, June 24, 1859, ended with the fall of the fortress Rocca, an Austrian loss.

16. A small village on Lago di Lecco, thirty-one miles north of Milan. The lake is a branch of Lake Como.

17. A public stagecoach, especially as formerly used in France.

18. Unidentified.

19. A major mountain pass connecting northern and southern Switzerland, named after Saint Gotthard of Hildesheim (died in 1038), patron saint of mountain passes. It is unclear what Emily meant by using the name "Vincent." Since this letter is a transcription in Emily's letter book copied probably by her mother, Mrs. Martin may have misinterpreted "Saint" for "Vincent."

20. Unidentified. Because this letter, like all in Emily's letter book, is a transcription of her letters, probably in her mother's hand, the accuracy of this name is highly suspicious.

21. Cunard Company, Royal Mail Steamship, Cuba. 7,000 tons, 600 horsepower. *New York Times*, December 3, 1864.

22. Unidentified.

23. The letter book transcription also erroneously dated this 1867. The hotel was built in 1855 as part of a sweeping revitalization of Paris. "A number of 'Grand Hotels'" were built at Napoleon III's request, and the Grand Hotel du Louvre was the first. "Hôtel de Louvre," Historic Hotels of the World, Then and Now, http://www.historichotelsthenandnow.com/louvreparis.html.

24. Camp de Chalons was a French military base also known as camp de Mourmelon at Mourmelon-le-Grand near Chalons-en-Champagne. Emily wrote her mother, "Emory left me last night for Chalons where the French Army are encamped. He was very anxious to go there before he left Europe." Emily to her mother, August 2, 1868, Emily's Letterbook (hereafter Letterbook).

25. Strategic intuition, a nebulous term coined by Carl von Clausewitz, eighteenth-century military strategist, indicates keen insight and quick military action on the part of a military leader to exploit an enemy's weakness.

26. Gen. Edmond Leboeuf (1809–1888) commanded the military camp at Chalons (Mourmelon) in 1868. He began his career as a colonel in the artillery, quickly rising through the ranks. In 1859 he fought at Solferino. In 1869 he became French minister of war. "Edmond Leboeuf, French General," *Encyclopedia Britannica*, last accessed May 9, 2016, http://www.britannica.com/biography/Edmond-Leboeuf.

27. This was probably the office of George Bowen, lawyer from 1852 until 1909. He served as president and director of the Holland Purchase Insurance Company, and was director since 1864 and vice president since 1900 of the First National Bank of Batavia. He was also Batavia town clerk, 1854–57; district attorney of Genesee County, 1857–89; Batavia postmaster, 1862–67; and state senator, 1870–73. He had an office in the Walker Building, Batavia. John William Leonard, ed., "George Bowen," *The Classified Who's Who in Finance* (New York: Joseph and Sefton, 1911), 528.

28. Upton's sister.

29. LeRoy is a town on the eastern (and therefore east of Batavia) county line of Genesee County.

30. Sara Kelsey Upton, Emory's sister. He relied heavily on her when Emily passed away. For many years, she became a helpmate in his household and his "social secretary." Upon his death, she became his executor and principal legatee. William Henry Upton, *Upton Family Records*, 309.

31. Unidentified.

32. Unidentified.

33. Possibly the wife of Col. Richard Irving Dodge, an 1848 graduate of West Point, who served successively with the 8th, 12th, 30th, 3rd, and 23rd Infantry Regiments from 1848 until he became aide-de-camp to General Sherman on January 1, 1881. He served with Sherman until June 1882. He began his army career as a second lieutenant in the 8th Infantry, July 1, 1848, and retired May 1891 as a full colonel. He died June 16, 1895. Heitman, *Register*, 1:377.

34. Wilson is unidentified. A Captain Eastman is mentioned in Octavius T. Howe and Frederick C. Matthews, *American Clipper Ships, 1833–1858*, vol. 1 (New York: Dover Publications), 155. "In 1866, her time (the *Electric Spark*) was 155 days, Captain Eastman reporting 42 days to the line and 40 days from the Pacific equator to port, she being within 90 miles of the Golden gate for 18 days." The U.S. Navy marked its presence on Key West beginning in 1823, when the federal government responded to piracy in the area. In 1845, Fort Zachary Taylor was established and later expanded in response to the Mexican War.

35. While in New Mexico Territory, in her journey between Fort Bascom and Fort Union, Eveline Alexander came across the 57th Regiment, U.S. Colored Troops. She recorded her reaction and those of local Mexicans who "appeared very much disgusted with the coming of the Negroes" characterizing them "as black as night." Eveline described them as "the most hideous blacks [she] had ever seen. There is hardly a mulatto among them; almost all are coal black, with frightfully bad places [?]. They must have been the refuse from the other states, for when Negroes were incorrigible they were sold south to the cotton plantations of Arkansas and Louisiana." Diary entry, August 11, 1866. Alexander, *Cavalry Wife*, 73. Most of the wives were either openly hostile or feared blacks. For a full discussion of racial feelings and relations, see Eales, *Bugles*, 130–34. On page 131, Eales reveals that Alice Grierson was the "only army wife" who "took a special interest in the well-being of black enlisted men."

36. The city of Colon, Panama, was originally called Aspinwall after shipping magnate William Henry Aspinwall (1807–1875), cofounder of the Pacific Mail Steamship Company and the Panama Canal Railway Company. Sending mail overland through the Panama isthmus to the West Coast was faster than directly through New Orleans or other southern continental ports. According to his obituary, "The way was opened to direct communication between Asia and America and Oceana and Australasia, besides an immense coastline extending from Panama to Bering's Straits." See "Obituary. William H. Aspinwall," *New York Times*, January 19, 1875.

37. Emory took Emily to Key West during the month of October 1868 and remained with her until mid-November. Her first extant letter to her mother from Key West was October 25, 1868.

38. Leeside refers to the sheltered side of the boat, as opposed to the windward side.

39. Eastman is identified in Emily's letter, October 30, 1868, to her mother.

40. Fanny, the wife of Maj. Jacob Beekman Rawles. Alexander, *Cavalry Wife*, 33–34. The Rawles were acquaintances of the Alexanders as well as the Uptons.

41. The steamship *Maryland* was built in 1864. *Proceedings of the Nineteenth Annual Meeting of the Board of Supervising Inspectors of Steam Vessels*, 127.

42. Possibly the Tacon Theater, which opened in 1838.

43. According to the Oxford English Dictionary, a "Volante" is "a two wheeled covered carriage drawn by a horse ridden by a postilion (freq. with another horse attached at the side), used in Spanish countries. Recent examples refer chiefly to Cuba." See also Ryder, "World on Wheels," 228.

44. Rear Adm. Henry K. Hoff was commander of the Atlantic Fleet. Civil War major general William Rosecrans served as U.S. minister to Mexico briefly from 1868 to 1869, when newly elected president Grant removed him.

45. "*Star of the West*—1172 tons, length 228.3ft × beam 32.7ft, wooden hull-side paddle wheels, two masts. Launched 17th Jun. 1852 by Jeremiah Simonson, New York for Vanderbilt, she started sailings between New York and San Juan de Nicaragua on 20th Oct. 1852 and continued this service for Charles Morgan from Jul. 1853 to Mar. 1856. She started New York—Aspinwall sailings for the United States Mail SS Co. in Jun. 1857 and in Sep. 1859 went onto the New York—Havana—New Orleans service. Chartered to the War Department in Jan. 1861, she was seized by Confederate forces and later burned." See "Steamships on the Panama Route," http://www.theshipslist.com/ships/descriptions/panamafleet.shtml.

46. Maj. Jacob Beekman Rawles was a classmate of Upton's. He graduated twenty-ninth in his class and was appointed second lieutenant, 3rd Artillery. He was later promoted to first lieutenant, 5th Artillery. He successfully became a captain, July 1866; a major, 4th Artillery, August 1887; a lieutenant colonel 1st Artillery, April 1897; a colonel 3rd Artillery, February 1899, and eventually brigadier general, April 1903. He retired that month. He died in 1919. Kirshner, *The Class of 1861: Custer, Ames, and Their Classmates after West Point*, 158 (hereafter Kirshner, *Class of 1861*); Heitman, *Register*, 1:817.

47. This letter and the following letter to her brother Jack are in another hand, probably Nelly's. Emily either was too ill to write these two letters and dictated them to Nelly, or Nelly wrote them both from whole cloth. Emily's handwriting is slanted to the left and often cramped; these two letters are clear, legible, and precise—closely resembling a penmanship exercise.

48. No family documentation has been discovered related to a marble bust.

49. Gen. Romeyn Beck Ayres, a West Point graduate in the class of 1847, was born in Montgomery County, New York, on December 20, 1825. His father had tutored him in Latin, making him an authority on the language at the academy. He served in the Mexican War, and when the Civil War broke out, he was advanced to captain in the 5th U.S. Artillery and commanded a battery at the First Bull Run. He went on to serve the entire war, participating in every major battle in the eastern theater. In 1866, he was appointed lieutenant colonel of the new 28th Regiment. He became a full colonel in 1879 as commander of the 2nd Artillery. He died December 4, 1888, and is buried at Arlington National Cemetery. Warner, *Generals in Blue*, 13–14; Heitman, *Register*, 1:177.

50. This is probably Thomas Hewson Neill, who graduated from the military academy in 1847, twenty-seventh in his class. A Philadelphia native born April 9, 1826, he served throughout the war along a similar track taken by Upton: Antietam, Fredericksburg, Salem Church (3rd Brigade, Howe's Division of Sedgwick's 6th Corps), Rappahannock Station, Mine Run, the Overland Campaign, and the Shenandoah Valley. Before the war he served with the 5th Infantry on frontier duty and served three years as an instructor at West Point. After the war he reverted to the rank of major of infantry from 1866–70. He replaced Upton as commandant of cadets in 1875 and transferred to the 8th Cavalry in 1879. He retired for health reasons in 1883 and passed away March 12, 1885, in Philadelphia. Warner, *Generals in Blue*. 342–43; Heitman, *Register*, 1:742.

51. This is probably Gen. William Montrose Graham, who rose through the ranks from second lieutenant with the 1st Artillery in 1855 to brevet brigadier general in March 1865. During the war he participated in the Peninsula Campaign, Antietam, and Gettysburg. He retired September 28, 1898, and was honorably discharged from the volunteers November 30 that year. He was one of those officers who was breveted as major general or brigadier general for services rendered during the war, but was not appointed to full rank. See Warner, *Generals in Blue*, 581 and 586; Heitman, *Register*, 1:469.

52. Edward Hatch was appointed captain of the 2nd Iowa Cavalry August 12, 1861. He rose to the rank of brevet major general of volunteers in December 1864 for gallant and meritorious service in the battles before Nashville, and achieved the rank of brevet brigadier general in the regular army in March 1867 for his service during the Battle of Franklin. Hatch mustered out of the volunteers in January 1866 and was given command of the 9th Colored Cavalry. He was a friend of the Alexanders also. Warner, *Generals in Blue*, 215–16. Heitman, *Register*, 1:510. Eveline Alexander reported in her diary March 29, 1867, that Hatch told her as he headed for the Texas frontier that his "regiment was finally armed and equipped. He did not say what part of Texas they were to be stationed in." Alexander, *Cavalry Wife*, 123. Hatch died April 11, 1889.

53. Upton led a cavalry division under Maj. Gen. James H. Wilson from December 1864 through mid-May 1865 through Alabama and Georgia. Wilson's raid, which occurred in the waning months of the war, was a tactical success, but it did little to further the outcome of the war.

54. Judge Lyman Tremain practiced law in Albany and served in the Forty-Third Congress, 1873–75. His wife was Helen Cornwall Tremain, and they had three children, Grenville, Helen, and Lyman. Lyman was seven years old when he died. Grenville married Eliza Williams Martin, Emily's sister. He died ten years later of typhus at age thirty-three.

55. Eveline Throop Martin Alexander was Emily's sister. Sometimes Upton spelled her name Evy.

56. Sedgwick Barracks, named for the admired Union general killed in action at the Battle of Spotsylvania, was in use from August 1864 to early 1874. Units stationed there included companies from the 1st U.S. Infantry, the 2nd U.S. Infantry, the 22nd U.S. Infantry, Battery G of the 5th Artillery (a.k.a. "The Alexander Hamilton Bodyguard," which had lineage going back to the Revolutionary War), and the famous 9th Cavalry Regiment, "Buffalo Soldiers." The camp of instruction served as a training ground for cavalry troops. According to official records, there were 2,641 cavalrymen in the camp as of June 1864. Breerwood, "Greenville Encampment," https://neworleanshistorical.org/items/show/639.

57. Willowbrook was the home of the Throop-Martin family on Lake Owasco, south of Auburn, New York, where Upton and Emily were married.

58. Classical allusion to Greek mythology. Leander, the lover of the priestess Hero, tried to swim the Hellespont to join her, but drowned in the attempt.

59. Bvt. Brig. Gen. Lewis Cass Hunt, graduate of West Point in 1847, was born February 23, 1824, at Fort Howard in Green Bay, Wisconsin. He was the son and grandson of regular army officers. His brother was Henry Jackson Hunt, who became an artillery expert involved with rewriting artillery tactics after the war. Lewis saw service in Mexico and the Pacific. He took part in the Peninsula Campaign and was badly wounded at Seven Pines.

After recovery, he finished out the war in the Carolinas. After the war he was posted to far-flung posts in the West, achieving the permanent rank of colonel of the 14th Infantry in 1881. He had suffered from chronic dysentery since the Mexican War, and he died six days after reporting to Fort Union, September 6, 1886. He is buried at Fort Leavenworth. Hunt's wife was a daughter of Gen. Silas Casey. Warner, *Generals in Blue*, 243; Heitman, *Register*, 1:556.

60. James F. Casey, the collector of customs in New Orleans, was appointed by Grant and later charged with stealing funds. Casey was Grant's brother-in-law. See Ron Chernow, *Grant*, 757.

61. Brig. Gen. John Thomas Croxton was one of the brigade commanders during Wilson's raid into Alabama and Georgia. A native of Kentucky, he received

exceptional educational experience, graduating from Yale in 1857, studying law at Georgetown in Kentucky, and later practicing in Paris, Kentucky. During the war he fought at Perryville, Tullahoma, and was severely wounded at Chickamauga. He fought at Atlanta and at Nashville, where he faced Nathan Forrest and John B. Hood. After a brief stint as commander of the military district of Southwest Georgia, he resigned his commission December 1866 and returned to law practice. He remained extremely active after the war establishing the Louisville *Commercial* and served as U.S. minister to Bolivia, where he died April 16, 1874. Warner, *Generals in Blue*, 104; Heitman, *Register*, 1:342.

62. Unidentified.
63. Possibly in Nelly's hand.
64. Unidentified.

Chapter 3

1. There was a two- to three-week delay in the post. On December 18, Emily complained to her mother "I have not heard from Emory since he reached Memphis. My last letters were from New Orleans; indeed, I have not heard a word for two weeks. A steamer from New Orleans has been due for the last five days, but no one has heard of it. It is a great discomfort to hear from my husband so seldom when I have nothing to do but think of him in the interval." Emily to her mother, December 18, 1868.

2. Unidentified.

3. The Overton Hotel, officially opened after the war in 1866, was demolished in 1925. "Historic Memphis Hotels," http://historic-memphis.com/memphis-historic/hotels/hotels2.html.

4. John William Leftwich, a Democrat but Unionist, served one term in the Thirty-Ninth Congress, 1866–67. He was a delegate to the Democratic National Convention in New York in 1868 and mayor of Memphis 1869–70. He disputed the election of William J. Smith to the Forty-First Congress, but he died en route to Washington to make his case. He was not, as Upton indicated, "congressman elect." *Biographical Directory of the American Congress*, 1452.

5. Upton's attempts are out of the ordinary particularly because of Emily's absence and condition. As a result, the Uptons do not represent a typical "frontier" army family as described in McInnis, *Wives*, chap. 6, "Imperial Gender Crossings: Officers' and Wives' Dress and Homemaking on the Edges of Empire," 119–47.

6. Samuel Nicoll Benjamin (1839–1886) from New York, was an Upton classmate. According to author Ralph Kirshner, Benjamin joined the artillery right out of West Point, and was "brilliant in the defense of Knoxville, was wounded at Spotsylvania, and won the Medal of Honor." He married Julia Kean Fish, the daughter

of Grant's secretary of state, Hamilton Fish (1808–1893). In later life, he served in the army's Department of the East, where he died in 1886. Kirshner, *Class of 1861*, 155.

7. The postwar army and navy were beleaguered by no-pay, slow-pay issues that went well into the 1870s, 80s, and 90s. They were constantly embroiled with the larger issue, which Upton addressed to no avail—army reorganization. See for example, "The Pay of the Army," *Army Navy Journal*, October 13, 1877, p. 152.

8. When Upton is settled, he will be five blocks from the Overton, where he takes his meals. He will walk five blocks each way; 10 blocks/meal × 3 meals/day = 30 blocks.

9. Brig. Gen. Andrew J. Alexander Upton's brother-in-law. See Myres, "Colonel's Lady," 26–38.

10. Upton's sister.

11. Unidentified.

12. Elizabeth Blair Lee (1818–1906) was the daughter of Francis Preston Blair. Her brother Francis P. Blair Jr. ran for vice president on the Democratic ticket led by Horatio Seymour of New York in 1868. Francis Jr. was a Martin friend who often visited Willowbrook and who was probably the reason Upton knew Betty Blair. See also Fitzpatrick, *Upton*. Mrs. Martin, writing to Emily: "I must tell you a great secret, Betty Blair expects to visit Key West this winter. Do not speak of this to anyone but Nelly." Mrs. Martin to Emily, November 29, 1868.

13. Paducah, Kentucky, where his horse Max was stabled.

14. According to Young's *Standard History of Memphis*, "Calvary Church has been called the Mother Church of the Episcopal faith in Memphis, the Parish having been organized in 1832, and the church existed for a number of years as the only one of this denomination in the city. The first church building stood on Second Street between Adams and Washington. In 1841 the present edifice on the corner of Adams and Second Street was erected and was much enlarged and improved in 1880, and now contains a seating capacity of 750. The early history of the church is rather obscure, but Rev. Thos. Wright seems to have been the first rector of the parish, followed by Rev. George Wells." Young, *Standard History of Memphis*, 508. Still in operation, it is the oldest public building in Memphis and on the National Register of Historic Places.

15. George White, DD, Calvary Church, Memphis, ordained 1843. *Journal of Proceedings of the 47th Annual Convention of the Protestant Episcopal Church*, 5.

16. Bishop Charles Todd Quintard, DD, LLD, Bishop of the Protestant Episcopal Diocese of Tennessee. Obituary, *New York Times*, February 16, 1898.

17. Unidentified.

18. Handkerchiefs in Turkey had special meaning. According to one author: "Throughout history, there have been very few items used for multiple purposes. Among them, handkerchiefs have an interesting story both as decoration and

clothing as well a means of communication between lovers." Ekinci, "Handkerchiefs," https://www.dailysabah.com/feature/2016/02/19/handkerchiefs-the-secret-language-of-love.

19. Probably De Witt Clinton Poole, of Wisconsin. Poole joined the army on May 17, 1861 as first lieutenant of the 1st Wisconsin Infantry. On October 31, 1861, he became lieutenant colonel of the 12th Wisconsin. He resigned his volunteer commission and was commissioned captain of the 25th Infantry, regular army, January 1867. He was unassigned April 26, 1869, and then assigned to the 22nd Infantry, October 1870. He retired September 28, 1892. Heitman, *Register*, 1:797.

20. The house was on a corner, and the other street is unnamed.

21. Bvt. Lt. Col. John Christopher, from Pennsylvania enlisted May 1861 as first lieutenant in the 16th Infantry; promoted to captain February 1862; transferred to the 25th Infantry September 1866; further transferred to the 18th Infantry April 1869. He was awarded brevet major in September 1863 for his service at Chickamauga, and brevet lieutenant colonel in March 1865 for his service during the war. Heitman, *Register*, 1:300.

22. Probably Emily's brother George Bliss Martin, 1852–1928.

23. Dr. and Mrs. William Kirkwood were friends of the Martin family. Dr. Kirkwood wrote Upton of Emily's last days in Nassau. See Michie, *Upton*, 236–37, for a copy of Kirkwood's letter June 26, 1870, to Emory. For thirty years he owned a home known as "Cascadia" in Nassau. He is mentioned in a promotional brochure (p. 25) titled "General Description of the City of Nassau . . . and Other Statistics of Interest to Invalids and Travelers," 1870. The piece touted a place where "the invalid (after a sea voyage of only four days) may enjoy the finest and most equable climate in the world." (p. 11). He provided Emily with a place to rest and recuperate. As she wrote to her sister Mary (called Molly), "Dr. and Mrs. Kirkwood are as good and kind to us as they can be, and will not hear of our going to a hotel." Emily to Molly, Feb. 25, 1869, Letterbook.

24. Weavings.

25. Wife of Bvt. Lt. Col. John Christopher.

26. Maj. Gen. James Harrison Wilson, Upton's commander January–May 1865 during Wilson's raid into Alabama and Georgia, March–April 1865.

27. New York silversmiths (1851–76).

28. Enos Throop Martin, Emily's eldest brother, was affectionately known as "Throop" (pronounced "Troop"). He was the fifth of eleven children and eldest son of Enos Thompson Throop and Cornelia Williams Martin. He served a stint in the navy but earned a degree in business from Union College in 1866. He eventually married Helen Tremain. At age forty, he, like Emily, succumbed to tuberculosis.

29. Upton's pet.

30. Unidentified.

31. Unidentified.

32. Fort Jefferson is on Garden Key. Construction on the fort began in 1846, and it was decommissioned during World War I. Immediately after the Civil War, it contained the infamous Dr. Samuel Mudd (1866–67) and three of the Lincoln conspirators: Edmund Spangler, Michael O'Laughlen, and Samuel Arnold. An epidemic of yellow fever killed O'Laughlen, but Mudd's medical expertise won his freedom when he Spangler and Arnold were pardoned by President Johnson.

33. This is the wife of Capt. Thomson Price McElrath, who originally joined the army from New York City in the 9th New York Infantry, May–June 1861. He was promoted to second lieutenant May 1861 in the 5th Artillery, and was promoted to first lieutenant March 1862. Served as regimental quartermaster from December 1862 to September 1867 when he was made a captain. He received a brevet captain's rank for his valor at Gaines Mill, and achieved major in March 1865 for meritorious service. He resigned his commission January 5, 1870. Heitman, *Register*, 1:664.

34. Probably Capt. Charles A. M. Estes. A Wisconsin native, he rose through the ranks during the Civil War from private to captain of the 25th Infantry in September 1866 and then transferred to the 18th Infantry in April 1869. He was brevetted a captain in September 1864 for gallant and meritorious service during the Atlanta Campaign and the Battle of Jonesboro. He was honorably discharged January 1, 1871, and died March 19, 1879. Heitman, *Register*, 1:408.

35. Possibly the widow of Col. J. W. A. Pettit, known as the father of free schools in the city of Memphis. Keating, *History of the City of Memphis*, 273.

36. From Shakespeare, Hamlet, act 1, scene 3, Polonius "Give every man thy ear but few thy voice. Take each man's censure but reserve thy judgment."

37. Brother-in-law Andrew Alexander.

38. Unidentified.

39. After a brief stay at Fort Jefferson on the Tortugas, Emily returned to Key West. She told her mother that she felt she had gotten stronger while there, and that she walked "around the breakwaters: a mile each day besides other shorter walks." Emily to her mother, December 18, 1868.

40. English equivalent of an American bathrobe, a lounging coat.

41. The daughter of Henry H. Martin, president of the Albany Savings Bank. She married Julien Tappan Davies on April 22, 1869. *Banker's Magazine and Statistical Register*, 787–800; *New England Historical and Genealogical Register, 1921*, lxvi–lxvii.

42. This is possibly James Hammond Baldwin, who originally joined the 35th Massachusetts Infantry as a first lieutenant in August 1862 and later transferred to the 1st Battalion Massachusetts Artillery in January 1863, where he rose to rank of captain. He resigned his volunteer commission October 1865 and joined the regular army as a second lieutenant, 16th U.S. Infantry in March 1866; transferred to the 25th Infantry in September 1866; became first lieutenant in July 1867; transferred to 18th Infantry in April 1869; and became regimental quartermaster

in May and June 1869. Baldwin retired November 30, 1892, and died November 11, 1894. Heitman, *Register*, 1:186.

43. Capt. and Asst. Surgeon William Scott Tremain enlisted in the army from Prince Edward Island, New York, as assistant surgeon of the 24th Massachusetts Infantry in August 1863. He was honorably discharged from volunteer service in April 1864, joining the 31st U.S. Regular Infantry as surgeon on May 2, until he resigned September 1, 1864 to rejoin the U.S. Volunteers until he mustered out June 1866. He was made a major surgeon on June 30, 1882, and retired on February 27, 1891. He died January 9, 1898. Heitman, *Register*, 1:970.

44. Wife of Capt. Charles A. M. Estes.

45. Orville Elias Babcock was an Upton classmate. Of all the famous and notorious graduates of May 1861 from the military academy (there were two graduations that year, May and June), none proved more controversial than Vermont native Orville Babcock. He served with distinction in the Corps of Engineers during the war and was brevetted brigadier general in the regular army at war's end. According to Ralph Kirshner, when Grant became president in 1869, he appointed Babcock his "influential private secretary" and quickly became the "center of controversy." During the Grant administration and its numerous scandals, Babcock became embroiled in the Whiskey Ring and was indicted December 1875. Grant "gave a deposition supporting Babcock, who was acquitted on February 28, 1876. After leaving the White House, Babcock became an inspector of lighthouses, drowning in Mosquito Inlet, Florida, on June 2, 1884." Kirshner, *Class of 1861*, 153–54; Warner, *Generals in Blue*, 581; Heitman, *Register*, 1:178. For a full narrative of the Whiskey Ring and Babcock's and Grant's role in it, see also McFeely, *Grant: A Biography*, 407–16; and Chernow's more recent and fuller accounting in *Grant*, 796–807.

46. Horace Porter graduated from the military academy in 1860. A native of Huntingdon, Pennsylvania, Porter came from a long line of American patriots, politicians, and military people dating back to the Revolutionary War. He graduated as a second lieutenant from the Academy in Ordnance. When the war ended, he had risen to the grade of lieutenant colonel. He participated in many of the important battles of the western theater, receiving the medal of honor for his "gallantry at Chickamauga, September 20, 1863 in rallying enough fugitives to hold the ground at a critical moment when the lines were broken under heavy fire long enough to facilitate the escape of numerous wagon trains and batteries." He resigned from the army December 31, 1873. Heitman, *Register*, 1:799. He served as aide-de-camp to Grant from 1866 to 1869, when he became Grant's personal secretary in the White House (1869–72). He served simultaneously as Sherman's aide-de-camp. He became embroiled in the Jay Gould–Black Friday gold scandal and then the Whiskey Ring investigation in 1876. He was never charged. See Chernow, *Grant*, 672–80 and 796–809. In later life he became CEO of the Pullman Palace

Car Company and later, president of the West Shore Railroad, was ambassador to France 1897–1905, and was instrumental in the construction of Grant's tomb. He died in New York on May 29, 1921. Obituary, General Porter, *New York Times*, June 3, 1921.

47. George Morton Randall, an Ohio native, rose in the ranks from private to brigadier general during the Civil War. He participated in nearly every major battle of the eastern theater from Antietam to Petersburg in 1865. He was appointed captain of the 4th Infantry, September 23, 1865. He also served with the 23rd, 4th, 8th, and 17th Infantry from 1865 to 1898. In 1873 and 1874, he saw extensive action in the West fighting Indians. Heitman, *Register*, 1:814. Upton's mother's maiden name was Randall.

48. The four "Grand" Armies of the Union—the Armies of the Tennessee, of the Cumberland, of the Ohio, and of Georgia held a reunion in Chicago on December 15 and 16, 1868. Generals Grant, Sherman, Thomas, Schofield, Slocum, and Howard were all expected to attend. The idea of a "grand" reunion of the western armies originated with Sherman. "The Army Reunion in Chicago," *New York Times*, December 15, 1868. The "grand" banquet was held at the Chicago Board of Trade. See *Army Reunion . . . December 15 and 16, 1868*.

49. Gen. Cyrus Ballou Comstock graduated from the academy in the class of 1855. Born February 3, 1831, in Wrentham, Massachusetts, he was accepted to West Point in 1851. Upon graduation, Comstock joined the Army Corps of Engineers. When war broke out, he worked on the fortifications surrounding the capital until he joined the Army of the Potomac. He served as chief engineer of the Army of the Tennessee and its successful siege of Vicksburg. Transferring back east, Grant appointed him to his staff as aide-de-camp. He was breveted major general in the volunteers and brevet brigadier general in the regular army at war's end. He was appointed to the military commission trying the Lincoln conspirators but was relieved from his post when he expressed doubt about the transparency of the proceedings. His postwar career was marked by developing innovations in physics as a member of the National Academy of Sciences. See C. B. Comstock Papers, 1847–1908, Library of Congress; Abbot, *Biographical Memoir of Cyrus Ballou Comstock*. Also, Heitman, *Register*, 1:319.

According to Sandra Myres, evidently Comstock was a close family friend. "Eveline Alexander's list of 'Letters sent and Received' frequently includes his name." Alexander, *Cavalry Wife*, 137n3.

50. Comstock died May 29, 1910, and was buried "by the side of his wife Elizabeth, daughter of Montgomery Blair. Their marriage had taken place in 1869 and her death and that of their infant occurred in 1872." Abbot, *Comstock*, 178. Upton refers to her as "Betty Blair."

51. Upton's family pet dog.

52. Upton's "servant."

53. Emily's eldest sister Mary Williams Martin (1838–1884), also called "Molly," was not cured. She died in a tuberculosis sanatorium in Glen Cove, Long Island, at age forty-five.

54. Brig. Gen. Martin Thomas McMahon. It was McMahon who brought the orders to Upton to charge the Salient at Spotsylvania, May 10, 1864. McMahon presented Upton with twelve handpicked regiments, selected the time and the target, and Upton did the rest. Supposedly Grant promoted Upton to brigadier general on the spot, an assertion not supported by documentation. McMahon's tale of Upton's battlefield promotion reached the public through Isaac O. Best's *Upton's Regulars: History of the 121st New York State Infantry*, published in 1921, sixty years after the war began. McMahon was certain that Upton received his star the following morning, May 11, and in one particular statement declared that Upton "cut off his eagles and we got some thread and had the stars sewed on his shoulder, and he rode directly to his command to show them his preferment." Dewitt Clinton Beckwith, "Three Years with the Colors of a Fighting Regiment in the Army of the Potomac, By a Private Soldier," *Mohawk Democrat*, January 31, 1894; and Best, *121st New York State Infantry*, 139. It must have been true, McMahon and Beckwith argued, after all, "General Grant, in his memoirs, mentions its commander (Upton) and it (the 121st New York Volunteers), an honor great because no other regiment was mentioned." Beckwith, "Three Years with the Colors," June 27, 1894. After the war, McMahon became a member of the New York Assembly in 1891 and then the state senate from 1892 to 1895. In 1896, he was elected judge of the Court of General Sessions, which he held until his death in 1906. "General Martin T. M'Mahon Dies of Pneumonia," *New York Times*, April 22 and 25, 1906. Heitman, *Register*, 1:676. See also Cilella, *Upton's Regulars*, 294–304.

55. Emory's brother.

56. Henry's wife.

57. Emily had Christmas dinner on the *Gettysburg*, which was docked at Havana. Emory had befriended the steamer's commander, Admiral Hoff, "a charming old gentleman," as Emily relayed to Evy. Hoff and the *Gettysburg* safely returned Emily to Key West. Emily to sister Evy, January 3, 1869.

58. Probably De Lancey Floyd-Jones, identified in the introduction.

59. An antimacassar, a small cloth placed on the backs or arms of chairs for protection from dirt.

60. There are two *Commentaries.Commentarii de Bello Gallico* deals with the Gallic Wars, and *Commentarii de Bello Civili* chronicled the recent Roman Civil War.

61. In the midst of Reconstruction, radical Republicans gained control of the Arkansas government. It raised a militia made up of black soldiers with white officers, as had been the practice during the war. Whites turned to the Ku Klux Klan. The two groups clashed well into the late 1870s and only stopped when

Reconstruction ended officially in 1876. Sesser, "Militia Wars of 1868–1869," https://encyclopediaofarkansas.net/entries/militia-wars-of-1868-1869-7904/.

62. Possibly American sculptor Franklin Simmons (1839–1913) of Maine. Before moving to Rome in 1868, he completed several commissions for American Civil War personalities and events, including an equestrian monument of Ulysses S. Grant and Gen. John Logan of Illinois. "Franklin Simmons Dead. American Sculptor Designed Grant and Logan Monuments," *New York Times*, December 9, 1913.

63. This is a strange passage, and it appears that Emily has omitted connecting ideas.

64. The steamer *Gettysburg* spent the summer of 1868 assisting in the laying of a telegraph cable from Havana to Key West. From August to early October she cruised between Haiti and Key West. During the war it served as a blockade enforcer.

65. Emily's experience was exciting and highly unusual. Ada Vogdes, wife of Lt. Anthony Wayne Vogdes, a Civil War veteran, was stationed at Fort Fetterman in Colorado near the Platte River. She described Christmas as a "glorious day" and far superior to any "in the south of France," a far cry from Emily's experience. It had snowed the day before and the air was crystal clear. The sutler "gave us a delightful party, the first I believe ever given here and we had a nice time even though there were only two ladies present," Ada wrote. Their celebratory supper consisted of "jellies, cakes of all kinds, chicken salad, roasted rabbit, tongue, sardines, raisins, almonds, candy, and the most delicious chicken I ever ate" followed by "cream, coffee and wines." She finished stating the "rooms were beautifully decorated with flags and evergreens and looking glasses." Vogdes, "Journal," December 25, 1869, pp. 9–10.

66. Emily and Nelly were witnessing the opening salvos of the Ten Years' War, Cuba's rebellion for its independence against Spain. After the Spanish-American war, Cuba finally became a free country in 1902.

67. Unidentified.

68. Probably an earlier suitor of Emily's.

69. Emily wrote her mother that Emory's house was most uncomfortable, but that would change with the "new quarters he will be living in when I join him. The new quarters will be very comfortable; four rooms all on the same floor, in addition there is a bathroom, dining room, kitchen and servants rooms, this you see will be quite a large house and as Emory's in command, will entail upon me, considerable entertaining." Emily to her mother, January 27, 1869.

Chapter 4

1. Emily's reaction was similar. She told her sister "Do you wonder I feel ready to fly when I think of him alone and know how much I could do for his comfort were I with him." Emily to Evy, January 3, 1869.

2. Upton misdated it "1868." This letter contains several names Upton related to Emily alerting her to the "society" she would join when the two were finally reunited. The issue or topic of "class" appears in many officers' wives' narratives. Terms such as "woman" and "lady" had different meanings. On the post–Civil War frontier, a lady was an officer's wife; a woman was a partner of a soldier. Complicating the social structure, soldiers who were promoted to officer carried with them the burden of their wife's original lower-class status. "A female from the lower classes who married an officer received only partial acceptance as a 'half-way' lady." McInnis, *Wives*, 69. Eveline Alexander wrote in her diary: "The 'womenkind' in this regiment are rather a queer set. Mrs. C. was a company washerwoman before her husband was promoted from the ranks. Mrs. K. and her daughter are very common. Mrs. H. and 'Patrita' are Mexicans." Then there were two child brides—one nineteen and "not highly educated," and a "child of fourteen that Lieutenant Carroll married . . . she seems an innocent little girl, ignorant alike of good or of evil." Alexander, *Cavalry Wife*, 36.

3. David Parkinson enlisted in the regular army from Michigan and mustered in as a private with the 2nd Battalion, 16th Infantry in April 1862. He was promoted to captain of the 25th Infantry in September 1866. He was honorably discharged in August 1870 at his own request. Heitman, *Register*, 1:771.

4. George J. Madden joined the regular army from Connecticut as an enlisted man and rose through the ranks during the Civil War. He was promoted to second and then first lieutenant in January 1866 and was assigned to the 25th Infantry. He transferred to the 18th Infantry in April 1869 and was dropped from the rolls March 1873. Heitman, *Register*, 1:683.

5. Upton may have been quoting English writer William Cowper, who wrote in 1790 of riding along in a coach to visit family and friends: "When I saw this moment a poor old woman coming up the lane opposite my window I could not help sighing, and saying to myself—'Poor but happy old woman! Thou art exempted by the situation in life from riding in chaises, and making thyself fine in a morning, happier therefore in my account than I who am under the cruel necessity of doing both.'" Cowper to his cousin Lady Hesketh, June 17, 1790. Cowper, *Works of William Cowper*, 133.

6. William Henry Bainbridge was born in Middlesex, Yates County, New York, on December 11, 1840, married at Auburn, New York in February 1868 to Emma Easterly of Auburn, who died in Chicago in February 1887. "Frank Mortimer McMath," http://www.ebooksread.com/authors-eng/frank-mortimer-mcmath /memorials-of-the-mcmath-family-including-a-genealogical-account-of-the -descenda-amc/page-10-memorials-of-the-mcmath-family-including-a -genealogical-account-of-the-descenda-amc.shtml. Auburn was Emily's hometown.

7. Recherché means sought out with care, very rare, exotic, of studied refinement, precious, or affected. Emily expressed surprise at Emory's New Year's party:

"Emory had quite a party on New Year's night—fifteen guests. I do not know how he entertained them." Emily to her mother, January 24, 1869.

8. William Conway, from New York City, joined the 74th New York Volunteers at the outbreak of the war, achieving the rank of captain when he was mustered out June 19, 1864. He rejoined the regular army as a second lieutenant in March 1866, eventually serving with the 25th and 22nd Infantry. He became a captain in July 1879 and was made brevet captain in February 1890 for gallant service in action against the Indians at Spring Creek, Montana, in October 1876. He retired in June 1894. Heitman, *Register*, 1:323.

9. William H. Hugo, from New York and Michigan, was appointed captain of the 70th New York Volunteers in June 1861, and mustered out of the volunteers to reenlist in the regular army as a second lieutenant with the 16th Infantry in May 1866. He transferred to the 25th in September 1866 and was promoted to first lieutenant in November 1868. On January 1, 1869, he was assigned to the 9th Cavalry. He was dismissed in November 1881. Heitman, *Register*, 1:553.

10. These were perhaps the parents of "Miss Morris," from New York, mentioned in a February 1869 social column in the *Memphis Appeal*. According to the paper, Miss Morris distinguished herself at the opening of the Peabody Hotel that year. It described her as "a sparkling gem of love and beauty, dressed in one of those bewitching styles, which leave the beholder in blissful uncertainty." *Memphis Appeal*, February 1869.

11. Unidentified.

12. Unidentified.

13. David Parkinson enlisted with the 16th Infantry (USA) in April 1862, just after Shiloh; he served with the 16th throughout the war. After Shiloh, the 16th was active at Murfreesboro, Chattanooga, and in the Atlanta Campaign. After the war, the 2nd Battalion of the 16th became the 25th Infantry (1862–1869). Parkinson was regimental quartermaster and then unassigned until he was discharged in August 1870. Heitman, *Register*, 1:771. See 283n3, this volume.

14. This is possibly William F. Houston from Pennsylvania, who served throughout the war in all three branches of service—artillery, infantry and cavalry. His last assignment was as a second lieutenant, 23rd Infantry, January 1867. Then he was promoted to first lieutenant in January 1869 but cashiered August 12 of that year. Heitman, *Register*, 1:545.

15. George J. Madden served along with Parkinson in the 16th Infantry, but he joined it late in the war. The 16th spent most of the war with the Army of the Ohio and then with the Army of the Cumberland. Madden transferred to the 25th and then the 18th after the war. Army reorganization after the war makes it difficult to track unit lineage accurately. The army expanded briefly in 1866 and then contracted in 1869. Heitman, *Register*, 1:683. See 283n4, this volume.

16. This is possibly William J. Kyle, Ohio. He joined the 25th Ohio in June 1861 and remained with the regiment until January 1865. He was commissioned in

January 1865, mustered out of the volunteer force June 1866, and transferred to the 25th Infantry in September 1866 and later to the 11th Infantry in January 1871. He was dropped from the rolls in February 1877. Heitman, *Register*, 1:610.

17. Gen. Gordon Granger, an 1845 graduate of the military academy, was appointed colonel of the 25th Infantry in July 1866. He served with distinction in the Mexican and Civil Wars. He was cited for gallant and meritorious service at Chapultepec in September 1847 and at Wilson's Creek in August 1861 and fought at Chickamauga, Chattanooga, and Mobile Bay. After a leave of absence from April to September 1867, he assumed command of the District of Memphis in September. He took leave again in February 1868 through October 1868, resuming command of the District of Memphis from October 1868 to March 1869. He died January 10, 1876. Cullum, *Biographical Register*, 239. Heitman, *Register*, 1:469.

18. New York banking firm established in 1852. J. P. Morgan apprenticed at the firm until he left to establish his own mega-financial business.

19. This is James H. Wilson, Upton's cavalry commander during the last four months of the Civil War. Upton is referring to Wilson's talk at the Grand Reunion of Western Armies in Chicago, December 15–16. See *Army Reunion . . . December 15 and 16, 1868*, 143–53. Upton is mentioned several times in glowing terms that are later evident in Wilson's introduction to Michie's biography. See Michie, *Upton*, ix–xxviii.

20. Emily was not keen to move to Nassau, but eventually became convinced that the climate of Key West was not conducive to her recovery. "I shall make rapid improvement," she told her mother. She had also grown tired of the social scene in Key West and looked forward to a change. Emily to her mother, January 17, 1869.

21. Thomson Price McElrath was a second lieutenant in the 5th Artillery in 1861—the same as Upton's first assignment. He was awarded a brevet captaincy June 27, 1862, for gallant and meritorious service at Gaines Mill, Virginia, and major in March 1865 also for meritorious service. He resigned his commission January 1870. Heitman, *Register*, 1:664.

22. For the story of Evy Alexander (Emily's sister) and her life out west as the wife of an army officer, see Myres, "Colonel's Lady," 26–38.

23. According to Emily, "Emory saw Gen. Comstock in Washington, he says 'Comstock told me the staff corps might be increased in which case he will do all he can for Alexander's transfer. He will soon set the ball in motion to that end.' I do hope he will be successful and Andrew may be ordered northeast in the spring." Emily to her mother, January 9, 1870.

24. Upton misdated this "1868."

25. Established in 1832. Casseday, *History of Louisville*, 186.

26. It is unclear which theater Upton attended or the name of the play. He may have attended Weisinger Hall, which was first located "over a meat market (1867)."

Casto, *Historic Theaters of Kentucky*, 51. Before the Amphitheater Auditorium was built in 1889, "the larger dramatic and operatic touring companies tended to bypass Louisville, as the city's theaters could not hold audiences sizeable enough to underwrite the costs of the productions." Gatton, "'Only for Great Attractions,'" 27–38. Quote from 27. Louisville's earliest theater, the City Theater, came on line "in 1808 before the first church had been built." Wallace, "Footlights and Curtain Calls," https://www.filsonhistorical.org/archive/news_v6n4_theater.html.

27. President Thomas Jefferson established the United States Coast Survey in 1807, which by 1868 had, through deep-sea exploration, dredging, and deep-sea research, produced usable information and data to shippers and scientists about the makeup of the country's shores and shoreline. The U.S. Coast Survey was the predecessor of the National Oceanic and Atmospheric Administration, NOAA.

28. This was Gen. Thomas Swords, an 1829 graduate of West Point. A New Yorker, Swords had a long career in the infantry and the dragoons during the 1830s. Promoted to captain in the quartermaster corps in 1838, he rose through the ranks to colonel assistant quartermaster general in 1861. He served all four years in the quartermaster corps. At war's end he served as chief quartermaster of the Department of the Cumberland in Louisville, March 1867 to April 1869. He officially retired in February 1869 and died in March 1886. Cullum, *Biographical Register*, 563; and Heitman, *Register*, 1:941.

29. This was Samuel Wylie Crawford. An assistant surgeon from Pennsylvania, Crawford had extensive service with the army from his enlistment in March 1851. He rose from major in the 13th Infantry in May 1861 to brigadier general in April 1862. He mustered out of the volunteers a year after war's end, in June 1866. During the war he participated in the most important battles of the eastern theater including Gettysburg, Grant's Overland (Wilderness) Campaign, Petersburg, and Five Forks. He received several promotions and brevets for gallant and meritorious service at Gettysburg, Five Forks, and the Wilderness Campaign. He retired in February 1873 and died November 3, 1892. Heitman, *Register*, 1:337.

30. See 290n16, this volume, for identification of Dr. Storrow.

31. Capt. John M. Dukehart, a Confederate Navy veteran piloted the *Cuba*, an 1,100-ton screw steamer between Nassau, Havana, and New Orleans for the Baltimore and Havana Steamship Company. Letter of Varina Davis, October 15, 1869, in Davis, *Papers of Jefferson Davis*, 390.

32. Published in Upton, *Correspondence*, 1:259. Emily and Nelly visited Havana for what was to be a four-day stint that turned out to be closer to a week. Bad weather prevented them from leaving the safe harbor of Havana. Emily found the city "one of the strangest places in the world and so thoroughly foreign" that it could have been in Africa. She was there "at a very unsettling time." They were detained by city authorities "as the insurrectionists were fighting within five miles" and she "could see the pickets in the surrounding hills." Spanish soldiers anticipated a

Christmas rebel attack that did not materialize. Emily to her father, December 28, 1868; Letterbook; and Emily to Sister Evy, January 3, 1869. Neither Emory or Emily wrote about or realized that this was the beginning of the so-called Ten Years' War, Cuba's attempt to throw off Spanish rule. See Gott, "War of Independence and Occupation, 1868–1902," chapter 3 in *Cuba: A New History.*

33. This was Bvt. Col. Peter Tyler Swaine, an 1852 graduate of West Point. From New York City, Swaine served five years prior to the war as a regimental quartermaster. When war broke out, he joined the 15th Infantry in May 1861. He transferred to the volunteers, to the 99th Ohio, as colonel in September 1862, mustering out December 1864 to rejoin the regular army as major of the 16th Infantry and then the 25th Infantry in September 1866. He rose to colonel of the 22nd Infantry in April 1884. He received brevets for meritorious service at the Battles of Shiloh and Murfreesboro. Swaine retired in January 1895. Heitman, *Register,* 1:938.

34. The Louisville *Courier-Journal* reported on September 4, 1868, "A military court martial is now in session at the District Headquarters in this city," and "Col. Hunter Brook(e), of Cincinnati, is in the city, attending an important military trial now in progress." The Department of the Cumberland, General Orders, Courts Martial Cases, 1866–1869 (LC), indicates that between November 1868 and April 1869, only one officer, Bvt. Col. Joseph B. Collins (major, 2nd Infantry) was tried and acquitted by court-martial "for conduct unbecoming an officer and a Gentleman" and "false claims" (General Order No. 7, January 7, 1869, Louisville.) Presiding were Bvt. Maj. Gen. S. W. Crawford and Bvt. Maj. Jacob Kline, judge advocate (LC). The trial was Collins's third in eleven months. In April 1868, he was charged with several counts of drunken conduct and acquitted. That September he was charged and acquitted for selling government property for personal gain. The court-martial to which Upton is referring was January and February 1869. See National Archives Record Group 153 (Army Courts Martial), 003074, 003514, and PP107 respectively.

35. Also in Upton, *Correspondence.* 1:260–61.

36. Although Upton identified himself as an abolitionist, it is unclear what his racial views were. According to editor Sandra Myres, Andrew Alexander's family "emancipated [their] slaves before the Civil War." The Martins "would appear to have been Unionist but not abolitionist." Myres argues that although Harriet Tubman lived in Auburn, "near Willowbrook, neither Evy nor any other family member mentions her in their published works." Alexander, *Cavalry Wife,* 145n16.

37. The Hotel Barberi, St. Marcs, and the Doges Palace in Venice are places Emily and Emory visited on their honeymoon.

38. To sister Maria, Translation by James and Sarah Lander and Lee Rast, Holland Land Office Museum (hereafter HLOM). First published in Upton, *Correspondence,* 1:261–62.

39. Upton wrote three letters in French to remain proficient in the language. Michie published only a small portion of the third letter, dated March 28, 1869. All three shed a warm light on Upton's brief marriage. Michie, *Upton*, 233–34.

40. The Royal Victoria Hotel.

41. Dr. Kirkwood wrote Upton of Emily's last days in Nassau. See Michie, *Upton*, 236–37, for a copy of Kirkwood's letter June 26, 1870, to Emory. For thirty years he owned a home known as "Cascadia" in Nassau. He is mentioned in a promotional brochure (p. 25) titled "General Description of the City of Nassau . . . and Other Statistics of Interest to Invalids and Travelers." 1870. The piece touted a place where "the invalid (after a sea voyage of only four days) may enjoy the finest and most equable climate in the world." (p. 11).

42. The "owners" of the Royal Victoria were former American officers during the war "Messers. Cleveland & Newell." (p. 17). Kirkwood was also a member of the Bahamian legislative council from 1844 until his death in 1889.

43. Unidentified.

44. This was perhaps the paddle-steamer *Eagle* built by Robert Steele and Company of Greenock, Scotland and refitted with a steam engine by the firm of Caird and Company, Glasgow.

45. This was probably Jacob Beekman Rawles, noted above.

46. Julia was the wife of Samuel Nicoll Benjamin. "K" refers to her middle name, Kean, and "F" to her maiden name, Fish.

47. Ball and Black was a New York City competitor of Tiffany's that manufactured and sold jewelry, clocks, silverware, furniture, and chandeliers. They occupied a five-story building on the corner of Broadway and Prince Streets which opened July 3, 1860. The owners topped the new facility with a "colossal gold eagle with spread wings, so long the emblem and trademark of this house." *New York Times*, July 2, 1860. "Make raise" is nineteenth-century slang for securing money.

48. This was Upton's publisher for his Army *Tactics* manual.

49. This was Maj. Gen. Alfred Thomas Archimedes Torbert, an 1855 graduate of West Point. A native of Delaware, Torbert served honorably as an officer during the Civil War in several regular army and volunteer regiments until he was mustered out of volunteer service January 1866. He was brevetted for gallant service at Gettysburg, Haw's Shop (Virginia), Winchester, and Cedar Creek. He resigned October 1866. He drowned at sea August 29, 1880. Heitman, *Register*, 1:965.

50. Upton bought the horse from Asst. Surgeon Charles Ravenscroft Greenleaf, who wrote to Upton on April 21, 1869, that he had been ordered west to the Department of the Columbia and that he would like Upton to pay for the horse. "Money will be a scarce commodity with me in taking a wife & family over the Pacific RR on $250 mileage, or I would not mention the matter to you." Greenleaf to Upton, April 21, 1869, Throop Martin Papers; Heitman, *Register*, 1:476.

51. A friend of Mrs. Martin.

52. After the Civil War, Upton floated the notion of starting a West Point–like academy in China. During his eighteen-month world tour, 1875–76, when he visited China, Upton tried to revive the idea. Both governments rejected the idea. See Upton, *Correspondence*, 1:280–81n.

53. Capt. M. R. Greene commanded the steamer *Eagle*. *New York Times*, March 9, 1870.

54. Postmaster.

55. Conflicts, clashes, disagreements.

56. Lt. William H. Hugo, from New York and Michigan, was appointed captain of the 70th New York Volunteers in June 1861 and honorably mustered out of volunteer service in July 1864 to accept a commission as second lieutenant in the 16th Infantry in May 1866, and then moved to the 25th Infantry in September of that year. He was assigned to the 9th Cavalry in January 1871 and was dismissed in November 1881. Heitman, *Register*, 1:553.

57. This was Rear Adm. Henry K. Hoff, commander of the Atlantic Fleet, which included the USS *Gettysburg*. *Executive Documents*, Report of the Secretary of the Navy, 31, 35. American steamer *Gettysburg* was built in 1858 and survived different commissionings and decommissionings as an American naval vessel, a Confederate naval vessel, and finally a Caribbean transport calling at Key West, Havana, and other ports. She was finally decommissioned in 1879. Mooney, *Dictionary of American Naval Fighting Ships*.

58. Unknown, but probably under the command of Rear Adm. Hoff.

Chapter 5

1. In 2018 dollars, $7,000 would be nearly $121,000; $200 would be $3,455; and Upton's yearly pay at $2,450 would be equivalent to $42,300 today.

2. Meaning—find society outside the home.

3. Unidentified.

4. Unidentified.

5. Col. Richard Irving Dodge. See 271n33, this volume.

6. This was perhaps either St. Brigid Catholic Church or St. Mary's, both built in 1870.

7. Yawning.

8. Emily's response to her mother was telling. "All winter I have found my great desire has been to make and buy things for my house. I have been interested and delighted with the accounts which Emory has sent me of all he was doing to make our home comfortable and pleasant. My riding horse as well as our pretty carriage and horses I have thought of with great pleasure." Emily to her mother, March 5, 1869.

9. Probably the *Army Navy Journal*.

10. This U.S. Army post was established July 4, 1799, and named after John Adams. In 1965, the fort and surrounding land was given to the state of Rhode Island.

11. This was possibly Algernon Godfrey Kingsford, an Anglican priest. Pert, *Red Cactus*, 24–26.

12. Bellagio, Italy, sits on a spit of land that juts into Lake Como. It is located in the Lombardy region near the Swiss border, just north of Milan. Upton may be referring to the Anglican Church of the Ascension across the lake from Bellagio in Cadenabbia di Griante.

13. After some bureaucratic delays and suggestions for improving his first draft, which was approved August 1, 1867, Upton worked through 1869 to gain approval. It was revised once again in July 1873 when it "assimilated" the tactics of all three branches of the army—infantry, artillery, and cavalry. See Upton, *Correspondence*, 1, chap. 7.

14. From the Sermon on the Mount in Matthew 6:34. In other words, each and every day has enough trouble on its own.

15. Arkansas governor Powell Clayton's militia, also known as (Robert) Catterson's militia, operated in Arkansas 1868–69. Both men were former Union officers who used the militia to combat violence stemming from the adoption of the 1868 Arkansas Constitution. Martial law was declared until it was lifted on March 21, 1869. Sesser, "Militia Wars of 1868–1869," https://encyclopediaofarkansas.net/entries/militia-wars-of-1868-1869-7904/.

16. Surgeon Samuel Appleton Storrow was a native of Culpeper County, Virginia, but joined the Union army as a member of the regular army medical staff. He served as an assistant surgeon from August 1861 until June 1876. He attained the rank of brevet captain and major in March 1865 for faithful and meritorious service during the war. He died at age fifty-one, July 12, 1879. Heitman, *Register*, 1:930.

17. This was Francis Asbury Davies, an Upton classmate at West Point. From Pennsylvania, he finished twenty-third in his class. He joined the 2nd U.S. Artillery as a second lieutenant ending the war in the 16th Infantry. He returned to the academy as infantry instructor and later professor of French. He resigned in 1868. He received a brevet major promotion for gallant and meritorious service at the Second Bull Run. After retirement, Davies worked in insurance and for the U.S. Postal Service. Davies died in 1889. Kirshner, *Class of 1861*, 157; Heitman, *Register*, 1:356.

18. Meaning "satiated," "overflowing," "awash," "loaded."

19. This was a nineteenth-century Memphis social club.

20. Biblical reference to two ancient, disparate Israeli cities.

21. Probably the Overton Hotel.

22. This particular section of Upton's letter bears a national context. In 1924, Maj. William A. Ganoe wrote his *History of the United States Army*, wherein he

labeled the period 1865 to 1880 as "The Army's Dark Ages" (chapter 9, 298–354). After demobilizing nearly one million men at war's end, the army shrank first to 50,000, then to 30,000, and finally to prewar numbers of 25,000. The army had been reduced from saviors of the nation to a constabulary force quelling labor riots, fighting Indians in the West, occupying the South during Reconstruction, and guarding travelers and entrepreneurs pushing westward. Some citizens even harbored the opinion that the military was now unnecessary. Joseph G. Dawson, in his *The Late 19th Century U.S. Army, 1865–1898*, introduction, 1–10, summarizes the state of the army in the last third of the century. See also Coffman, *Old Army*, especially chap. 5, "'Promotion's Very Slow': Officers, 1865–1898," 215–86, and chap. 6, "'The Roving Life We Led': Women and Children, 1865–1898," 287–327; and Wooster, *Military and United States Indian Policy*, introduction, 1–12 and chapter 1, *The Military after 1865*, 13–40. Upton drew on many of these personal stories and his own when he wrote his two major works, *The Armies of Asia and Europe* (1878) and his posthumously published *The Military Policy of the United States*. A year before he died, he published "Facts in Favor of Compulsory Retirement," *The United Service: A Monthly Review of Military and Naval Affairs* 2 (March 1880): 269–88; 3 (December 1880): 649–66; and 4 (January 1881): 19–32.

23. On her honeymoon, Emily wrote her mother that for ten days straight, she had no energy and lay in bed. She admitted that her letters home were more "hope" than practical results, "but now thanks to the advice of an English physician [de Cosson], here and the warm pure air of Sorrento, I have improved very much." Emily to her mother, May 3, 1868, Letterbook.

24. The Uptons depended on the mail service via steamers. Emily described the routine to her father: "In regard to the mail steamers leaving Baltimore, there are only two, the *Cuba* and the *Maryland*, one leaving every two weeks arriving here the fifth day, then going to Havana and New Orleans, returning here on the home trip in about two weeks. We have also two vessels a month from New York but they bring no mail. A regular mail for Key West is brought to Havana every Tuesday by the line of steamers from New York. Here it remains till they have a chance to send it over, often the same day, by some stray fishing smack steamer or schooner." Emily to her father, November 19, 1868. According to Webster's Dictionary, a smack is a small fishing vessel "equipped with a well for keeping the caught fish alive." The more common British definition is a "single-masted sailboat used for fishing or coastal commerce."

25. Emily's brother "Troop." See chapter 3, n29.

26. Maj. Gen. George Sykes, an 1842 graduate of the military academy, served brilliantly in the Mexican War and Civil War as an infantry officer. He was promoted to brigadier general of volunteers September 1861 and major general one year later. He was mustered out of the volunteers in January 1866. He was made brevet captain for gallant service at Cerro Gordo in April 1847; colonel for

service at Gaines Mill, Va. in June 1862; and brigadier general in March 1865 for gallant service at the Battle of Gettysburg. Sykes died February 8, 1880. Heitman, *Register*, 1:941–42.

27. Christian sect founded in the eighteenth century, which was and remains extremely progressive, allowing each member to find his or her own path to sanctification.

28. Also known as cotton flannel.

29. In high spirits.

30. Their honeymoon.

31. From the *New York Times*, January 1, 1865:

> The new steamer *Moro Castle*, Capt. ADAMS Commander, built expressly for the Havana trade, arrived here a few days ago, having made the voyage from New York in five days and four hours. The *Moro Castle* is a side-wheel steamer, having an engine of 350-horse power, and an 80-inch cylinder. It was built at Jacob Westervelt's shipyard, and the machinery comes from the Allaire Works. It is 272 feet long, 40 feet wide, and 25 feet deep; tonnage, 2,000 tons, actual measurement, but registered at 1,680 tons. For comfort and elegance, the *Moro Castle* leaves nothing to be desired, and the traveling public of Havana, as well as its commercial classes, are under great obligations to the owners, Messrs. Spofford, Tileston & Co., for this addition to the steamers that ply between New-York and Havana. It is only a few years ago that the above-named firm built the *Eagle* for the Havana trade, which, from the commencement of its career, was the especial favorite of the Habaneros, and we are now indebted to the same company for another new steamer, even more commodious and elegantly fitted up than its predecessor. There is no doubt that it will be as complete a success, and that the *Moro Castle*, like the *Eagle*, will compensate its owners, very shortly, for whatever expenses may have been incurred. We wish its enterprising owners and able commander all the prosperity that they deserve. The *Moro Castle* brought out sixty-six passengers, and would have made the passage in a much shorter time, but from the newness of the machinery, it worked to a disadvantage, which will not be the case in a second voyage. There is accommodation in the state-rooms for two hundred and fifty passengers, both these and the saloons being large and commodious—particularly the latter, which are furnished in the most elegant and luxurious manner.

32. Unidentified.

33. Unidentified.

34. Frank Lane Wolford, lawyer, Union officer, and congressman, was born in September 1817, and died in August 1895. He studied law under Hiram Thomas, was admitted to the bar in Casey County, and practiced law in Liberty, Kentucky.

During the Mexican War, Wolford served under Col. William R. McKee. In 1847 he returned to Kentucky and was elected to the Kentucky House, serving from 1847 until 1849. From 1849 until the outbreak of the Civil War, Wolford earned a reputation as one of the best criminal lawyers in the Green River region.

During the Civil War, Wolford recruited for the 1st Kentucky Cavalry, serving as colonel. He spent most of his time in the 1st Cavalry chasing Gen. John Hunt Morgan of the Confederate cavalry until Morgan's capture in July 1863. In March 1864, Wolford was dishonorably discharged from the army by President Lincoln after publicly criticizing his presidency and was arrested and jailed several times by Gen. Stephen T. Burbridge until Lincoln intervened and ended the matter in 1865.

Wolford returned to the Kentucky House from 1865 to 1867. In 1865 and 1869, he was a Kentucky presidential elector, voting for Gen. George B. McClellan and Horatio Seymour, respectively. In 1867, he was appointed adjutant general by Governor John W. Stevenson (1867–71), serving until 1868. He practiced law in Liberty until 1879. He was elected to the U.S. Congress, where he represented the Eleventh Congressional District, serving two terms (March 4, 1883, to March 3, 1887).

Wolford was married twice: to Nancy Dever on November 2, 1849, and to Elizabeth Bailey on April 6, 1865. Tapp, "Incidents in the Life of Frank Wolford," 82–100; Kleber, *Kentucky Encyclopedia*, 963.

35. Unidentified.

36. It is debatable whether a posting to Arizona would have saved Emily's life. The arid atmosphere would have certainly been beneficial, but given the innumerable hardships of frontier life, the move might have been more detrimental than helpful. See Summerhayes, *Vanished Arizona*.

37. Congress passed the Army Reorganization Act on July 28, 1866, "but failed to provide resources to fund the Army at the levels authorized" by the act. So in 1869, "it further reduced the number of infantry regiments to twenty-five and authorized strength to 45,000." Brown, *Historical Dictionary of the U.S. Army*, 39.

38. This was probably Adelbert Ames, another Upton classmate. Ames, who eventually became a senator from Mississippi, was born in Rockland, Knox County, Maine, on October 31, 1835. He attended the common schools and graduated from the United States Military Academy at West Point in 1861. During the Civil War he served with the Union army from 1861 to 1865 as lieutenant, colonel, and brigadier general; was breveted colonel; and received the Congressional Medal of Honor for gallantry at the Battle of Bull Run. He was captain of the 5th Artillery in the regular army 1864–66. In that latter year he was promoted to lieutenant colonel of the 24th U.S. Infantry, where he served until his resignation in 1870. President Grant appointed him provisional governor of Mississippi on March 15, 1868, and on March 17, 1869, he was elevated to the command of the Fourth Military District (Department of Mississippi). Upon the readmission of the state of Mississippi

to representation, Ames was elected as a Republican to the U.S. Senate, serving from February 23, 1870, until January 10, 1874, when he resigned, having been elected governor in 1873. He also served as chairman of the Committee on Enrolled Bills (Fifty-Third Congress). He was governor of Mississippi from January 4, 1874, until March 29, 1876, when he resigned. At that point he moved to New York City and later to Lowell, Massachusetts. He engaged in the flour business with mills in Minnesota and took part in various manufacturing industries in Lowell. He was appointed brigadier general of volunteers in the war with Spain 1898–99; then discontinued active business pursuits and lived in retirement in Lowell, Massachusetts. He died at his winter home in Ormond, Florida, April 12, 1933; with interment in Hildreth Cemetery, Lowell, Massachusetts. *Biographical Directory of the American Congress*, 778–79. Heitman, *Register*, 1:162.

39. Emily was not only surprised but also dismayed by the news. In addition to this letter, Emory sent Emily an erroneous telegram. She wrote her father "I must confess that I was surprised by Emory's telegraph. 'Leave last of March. Regiment post to California,' for I really thought despite my knowledge of Army life, that we were to remain in Memphis for some time. I will not deny that it was without a heartache that I relinquished all my bright anticipations of the pleasant home in Memphis" that he, her mother, and Emory "had been preparing for [her] return." She acknowledged that it was "about time that I should commence my soldier life and take some of the hardships with the rest." She expressed gratitude that they were not singled out for reassignment, but that the entire regiment had been assigned the change. Emily to her father, March 3, 1869.

40. Nickname for Emily, whom he calls "pet."

Chapter 6

1. Emily confided in her mother "It was rather sad, dear mother, to spend this first anniversary so far from my husband, but I was very much pleased to find that the day had not been forgotten for in the morning, Dr. Kirkwood presented me with a token of Emory's thoughtful love, a beautiful amethyst ring like yours, which he had sent down sometime before to be presented on that day." Emily to her mother, March 5, 1869.

2. Upton is referring to Emily's mother's aid in the missionary work in the West, which consisted mainly of providing Bibles to western army posts.

3. Mrs. Christopher.

4. This was probably the wife of Capt. William Conway, who joined the 74th New York at the beginning of the war, in June 1861, as first lieutenant rising to the rank of captain, until he mustered out in June 1864. He later joined the 16th Infantry in March 1866, then transferred to the 25th Infantry in September. He was unassigned in April 1869, but later assigned to the 22nd Infantry in

April 1870. He was breveted for gallant service against the Indians at Spring Creek, Montana, in October 1876. Conway retired June 1894. Heitman, *Register*, 1:323.

    5. Probably the wife of Lt. William H. Hugo.

    6. Probably the wife of Charles A. M. Estes.

    7. Grant was inaugurated two days later. Upton could not understand Grant's reluctance to be president. Grant was on the record that he felt compelled to run and accept the role because he had little faith in the career politicians. He also believed that he had a duty to protect the victory he achieved keeping the Union intact.

    8. Elizabeth (Betty) Blair married Gen. Cyrus B. Comstock early in 1869.

    9. It is unclear which Mrs. Tremain Upton is referring to: Dr. Tremain's wife in Memphis; or Helen Cornwall Tremain, wife of Lyman Tremain of Albany. Emily's sister Eliza Williams Martin was married to Grenville Tremain, Lyman and Helen's son. He probably means Mrs. William Scott Tremain.

    10. An eighteenth and nineteenth-century quadrille dance for eight or sixteen couples.

    11. Mrs. J. W. A. Pettit was the sister of Captain Estes.

    12. This second letter, dated March 4, may be misdated.

    13. "Sufficient unto the day is the evil thereof." From the Sermon on the Mount, Gospel of Matthew, 6:34.

    14. Alexander Turney Stewart (1803–1876) was an Irish born entrepreneur who built his fortune on wholesale and retail merchandise. His department store, the Marble Palace on Broadway in New York City, sold women's high fashion. His business acumen attracted the attention of newly elected President Grant, who nominated him as his secretary of the Treasury, without properly vetting him. Stewart was not confirmed by the Senate under an "antiquated statute," which barred a Treasury nominee who was "directly or indirectly involved in trade or commerce." *Cernow, Grant*, 627 and 634. Stewart may have been rejected for his close association with the Tweed Ring. At his death, Stewart's wealth was estimated at $50 million. See also *New York Times*, April 22 and 24, 1876.

    15. HLOM, translation by James and Sarah Lander and Lee Rast, first appeared in Upton, *Correspondence*, 1:264–66.

    16. The Act of March 3, 1869, reduced the number of regular army regiments from forty-five to twenty-five. The consolidated 39th and 40th Regiments became the 25th Infantry—a colored unit. See Ganoe, *History of the United States Army*, 324; and Connelly, *John M. Schofield*, 218.

    17. The orders to Arizona were rescinded in favor of Atlanta, which Upton erroneously thought would improve Emily's health. Emory met Emily at the end of March in New Orleans, and in April and May they were at McPherson Barracks (later Fort McPherson). On June 30 she returned to Willowbrook.

    18. The Upton Brothers had established a machine shop in Battle Creek and Benton Harbor, Michigan, that eventually became the Whirlpool Corporation.

19. Upton's income, including his lucrative royalties, gave the couple a higher standard of living than most postwar officers and their families. Alice Blackwood Baldwin's letters and reminiscences are replete with financial anxiety. Alice continually complained of extended poverty, reliance on the charity of family and even strangers, and most of all—debt. "I am sick and soul sick of being eternally in debt," she wrote her husband Frank. Three years later she told him bluntly: "Our purse is not adequate to our station." Alice to Frank, December 3, 1870, and January 24, 1873, Baldwin, *Memoirs*, 7–8.

20. Robert S. Brown.

21. For an excellent discussion of postwar army promotions, see Coffman, *Old Army*, chap. 5, "'Promotion's Very Slow': Officers, 1865–1898," 215–86.

22. William Denison Whipple, appointed to the military academy in 1847, graduated in the class of 1851, ranking near the bottom of his class. This low standing was belied by future assignments and achievements. He was born in Madison County, New York, in the hamlet of Nelson, August 2, 1826. He performed routine duty on the frontier in New Mexico and Texas, and in 1861 was on quartermaster duty at Indianola, Texas, when that post was captured by Texan insurgents. He escaped through the enemy's lines and made his way east in time to participate in the Battle of First Manassas as assistant adjutant general in Hunter's Division. He served as a staff officer during and after the Civil War and was successively promoted to captain, major, brigadier general of volunteers (July 17, 1863), and colonel. He also won the brevet of major general, United States Army, for "gallant and meritorious services in the field" during the war.

He served in the Departments of Pennsylvania and Virginia, Middle Military Department, 8th Corps, and sundry other posts. In November 1863 he became assistant quartermaster general of the army and Department of the Cumberland, and the following month he was appointed George H. Thomas's chief of staff. He participated in the Chattanooga and Atlanta Campaigns as well as the opposition to John Bell Hood's invasion of Tennessee at Franklin and Nashville. He continued with Thomas after the war, until the latter's death in San Francisco in 1870, when Whipple was appointed aide-de-camp to General Sherman, whom he served for five years. From 1878 until his retirement in 1890 he was adjutant general of the Division of the Missouri, Division of the Atlantic, and Department of the East. He died in New York City, April 1, 1902. He was buried at Arlington National Cemetery. "William Denison Whipple," http://www.arlingtoncemetery.net/wwhipple.htm; Heitman, *Register*, 1:1026.

23. Emerson Hamilton Liscum age nineteen, of Burlington, enlisted May 1861 and mustered in as corporal, Company H, 1st Vermont Volunteer Infantry, May 1861. He mustered out with the regiment on August 1861. He was engaged in the Battle of Big Bethel.

He served as corporal, sergeant and first sergeant of Companies E and A, 2nd Battalion, 12th U.S. Infantry, from February 1862 to March 1863. He was commissioned second lieutenant in March 1863 and first lieutenant in May 1863. He was wounded at Cedar Mountain. With the 12th Infantry, he was present at Chancellorsville and Gettysburg, where he was severely wounded near Round Top on July 2. He was also present at Bethesda Church and Hatcher's Run. He was breveted captain "for gallant and meritorious services in the field" to date from August 1, 1864. He was regimental quartermaster from February to October 1865.

After the war, Liscum transferred to the 30th U.S. Infantry in September 1866. He accepted a captaincy in the 25th U.S. Infantry in March 1867. In July 1870, he was assigned to the 19th U.S. Infantry. He was promoted to major in May 1892 while attached to the 22nd U.S. Infantry, and was promoted to lieutenant colonel, 24th U.S. Infantry, in May 1896. He was promoted to brigadier general, U.S. Volunteers, in July 1892, from which he was discharged in December 1898. Returning to the regular army, he was promoted colonel and assigned to command the 9th U.S. Infantry in April 1899. He was killed in action at the Battle of Tientsin, China, on July 13, 1900. "Emerson Hamilton Liscum," https://www.fold3.com/page /637052621-emerson-hamilton-liscum. Heitman, *Register*, 1:634.

24. According to army historian William Ganoe, the very day U. S. Grant took office, March 3, 1869, Congress's appropriation bill "decreased the 45 regiments of infantry to 25." It froze all commissions, promotions, and enlistments. The minimum enlistment "for all troops was to be for five years." Ganoe, *Army*, 324.

25. HLOM, portion in Michie, *Upton*, 233–34, translation by James and Sarah Lander and Lee Rast, first printed in Upton, *Correspondence*, 1:266.

26. The official orders were dated March 15, 1869, General Orders No. 17, "Reorganization of the Infantry of the Army." The order was designed to implement General Orders No. 16, March 10, 1869, intended to consolidate army infantry regiments and to make "the transfers demanded by the necessities of the service as economically as possible." The 18th and 25th Regiments were merged and ordered to Atlanta. The field officers were to be Thomas H. Ruger, colonel; Upton, lieutenant colonel; and James Van Voast, major. Letters Received by the Office of the Adjutant General, 1861–1870, RG 94, M619, Roll 666, National Archives Building, Washington, D.C. (hereafter NAB). See also "Reorganization of the Army," *Report of the Secretary of War to 41st Congress, Second Session*, vol. 1, Executive Doc. I, Pt. 2, 237.

27. Emily was "glad" that she was "going to Atlanta instead of Arizona and [felt] as happy as possible in anticipating the imminent move. Emory seems crazy to have no more moves and I am wild to get to him," she wrote. "I do not know whether I am going to Memphis or Atlanta. I don't much care." Emily to her mother, April 2, 1869.

Chapter 7

1. Along with the *Cuba*, the *Liberty* plied the waters between Baltimore and Havana in the late 1860s, making stops along the way, including Key West. The *Liberty* was built in Philadelphia in 1864.

2. Probably Brig. Gen. Morris Smith Miller, from New York, a graduate of the academy in 1834. By the time the Civil War broke out, Miller had served in many capacities in the regular army as an officer, primarily in the artillery. He joined the army quartermaster corps in September 1845 and was a major in the corps May 1861. He served the entire war in the quartermaster corps, and was finally breveted colonel and brigadier general for his service, March 13, 1865. Miller died March 11, 1870. Heitman, *Register*, 1:711–12.

3. This was Capt. G. B. Balch of the USS *Contoocook*. With its thirteen guns, the USS *Contoocook* was considered the flagship of the North Atlantic Squadron. Balch was vulnerable to a reduction in service. "During the year 1867 there were 11,900 men employed in the naval and coast survey service, but this number was reduced in 1868 to 8,500 men." Camp, *American Yearbook and National Register*, 139. Also see *Register of the Commissioned, Warrant, and Volunteer Officers of the Navy of the United States including Officers of the Marine Corps and Others to January 1, 1870*, 9 (hereafter *Navy Register*).

4. Possibly Henry A. Bartlett, marine captain. *Navy Register*, 120.

5. Possibly Francis M. Greene, from New Hampshire. "List of Lieutenants," in Camp, *American Yearbook and National Register*, 134.

6. This was Edward Van Slice, master of the SS *Columbia*. "Immigrant Ships Transcribers Guild: SS Columbia," http://immigrantships.net/v6/1800v6/columbia 18680410.html.

7. Emily's servant.

8. Nineteenth-century traveler Joseph J. Dimock experienced much the same introduction to Cuba hotels when he wrote in his diary, "On waking this morning about daybreak found our steamer in her dock in the harbor of Havana just back of Mrs. Almy's hotel" (p. 107). And in another entry he refers to the longer name, "Madame Almy's Hotel d'Luz" (p. 4). Dimock, *Travel Diary of Joseph J. Dimock*, 4, 5, 107–8. Dimock served as a major in the 82nd New York Volunteers and died of typhoid during McClellan's Peninsula Campaign in 1862. Ibid., xv.

9. Rear Adm. Henry K. Hoff, commander of the North Atlantic Fleet. *Navy Register*, 92.

10. SS *Columbia* may have been one of two ships with the same name. One was built in 1862 by Archibald Denny of Dumbarton, and the other was a passenger/cargo vessel built by Alexander Stephen and Sons of Glasgow in 1866. List of Ships Named SS *Columbia*, Wikipedia, last accessed June 7, 2018, https://en.m.wikipedia.org/wiki/List_of_ships_named_SS_Columbia.

11. This letter is a handwritten copy, possibly executed by Mrs. Martin, but unlike her handwriting. As Emily explained in her later letter on May 17, she sent the letter first to her mother, who sent it on to Mr. Smith. According to editor Sandra Myres, the Martins were "more ecumenical than denominational." Brother Edward claimed his mother was "full of religion" informed "by her church associations." She was not "really sectarian." Her goal was "to save the world." Alexander, *Cavalry Wife*, 127n2.

12. The Reverend T. Ralston Smith was the corresponding secretary of the American Bible Society at the Bible House in Astor Place in New York City. *Bible Society Record*, July 20, 1871, p. 109. He carried on a brief correspondence with Mrs. Martin in the late 1860s. See Throop-Martin Papers, Series 2, Box 5, Pt. 1.

13. Edward Sanford Martin (1856–1939) was Emily's brother. Although he was a lawyer, he established his reputation as a man of letters contributing essays to *Harper's Monthly*. He founded the *Harvard Lampoon* and was the first editor and cofounder of *Life* Magazine in 1883. In 1923 he was honored by the Harvard Club for his twenty-five years at Harper and Brothers, Publishers. Famed federal judge Learned Hand, members of the Harvard, Century, and University Clubs, and former members of the staff of *Life* attended his funeral. His obituary proclaimed: "He attained unusual journalistic prestige, for he was never commonplace and his humor was of the subtlest." He was buried in Hillside Cemetery, Wilton, Connecticut. "Edward S. Martin, Editor and Writer," and "Edwin S. Martin Rites," *New York Times*, June 14 and 17, 1939.

14. Possibly a Martin horse.

15. Emily was referring to St. Philip's Church, established in 1846. By 1875, it had grown into the largest Episcopal parish in Georgia. "A History of the Cathedral of St. Philip," https://www.stphilipscathedral.org/About/History/.

16. Gen. George Gordon Meade replaced Maj. Gen. John Pope as commander of the Third Military District consisting of Georgia, Alabama, and Florida. Meade, under congressional Reconstruction, 1867–68, fired Georgia governor Charles Jones Jenkins and replaced him with a military governor, Maj. Gen. Thomas Howard Ruger. See Bragg, "Reconstruction in Georgia," http://www.georgiaencyclopedia.org/articles/history-archaeology/reconstruction-georgia. It was this historical development that led Emory Upton and Thomas Ruger to become friends. Later, between 1870 and 1875, Upton served as commandant of cadets at West Point, and Ruger served as superintendent.

17. John Livingston Nevius (1829–1893), *China and the Chinese* (Harper, 1869). Nevius was an American Protestant missionary who wrote extensively on his experiences in China. Like Upton, he was a native of upstate New York. He was born on farm in the Finger Lakes region.

18. Bvt. Maj. Gen. Alfred Howe Terry, once colonel of the 2nd Connecticut Volunteers during the Civil War, was a strong opponent of the KKK. He assumed command of the Third Military District in Atlanta in December 1869. During the

war, Terry served as brigadier and major general and is best remembered as leading the successful charge against Fort Fisher and the capture of Wilmington, North Carolina, cutting off the last major open port of entry for the Confederacy. He served out west after the war and was General Custer's commander at the time of the Battle of Little Big Horn. Terry died December 16, 1890. Heitman, *Register*, 1:951.

19. Maj. Gen. Thomas Howard Ruger was a native of Lima, New York, but moved west, serving during the war with the 3rd Wisconsin Regiment from Janesville. He graduated from the academy in 1854 and resigned his commission in 1855 to study law. During the war he participated in all major battles in the eastern theater and then led a brigade of the 20th Corps during Sherman's Atlanta Campaign. He was appointed governor of Georgia, served with the Freedman's Bureau in Alabama, and was superintendent of the academy from 1871 to 1876, coinciding with Upton's term as commandant of cadets, 1870–75. He retired as a major general in the regular army in 1897 and died June 3, 1907. He is buried at West Point. Heitman, *Register*, 1:850.

20. Henry Lane Kendrick, professor of chemistry, mineralogy and geology 1857–1880. *Centennial of the United States Military Academy at West Point, New York: 1802–1902*, 2:289. Hereafter *Centennial*.

21. This is probably Albert E. Church, military academy class of 1828, who became professor of mathematics in March 1838, and was an artillery officer from 1828 to 1836. Church died March 30, 1878. *Centennial*, 2:216; Heitman, *Register*, 1:301.

22. Probably Henry Jackson Hunt from the military academy class of 1839. Hunt fought in the Mexican War at Contreras, Churubusco, and Chapultepec in 1847. During the Civil War, he became the chief of artillery, earning honors at Gettysburg and the siege of Petersburg. He attained the rank of colonel of the 5th U.S. Artillery in 1866. Heitman, *Register*, 1:556. Hunt crossed swords with Upton over the writing of the tactical manual for the artillery. See Upton, *Correspondence*, Upton to General Sherman, February 6, 1875, 1:354–56. Hunt died February 11, 1889.

23. Maj. James Van Voast was from New York City. He joined the 3rd Artillery upon graduation from West Point in 1852. He was promoted to first lieutenant in the 9th Regular Army Infantry in March 1855. He became a regimental quartermaster in July 1855, a position he held until June 1858. Van Voast served as a captain and then major in the 18th Infantry in December 1863. By August 1871 he had become a colonel with the 16th Infantry, and then colonel of the 9th Infantry in February 1882. He retired April 2, 1883. Heitman, *Register*, 1:984.

24. County seat of Warren County, southeast of Atlanta. Russell K. Brown, "Warrenton," New Georgia Encyclopedia, last edited August 15, 2013,

https://www.georgiaencyclopedia.org/articles/counties-cities-neighborhoods/warrenton.

25. Possibly the daughter of American socialite Bradley Martin (1841–1913).

26. Bradley Martin, New York socialite and entrepreneur. Although she refers to him as Uncle Bradley, the relationship to Emily is unclear.

27. Camp McDowell was renamed Fort McDowell in Maricopa County, Arizona, in 1866 for Maj. Gen. Irvin McDowell.

28. This was the wife of Maj. Gen. George Stoneman Jr. (1822–1894), who graduated from the academy in 1846 and gained fame as a cavalry officer and Civil War general. During the war he led a futile cavalry expedition against Richmond. He was honored with brevets for service at Fredericksburg, for the capture of Salisbury, North Carolina, and generally for service during the war. In July 1866 he was promoted to colonel in the regular army and given command of the 21st Infantry. He took command of the Department of Arizona, First Military District. Stoneman retired February 1891 and died three years later, September 4, 1894, in Buffalo, New York. Heitman, *Register*, 1:930. See also Waugh, *Class of 1846*.

29. This letter, to her brother George, and the following were transcribed into Emily's letter book, which was maintained by Mrs. Martin, but it does not to appear to be in her handwriting.

30. Brother George Martin.

31. Brother Enos Throop Martin.

32. Evy and Andrew Alexander's daughter. Her given name was Myra Madison Alexander and she was nicknamed "Midge." In 1870, after Emily's death, Midge was renamed Emily Upton Alexander. Myres, "Colonel's Lady," 38. See also Alexander, *Cavalry Wife*.

33. Catherine Thompson, aged fifty-seven, died the next day, October 26, 1869, according to the records of Fort Hill Cemetery, and is buried in section Ridgeland, lot 19, grave 7. "Fort Hill Cemetery," http://www.interment.net/data/us/ny/cayuga/fort-hill-cemetery/records-t.htm.

34. Brother-in-law Grenville Tremain (1845–1878).

35. Unidentified.

36. Probably a relative. Emily's mother was a Williams.

37. Nelly also wrote her mother and fairly echoed Emily's own assessment of health. "Emily is getting on as nicely as we could possibly expect. The first two weeks she improved wonderfully after that for a week, she felt rather miserable, but now she has taken a start again. Upton will tell you all about her room and how comfortable she is and how kind the Kirkwoods are to her. She can be as quiet and as gay as she pleases." Nelly to her mother, December 12, 1869.

38. She meant their wedding anniversary, February 19.

39. In December 1869.

40. Probably Bvt. Maj. Gen. Cyrus Ballou Comstock, 1855 West Point graduate.

41. The full title is "The Cricket on the Hearth: A Fairy Tale of Home." This Charles Dickens novella was published just before Christmas 1845.

42. Brother Edward Martin.

43. Emily's sister Violet Blair Martin Wilder (1860–1919) was the youngest Martin child. She married West Point graduate Wilber Elliott Wilder, class of 1877. As a first lieutenant with the 4th U.S. Cavalry, Wilder rescued Pvt. Edward Leonard, who was severely wounded at Horseshoe Canyon, New Mexico, April 23, 1882, while he was under heavy fire. Heitman, *Register*, 1:1035.

44. Unidentified.

45. This is the last known letter written by Emily before her death the following month. It was written on her second (and last) wedding anniversary, and her mood is upbeat and optimistic making her handwriting stronger and clearer than other examples.

46. A. D. Kirkwood to Mrs. Martin, Throop Martin Papers, Princeton University Library, PUL C0055, Box 5, Part 1.

47. Emily's siblings Edward Sanford Martin and Violet Blair Martin Wilder.

48. Mrs. Peabody to Mrs. Martin, March 26 and April 1, 1870, Letterbook. The family spelled Nelly's name with a "y" and the decision was made to leave this letter as written without inserting brackets with each mention of "Nellie."

49. Mary Lindley to Mrs. Martin, April 1, 1870.

50. Joanna Boyd to Mrs. Martin, April 1, 1870. It is unknown if Upton saw the condolence letters vividly detailing his wife's last hours addressed to Mrs. Martin. Later correspondence between Upton and his mother-in-law indicate that they remained close and it is entirely likely that she shared those letters with him.

51. Wilson Papers, LC. Published in Upton, *Correspondence*, 1:282–83.

52. Upton's friends, in addition to Wilson, wrote letters of support and condolences to Upton. Classmate Orville Babcock wrote from Washington, where he was President Grant's private secretary. Babcock to Upton, April 11, 1870; Samuel R. Brown, DD, an American missionary of the Reformed Church of America from Yokohama, Japan. Brown to Upton, October 20, 1870; Capt. Jacob B. Rawles, 5th Artillery, from his post at Fort Warren, Massachusetts, to Upton, June 13, 1870; and Ella D. Anderson, stationed in Atlanta at McPherson Barracks, May 1, 1870. Emory Upton Collection, William L. Clements Library, University of Michigan.

53. Maj. Gen. William Worth Belknap was secretary of war under Grant October 1869 to March 1876, preceded by John Rawlins. Warner, *Generals in Blue*, 29–30. His father was a distinguished veteran of the War of 1812 and Indian and Mexican Wars. Belknap carried on his father's reputation, earning the rank of brevet major general during the Civil War. After the war he returned to his adopted state of Iowa, but then President Grant named him his secretary of war. Belknap

resigned under a cloud of impeachment for malfeasance in office. Purportedly he received $24,450 in payments to facilitate a trading establishment at Fort Sill. He was to be convicted, but he resigned, making the impeachment effort moot. "Belknap's Sudden Death. His Lifeless Body Discovered in His Room." *New York Times*, October 14, 1890.

54. Upton to his parents. Michie, *Upton*, 239–40. Location of original unknown.

55. Upton to his sister, probably Sara. Michie, *Upton*, 240–41. Location of original unknown.

56. Dr. Kirkwood to Emory Upton, June 26, 1870. In Michie, *Upton*, 236–37. Location of original unknown.

57. Emory to Emily, March 20, 1870. United States Military Academy, Manuscripts Department, Upton Papers. Upton's last letter to Emily was March 20, 1870, reaching her just before she died. According to the Upton Papers (USMA), sister Nelly read the letter to Emily on her deathbed. There is a handwritten transcription probably in Nelly's hand of Emory's last letter. There is also a transcription of a letter to Emory from Nelly dated March 31, 1870, expressing her condolences to her brother-in-law. To her attending physician Dr. Kirkwood, Emily professed her relief that Upton was not there: "Oh, I am so glad that Upton is not here to witness this, it would add so much to our pain in parting!" Michie, *Upton*, 237. Location of originals unknown. Published in Upton, *Correspondence*, 1:281–82.

58. Anna Peabody was with Emily to the end. She and a Mary E. Lindley and a Joanna M. Boyd wrote letters March 26, March 27, and April 2, 1870 respectively from Nassau to Emily's mother describing her last days. Someone, probably Mrs. Martin, had the letters transcribed and printed with a black mourning border and included them in Emily's diary.

Epilogue

1. Nelly to her mother, April 14, 1870.
2. Schlereth, *Victorian America*, 290–91.
3. Upton to Gen. Francis Winslow, July 7, 1865, Francis Edward Winslow Papers, 1862–1917, University of Iowa Libraries, Special Collections Department, MSC 424; Upton to "Dear Sir," December 8, 1865, HLOM, published in Upton, *Correspondence*, 1:232–33; see Upton's letter to Gen. George Leet, Grant's assistant adjutant general, April 6, 1867, in Upton, *Correspondence*, 1:239–42; Upton to Sherman, November 8, 1867, William T. Sherman, Papers, Roll 13, LC. Sherman or an aide penciled in the notation "Ansd." (answered) in Upton, *Correspondence*, 1:245.
4. Fellman, *Citizen Sherman*, 291. See also Upton, *Correspondence*, 1:245n64. Sherman biographer Lee Kennett argues that the common wisdom regarding the Sherman-Upton relationship is that "Upton did the spade work and writing."

Kennett disagrees with that sentiment. He maintains, "recent research suggests that Sherman's input was greater than generally thought." Kennett, *Sherman*, 315. Stephen Ambrose argues that Sherman and Upton were as mentor and mentee. Sherman was nineteen years older than Upton, and Sherman "treated him . . . as a protégé and a spokesman," adding that the two "had a beneficial relationship." Ambrose, *Upton*, 76. John Marszalek calls Upton "Sherman's pet." Marszalek, *Sherman*, 463.

5. Marszalek, *Sherman*, 430–37.

6. Correspondence Files of the Adjutant General's Office, 1812–1917; Letters Received by the Office of the Adjutant General, 1861–1870, RG 94, M666, Roll 576, NAB.

7. October 10, 1866. Correspondence Files of the Commission Branch, 1863–1870 and the Appointment, Commission, and Personal Branch, 1871–1894, Commission Branch, 1863–1870, M1064, RG 94, M1395, ACP000196 (hereafter ACP).

8. Upton to DuPont, July 6, 1880; September 8, 1880. DuPont Papers, Hagley.

9. Dr. Samuel Powel to Mrs. Martin (presumably), Philadelphia, May 12, 1881, as cited in Michie, *Upton*, 486–87.

10. Upton to DuPont, September 22, 1880, and Upton to Maria, September 22, 1880, HLOM, and in Michie, *Upton*, 484. In November, Upton assured Maria that he was not suffering and that the "cautery has been applied once since my return (from New York) and the Dr. says he is about through with it." Upton to Maria, November 3, 1880, HLOM.

11. Michie, *Upton*, 482–83.

12. Upton to Maria, January 23, 1881, HLOM.

13. Thompson, *Presidio*, no page numbers.

14. Upton to DuPont, February 4, 1881, DuPont Papers, Hagley. He also wanted to return east to have easy access to Dr. Allen. Upton to Sara, December 26, 1880, HLOM. Upton was reunited with a classmate, Col. Henry Hasbrouck, who testified to the fact that when Upton "first joined the regiment he told me he was sorry to come out West; that he particularly desired to remain east, in order to avail himself of the services of a specialist whom he had consulted about a catarrhal trouble that worried him." Michie, *Upton*, 491.

15. For an abbreviated version of the events surrounding Upton's death, see Upton, *Correspondence*, 2:321–24.

16. Hasbrouck's complete testimony at Upton's inquest was published in *The Evening Auburnian*, Monday, March 28, 1881. It was excerpted in several other papers.

17. "The Late General Upton," *Army Navy Journal*, March 26, 1881, p. 707; "The Late Gen. Upton," *San Francisco Call*, March 16, 1881, reprinted in the *New York Times*, March 24, 1881.

18. "The Late General Upton," *Army Navy Journal*, March 26, 1881, p. 707.

19. "The Late Gen. Upton," *San Francisco Call*, March 16, 1881, reprinted in *New York Times*, March 24, 1881.

20. "Gen. Upton's Death," *New York Times*, March 17 and 19, 1881; Upton Papers, GCHD.

21. *Syracuse Standard* as cited in unknown clipping, Upton Papers, GCHD; Shaler to Hancock, March 18, 1881, in an unknown newspaper, possibly the *Evening Auburnian*, Upton Papers, GCHD; Clipping, Upton Papers, GCHD. The *Army Navy Journal* cited an erroneous source from San Francisco that Upton's body would go to Batavia. *Army Navy Journal*, March 26, 1881, p. 707.

22. Upton Papers, most from undated clippings from the *Evening Auburnian*, GCHD.

23. Upton Papers, probably from the *Evening Auburnian*; last quote from the *Auburnian*, March 29, 1881, GCHD.

24. Alexander to McDowell, March 19, 1881; and McDowell to Alexander, March 19, 1881, ACP, 1863–70, M1395, ACP000196, both sources in Upton Papers, GCHD; *Evening Auburnian*, March 28, 1881; General Order No. 3, March 17, 1881, Upton Papers, GCHD; *Bay City Tribune*, March 15, 1881, Upton Papers, GCHD; Sara Upton to Mrs. Martin, March 6, 1882, Princeton University Library.

25. Upton Papers, most from undated clippings from the *Evening Auburnian*, GCHD; Upton Papers, clipping citing the *Pioneer-Magnet* of Big Rapids, Michigan, no date, GCHD.

26. Upton Papers, newspaper clippings, GCHD; "Secret of Upton's Death. A Law Made Under Grant the Cause," Upton Papers, unknown newspaper clipping, GCHD.

27. Coffman, *Old Army*, 273–74; Weigley, *American Way of War*, 125, 169. Author Jeffrey Hice explores Upton's religious training and its relation to the serious action of suicide and eventually agrees with the initial assessment, that Upton's mucocele impaired his thought processes. See Jeffrey N. Hice, "Utmost Devotion to Duty"; Tidball, *Life of John C. Tidball*, 442.

28. Hyson et al., "Suicide of General Emory Upton," 445–52. See also Fitzpatrick, *Upton*, 239–42. Fitzpatrick states "After an autopsy..." (p. 240). There is no evidence that the inquest required an autopsy or that one was ever requested by the family and ever done. In more than one news account the body was embalmed almost immediately. Biographer Stephen Ambrose does not mention an autopsy. Ambrose, *Upton*, 136–50. Biographer Michie reprints a letter of Dr. Allen's to Michie stating: "The report of the surgeons who made the *post mortem* examination would be valuable in this connection," to which Michie added a revealing footnote: "None was made." Michie, *Upton*, 490.

29. Unidentified newspaper clippings: "Gen Upton's Will: Providing for the Education of Nephews and Nieces—Disposing of Battle Swords and Papers,"

dateline Batavia, May 10 (1882); and "The Will of General Upton: A Provision for Ambitious Genesee County Students," no dateline. Upton Papers, GCHD.

30. Robert Pickering to Mrs. Martin, March 11, 1881; Robert Pickering to Mrs. Martin, July 5, 1881; HB&B (Heaton, Butler, and Bayne) to Pickering, undated; HB&B to Mr. D. Appleton, October 4, 1881; D. Appleton to Mrs. Martin, November 12, 1881.

BIBLIOGRAPHY

Manuscript Collections

Genesee County History Department, Batavia, N.Y.
 Upton Family Papers
Holland Land Office Museum, Batavia, N.Y.
 Emory Upton Letters
Library of Congress
 C. B. Comstock Papers
 William T. Sherman, Papers
 Emory Upton, Papers
 James Harrison Wilson, Papers
 Department of the Cumberland, General Orders, Courts Martial Cases, 1866–1869
Massachusetts Historical Society Museum
 Emory Upton, Letters
National Archives Building, Washington, D.C.
 Correspondence Files of the Commission Branch, 1863–1870 and the Appointment, Commission and Personal Branch, 1871–1894. Commission Branch, 1863–1870, M1064.
 Correspondence Files of the Commission Branch, 1863–1870 and the Appointment, Commission and Personal Branch, 1871–1894. Appointment, Commission, and Personal Branch, 1871–1894, M1395.
 Correspondence Files of the Adjutant General's Office, 1812–1917; Letters Received by the Office of the Adjutant General, 1861–1870, M619.
 Correspondence Files of the Adjutant General's Office, 1812–1917; Letters Received by the Office of the Adjutant General, 1871–1880, M666.
 Correspondence Files of the Adjutant General's Office, 1812–1917; Letters Received by the Office of the Adjutant General, 1881–1889, M689.

Letters Received by the Headquarters of the Army, 1800–1899, RG 108, M635, Roll 111.
Records of the Judge Advocate General (Army), Army Courts Martial, RG 153.
The New-York Historical Society, New York, N.Y.
Campbell-Mumford Papers.
Martin, Cornelia Eliza. "What Might Have Been Expected: Album, 1837–1870."
Gilder Lehrman Institute, Upton Letters.
Pierpont Morgan Library, New York.
Emory Upton, Letters
Princeton University Library, Princeton, N.J.
Throop-Martin Papers (includes Emily's Letterbook, Series 7)
University of Iowa Libraries, Special Collections Department.
Winslow, Francis Edward Papers, 1862–1917, MsC 424.
University of Michigan, William L. Clements Library
Emory Upton Collection
University of Rochester, River Campus Libraries. Rochester, N.Y.
William Seward Digital Archive.
U.S. Army Heritage and Education Center, Carlisle, Pa.,
Upton Papers,
U.S. Military Academy Archives, West Point, N.Y
Upton, Emory, Papers.
U.S. Military Academy Library, West Point, N.Y.
Upton, Emory, Papers.
U.S. Military Academy Museum, West Point, N.Y.
Upton, Emory, Papers.

Books, Articles, Theses, and Dissertations

Abbot, Henry L. *Biographical Memoir of Cyrus Ballou Comstock, 1831–1910. Presented to the Academy at the April Meeting, 1911*. National Academy of Sciences, Biographical Memoirs, vol. 7. Washington, D.C.: National Academy of Sciences, July 1911.

"The Academy of Fine Arts, Venice, 1750–2010: Historical Background." Accademia di Belle Arti di Venezia, last accessed June 27, 2019, https://web.archive.org/web/20140606205051/http://www.accademiavenezia.it/accademia.php?id=1&type=eng.

Alexander, Eveline M. *Cavalry Wife: The Diary of Eveline M. Alexander, 1866–1867*. Edited by Sandra L. Myres. College Station: Texas A&M Press, 1977.

Ambrose, Stephen. *Upton and the Army*. Baton Rouge: Louisiana State University Press, 1964 and 1992.

American Bible Society. *Fifty-fifth Annual Report of the American Bible Society, Presented May 11, 1871 . . . and Also of the Life Directors and Members of the Society.* New York: American Bible Society, 1871.

Anderson, Scott W. *Auburn, New York: The Entrepreneur's Frontier.* Syracuse: Syracuse University Press, 2015.

Annual Cyclopedia and Register of Important Events of the Year 1869. Vol. 9. New York: Appleton, 1870.

Annual Reunion. *Third Annual Reunion of the Association of the Graduates of the United States Military Academy at West Point, New York, June 17, 1871; Tenth Annual Reunion, June 12, 1879; Eleventh Annual Reunion, June 17, 1880; Twelfth Annual Reunion, June 9, 1881; Twenty-Third Annual Reunion, June 9th, 1892.* Various Printers.

Anonymous. "Emory Upton Obituary and Eulogy." *Annual Report.* West Point: United States Military Academy. Annual Reunion, June 9, 1881.

The Army Reunion: With Reports of the Meetings of the Societies of the Army of the Cumberland, the Army of the Tennessee, the Army of the Ohio, and the Army of Georgia; Chicago, December 15 and 16, 1868. Chicago: S. C. Griggs, 1869.

Backman, Milton V., Jr. "Awakenings in the Burned-Over District: New Light on the Historical Setting of the First Vision." *BYU Studies* 9, no. 3, 1969.

Baker, Anni P. "Daughters of Mars: Army Officers' Wives and Military Culture on the American Frontier." *The Historian* 67 (2005): 20–42.

Baldwin, Alice Blackwood. *An Army Wife on the Frontier: The Memoirs of Alice Blackwood Baldwin, 1867–1877.* Edited by Robert C. Carriker and Eleanor R. Carriker. Salt Lake City: Tanner Trust Fund, University of Utah Library, 1975.

The Banker's Magazine and Statistical Register, from July 1885 to June 1886, Inclusive. Vol. 40. New York: Homan's Publishing, 1885–86.

Barnitz, Albert and Jennie. *Life in Custer's Cavalry: Diaries and Letters of Albert and Jennie Barnitz, 1867–1868.* Edited by Robert M. Utley. Lincoln: University of Nebraska Press, 1977.

Beers, F. W., ed. *Gazetteer and Biographical Record of Genesee County, N.Y. 1788–1890.* Syracuse: J. W. Vose, 1890.

Best, Isaac O. *History of the 121st New York State Infantry.* Chicago: Lt. Jas. H. Smith, 1921.

Bible Society Record Containing Correspondence, Receipts, etc., of the American Bible Society (New York) 16, no. 7 (July 20, 1871).

Biographical Directory of the American Congress, 1774–1949. Washington, D.C.: GPO, 1950.

Blaugund, Annette. "The Old Boy Network in Rome: Tenth Street Studio Artists Abroad." Chap. 16 in *The Italian Presence in American Art, 1760–1860,* edited by Irma B. Jaffe. New York: Fordham University Press, 1989.

Bragg, William Harris. "Reconstruction in Georgia." New Georgia Encyclopedia, last accessed October 26, 2018, http://www.georgiaencyclopedia.org/articles/history-archaeology/reconstruction-georgia.

Breerwood, Rhett, "Greenville Encampment: Union Cavalry and Barracks," New Orleans Historical, last accessed June 25, 2019, https://neworleanshistorical.org/items/show/639.

Brown, Jerold E., ed. *Historical Dictionary of the U.S. Army*. Westport, Conn.: Greenwood Publishing, 2001.

Brown, Russell K. "Warrenton." New Georgia Encyclopedia, last accessed August 15, 2013, https://www.georgiaencyclopedia.org/articles/counties-cities-neighborhoods/warrenton.

Camp, David N., ed. *The American Yearbook and National Register for 1869*. Vol. 1. Hartford: O. D. Case, 1869.

Casseday, Ben. *The History of Louisville, from Its Earliest Settlement Till The Year 1852*. Louisville, Ky.: Hull and Brother, 1852.

Casto, Marilyn. *Actors, Audiences, & Historic Theaters of Kentucky*. Lexington: University Press of Kentucky, 2000.

Centennial History of Missouri (The Center State): One Hundred Years in the Union, 1820–1921. Vol. 3. St. Louis: S. J. Clarke, 1921.

The Centennial of the United States Military Academy at West Point, New York: 1802–1902. 2 vols. Washington, D.C.: GPO, 1904.

Chapman, Helen. *The News from Brownsville: Helen Chapman's Letters from the Texas Military Frontier, 1848–1852*. Edited by Caleb Coker. Austin: Texas Historical Association, 1992.

Chernow, Ron. *Grant*. New York: Penguin Press, 2017.

The Christian World: Magazine of the American and Foreign Christian Union. Vol. 18, January to December 1867. New York: American and Foreign Christian Union, 1867.

Cilella, Salvatore G., Jr. *Upton's Regulars: The 121st New York Infantry in the Civil War*. Lawrence: University Press of Kansas, 2009.

Coffman, Edward M. *The Old Army: A Portrait of the American Army in Peacetime, 1784–1898*. New York: Oxford University Press, 1986.

Connelly, Donald B. *John M. Schofield and the Politics of Generalship*. Chapel Hill, University of North Carolina Press, 2006.

Convis, Charles L. *The Honor of Arms: A Biography of Myles W. Keogh*. Tucson: Westernlore Press, 1990.

Corbusier, Fanny Dunbar. *Fanny Dunbar Corbusier: Recollections of Her Army Life, 1869–1908*. Edited by Patricia Y. Stallard. Norman: University of Oklahoma Press, 2003.

Corbusier, William Henry. *Soldier, Surgeon, Scholar: The Memoirs of William Henry Corbusier, 1844–1930*. Edited by Robert Wooster. Norman: University of Oklahoma Press, 2003.

Cowper, William. *The Works of William Cowper. Comprising His Poems, Correspondence, and Translations with a Life of the Author*. Vol. 4 of 8 vols. Edited by Robert Southey. London: H. G. Bohn, 1853.

Cropper, Elizabeth. "Domenichino." *Grove Art Online. Oxford Art Online* 22, March 2011.

Cullum, George W., Brevet Major-General, Colonel of Engineers. *Biographical Register of the Officers and Graduates of the U. S. Military Academy at West Point, N. Y. from Its Establishment in 1802 to 1890 with the Early History of the United States Military Academy*. 7 vols. Boston and New York: Houghton and Mifflin, 1891.

Davis, Jefferson. *The Papers of Jefferson Davis, June 1865–December 1870*. Vol. 12. Baton Rouge: LSU Press, 2008.

Dawson, Joseph G. *The Late 19th Century U.S. Army, 1865–1898*. New York: Greenwood Press, 1990.

De Tocqueville, Alexis, Gustave de Beaumont, Arthur Goldhammer, and Olivier Sunz. *Alexis de Tocqueville and Gustave de Beaumont in America: Their Friendship and Their Travels*. Charlottesville: University of Virginia Press, 2010.

Dimock, Joseph J. *Impressions of Cuba in the Nineteenth Century: The Travel Diary of Joseph J. Dimock*. Edited by Louis A. Perez. Lanham, Md.: Rowman and Littlefield, 1998.

Eales, Anne Bruner. *Army Wives on the American Frontier: Living by the Bugles*. Boulder: Johnson Books, 1996.

Ekinci, Ekrem Buğra. "Handkerchiefs: The Secret Language of Love." *Daily Sabah*, last accessed July 1, 2018, https://www.dailysabah.com/feature/2016/02/19/handkerchiefs-the-secret-language-of-love.

"Emerson Hamilton Liscum," Fold 3, last accessed October 25, 2018, https://www.fold3.com/page/637052621-emerson-hamilton-liscum.

Executive Documents. Report of the Secretary of the Navy. House of Representatives, 2nd Session, 41st Congress, 1869–70. Washington, D.C.: GPO, 1870.

"Experience the Civil War Walking Tours of Memphis." Memphis Travel, last accessed July 29, 2018, https://www.memphistravel.com/memphis-civil-war-walking-tour.

Faust, Drew Gilpin. *This Republic of Suffering: Death and the American Civil War*. New York: Alfred A. Knopf, 2008.

Fellman, Michael. *Citizen Sherman: A Life of William Tecumseh Sherman*. Lawrence: University Press of Kansas, 1995.

Fitzpatrick, David John. "Emory Upton: The Misunderstood Reformer." PhD dissertation, University of Michigan, 1996.

———. *Emory Upton: The Misunderstood Reformer*. Norman: University of Oklahoma Press, 2017.

Foote, Shelby. *The Civil War: A Narrative*. Vol. 3, *Red River to Appomattox*. New York: Random House, 1974.

"Fort Hill Cemetery." Interment.net, last accessed November 22, 2016, http://www.interment.net/data/us/ny/cayuga/fort-hill-cemetery/records-t.htm.

"Frank Mortimer McMath." eBooksRead.com, last accessed August 26, 2016, http://www.ebooksread.com/authors-eng/frank-mortimer-mcmath/memorials-of-the-mcmath-family-including-a-genealogical-account-of-the-descenda-amc/page-10-memorials-of-the-mcmath-family-including-a-genealogical-account-of-the-descenda-amc.shtml.

"Frederick Townsend." In *The National Cyclopedia of American Biography Being the History of the United States*. Vol. 4. New York: James T. White, 1895.

Ganoe, William Addleman. *The History of the United States Army*. New York: D. Appleton, 1924.

Gates, John M. "The Alleged Isolation of U.S. Army Officers in the Late Nineteenth Century." *Parameters: Journal of the U.S. Army College* 10 (September 1980): 32–45.

Gatton, John S. "'Only for Great Attractions': Louisville's Amphitheater Auditorium." *Register of the Kentucky Historical Society* 78, no. 1 (Winter 1980): 27–38.

Gott, Richard. *Cuba: A New History*. New Haven: Yale University Press, 2004.

Grierson, Alice Kirk. *The Colonel's Lady on the Frontier: The Correspondence of Alice Kirk Grierson*. Edited by Shirley A. Leckie. Lincoln: University of Nebraska Press, 1989.

Griffis, William Elliot. *The Rutgers Graduates in Japan*. 2nd ed. New Brunswick, N.J.: Rutgers College, 1916.

Heitman, Francis. *Historical Register and Dictionary of the U.S. Army 1789–1903*. 2 vols. Washington, D.C.: GPO, 1903.

Hice, Jeffrey N. "The Utmost Devotion to Duty: Rediscovering the Faith and Character of General Emory Upton." MA Thesis, St. Bonaventure College, 1996.

"Historic Center of Rome . . . and San Paolo Fuori le Mura." UNESCO World Heritage Center, last accessed July 16, 2018, http://whc.unesco.org/en/list/91/.

Historic Hotels of the World: Then and Now, last accessed June 27, 2019, http://www.historichotelsthenandnow.com.

"Historic Memphis Hotels: The Smaller Hotels of the City." Historic Memphis, last accessed October 16, 2016, http://historic-memphis.com/memphis-historic/hotels/hotels2.html.

"A History of the Cathedral of St. Philip." Cathedral of St. Philip, last accessed June 27, 2019, https://www.stphilipscathedral.org/About/History/.

Hyson, John M., George E. Sanborn, Joseph W. A. Whitehorne, and William H. Mosberg. "The Suicide of General Emory Upton: A Case Report." *Military Medicine* 155, no. 10 (October 1990): 445–52.

"Immigrant Ships Transcribers Guild: SS Columbia—Havana, Cuba and Nassau, Bahamas Island to New York, 10 April 1868." From M237, Roll 292, List 276, National Archives and Records Administration. Transcribed by Phil Buckley,

May 17, 2004. Immigrant Ships Transcribers Guild, last accessed July 1, 2018, http://immigrantships.net/v6/1800v6/columbia18680410.html.

Jones, James Pickett. *Yankee Blitzkrieg: Wilson's Raid through Alabama and Georgia.* Athens: University of Georgia Press, 1976.

Journal of Proceedings of the 47th Annual Convention of the Protestant Episcopal Church in the Diocese of Tennessee Held in St. Peter's Church, Columbia on the 14th, 15th, and 16th of May 1879. Memphis: S. C. Toof, 1879.

Journal of the Executive Proceedings of the Senate of the United States from December 5, 1864 to February 6, 1866, Inclusive. Vol. 14, Part 1. Washington, D.C.: GPO, 1887.

Keating, J. M. *History of the City of Memphis, Tennessee.* Syracuse: D. Mason, 1888.

Kennett, Lee. *Sherman: A Soldier's Life.* New York: Harper Collins, 2001.

Kirshner, Ralph. *The Class of 1861: Custer, Ames and Their Classmates after West Point.* Carbondale: Southern Illinois University Press, 1999.

Kleber, John E., ed. *The Kentucky Encyclopedia.* Lexington: University Press of Kentucky, 1992.

Laqueur, Thomas W. *The Work of the Dead: A Cultural History of Mortal Remains.* Princeton: Princeton University Press, 2015.

Leonard, John William, ed. "George Bowen." In *The Classified Who's Who in Finance.* New York: Joseph and Sefton, 1911.

Longacre, Edward G. *Grant's Cavalryman: The Life and Wars of General James H. Wilson.* Mechanicsburg, Pa.: Stackpole, 1972.

Lookingbill, Brad L., ed. *A Companion to Custer and the Little Bighorn Campaign.* New York: John Wiley Sons, 2015.

Marsh, George P. *Correspondence: Images of Italy, 1861–1881.* Edited by Lucia Ducci. Madison, N.J.: Fairleigh Dickinson University Press, 2009.

Marszalek, John F. *Sherman: A Soldier's Passion for Order.* New York: Macmillan, 1993.

McFeely, William S. *Grant: A Biography.* New York: W. W. Norton, 1981.

McInnis, Verity. *Women of Empire: Nineteenth-Century Army Officers' Wives in India and the U.S. West.* Norman: University of Oklahoma Press, 2017.

McPherson, James. *Battle Cry of Freedom: The Civil War Era.* New York: Oxford University Press, 1988.

Michie, Peter S. *The Life and Letters of Emory Upton, Colonel of the Fourth Regiment of Artillery, and Brevet Major-General, U.S. Army.* New York: D. Appleton, 1885.

Mooney, James L. *Dictionary of American Naval Fighting Ships.* Navy Dept., Office of the Chief of Naval Operations, Naval History Division, 1959–81.

Myres, Sandra L. "Army Women's Narratives as Documents of Social History: Some Examples from the Western Frontier, 1840–1900." *New Mexico Historical Review* 65 (April 1990): 175–98.

———. "Evy Alexander: The Colonel's Lady at McDowell." *Montana: The Magazine of Western History* 24, no. 3 (Summer 1974).
———. "Frontier Historians, Women, and the 'New' Military History." *Military History of the Southwest* 19 (Spring 1989): 27–37.
The New England Historical and Genealogical Register, 1921. Vol. 75. Boston: Published by the Society, 1921.
New York State. Adjutant General's Office. *Annual Report of the Adjutant General of the State of New York. 1861–1868*. Albany: Various Government Printers. (Also published as Assembly Documents No. 80, 25, 49, 22, 24, and 38.)
———. Adjutant General's Office. *Annual Report of the Adjutant General of the State of New York for the Year 1903. Registers of New York Regiments in the War of the Rebellion (Supplementary Volumes to the Annual Reports of the Adjutant General for 1893–1905)*. Serial number 36. Albany: Oliver A. Quayle, State Legislative Printer, 1904.
———. Adjutant General's Office. *A Record of the Commissioned Officers, Non-Commissioned Officers and Privates, of the Regiments Which Were Organized in the State of New York and Called into the Service of the United States to Assist in Suppressing the Rebellion Caused by the Secession of Some of the Southern States from the Union, A. D. 1861. As Taken from the Muster-In Rolls on File in the Adjutant General's Office, S. N. Y.* Albany: Comstock and Cassiday, 1864.
North, Safford E., ed. *Our County and Its People: A Descriptive and Biographical Record of Genesee County, New York*. Boston: Boston History Company, 1899.
Pemble, John. *The Mediterranean Passion: Victorians and Edwardians in the South.* Oxford: Clarendon Press, 1987.
Perez, Louis A., Jr. *Cuba: Between Reform and Revolution*. New York, Oxford University Press, 1988.
Pert, Alan. *Red Cactus: The Life of Anna Kingsford*. Watsons Bay, Australia: Books and Writer Network, 2006.
Proceedings of the Nineteenth Annual Meeting of the Board of Supervising Inspectors of Steam Vessels, Held at Washington, DC, January 1871. Washington, D.C.: GPO, 1871.
Register of the Commissioned, Warrant, and Volunteer Officers of the Navy of the United States including Officers of the Marine Corps and Others to January 1, 1870. Washington, D.C.: GPO, 1870.
Roe, Frances M. A. *Army Letters from an Officer's Wife: 1871–1888*. Lincoln: University of Nebraska Press, 1981.
Rome and the Vatican. Rome: Arts Italia Editrice sri, 1998.
Ryder, Tom. "The World on Wheels: The Cuban Volante." *The Carriage Journal* 43, no. 5 (October 2005).
Schlereth, Thomas J. *Victorian America: Transformations in Everyday Life, 1876–1915*. New York: Harper Collins, 1991.

Sesser, David. "Militia Wars of 1868–1869." The Encyclopedia of Arkansas, last accessed December 11, 2018, https://encyclopediaofarkansas.net/entries/militia-wars-of-1868-1869-7904/.

"Steamships on the Panama Route—Both Atlantic and Pacific," The Ships List, last accessed February 5, 2005, http://www.theshipslist.com/ships/descriptions/panamafleet.shtml.

Starr, Merritt. "General Emory Upton—His Brothers, His Career." *The Oberlin Alumni Magazine* 18 (May 1922): 12–15, 31–36.

Summerhayes, Martha. *Vanished Arizona: Recollections of the Army Life by a New England Woman.* Sioux Falls: NuVision Publications, 2007.

Tapp, Hambleton. "Incidents in the Life of Frank Wolford, Colonel of the First Kentucky Union Cavalry." *Filson Club Historical Quarterly* 10 (April 1936): 82–100.

Thompson, Erwin N. *The Presidio of San Francisco: A History from 1846 to 1995.* Denver Service Center, National Park Service: Historic Resource Study, July 1997 (NPS-330).

Tidball, Eugene. *The Life of John C. Tidball: "No Disgrace to My Country."* Kent, Ohio: Kent State University Press, 2002.

Twenty-Sixth Annual Reunion of the Association Graduates of the United States Military Academy, at West Point, New York, June 10th, 1895. Saginaw, Mich.: Seemann and Peters, 1895. (Stoneman Obituary, 25–36.)

U.S. Adjutant General's Office. *Official Army Register of the Volunteer Force of the United States Army for the Years 1861, '62, '63,' 64, '65.* Part 2. New York and New Jersey. Washington, D.C.: Government Printing Office, 1865.

U.S. Military Academy. *Register of the Officers and Cadets of the Military Academy.* N.p., 1818–37 and 1855–70.

Upton, Emory. *The Armies of Asia and Europe: Embracing Official Reports on the Armies of Japan, China, India, Persia, Italy, Russia, Austria, Germany, France, and England. Accompanied by Letters Descriptive of a Journey from Japan to the Caucasus.* New York: D. Appleton, 1878.

———. *Correspondence of Major General Emory Upton.* Vol. 1, *1857–1875.* Vol. 2, *1875–1881.* Edited by Salvatore G. Cilella. Knoxville: University of Tennessee Press, 2017.

———. "Facts in Favor of Compulsory Retirement." *The United Service: A Monthly Review of Military and Naval Affairs.* Philadelphia: L. R. Hamersly. Vol. 2 (March 1880): 269–88; vol. 3 (December 1880): 649–66; vol. 4 (January 1881): 19–32.

———. *The Military Policy of the United States.* Washington, D.C.: GPO, 1904.

Upton, William Henry. *Upton Family Records: Being Genealogical Collections for an Upton Family History.* London: Mitchell and Hughes, 1893.

Utley, Robert M. *Frontier Regulars: The United States Army and the Indian, 1866–1891.* New York: Macmillan, 1973.

Vinton, John Adams. *The Upton Memorial: A Genealogical Record of the Descendants of John Upton of North Reading, Mass*. Bath, Maine: E. Upton and Son, 1874.

Vogdes, Ada A. "The Journal of Ada A. Vogdes, 1868–71." Edited by Donald K. Adam. *Montana: The Magazine of Western History* 13 (Summer 1963): 2–17.

Wallace, Robin L. "Footlights and Curtain Calls: Theater Since the 1800s." *The Filson Newsmagazine* 6, no. 4. Last accessed November 3, 2017, https://www.filsonhistorical.org/archive/news_v6n4_theater.html.

Warner, Ezra J. *Generals in Blue: Lives of the Union Commanders*. Baton Rouge: Louisiana State University Press, 1964.

———. *Generals in Gray: Lives of the Confederate Commanders*. Baton Rouge: Louisiana State University Press, 1959.

Waugh, John G. *The Class of 1846, From West Point to Appomattox: Stonewall Jackson, George McClellan and Their Brothers*. New York: Warner Books, 1994.

Weigley, Russell F. *The American Way of War: A History of United States Military Strategy and Policy*. Bloomington: Indiana University Press, 1973.

———. "Emory Upton." *The Dictionary of American Military Biography*. Westport, Conn.: Greenwood Press, 1984.

———. *Towards An American Army: Military Thought from Washington to Marshall*. New York: Columbia University Press, 1962.

"William Denison Whipple." Arlington National Cemetery, last accessed October 25, 2018, http://www.arlingtoncemetery.net/wwhipple.htm.

Williams, Mary L. "Ladies of the Regiment: Their Influence on the Frontier Army." *Nebraska History* 78 (Winter 1997): 158–64.

Williams, Roy. "Boardman, William Edwin (1810–1886)." Wiley Online Library, first published November 25, 2011, last accessed July 1, 2018, https://onlinelibrary.wiley.com/doi/pdf/10.1002/9780470670606.wbecc1561.

Wilson, James Harrison. *Under the Old Flag: Recollections of Military Operations in the War for the Union, the Spanish War, the Boxer Rebellion, etc*. New York: D. Appleton, 1912.

Winship, Kihm. "Elizabeth T. Porter Beach." *Skaneateles: The Character and Characters of a Lakeside Village* (blog), last accessed May 24, 2010, https://kihm6.wordpress.com/2010/05/24/elizabeth-t-porter-beach/.

Wood, Leonard. *Our Military History: Its Facts and Fallacies*. Chicago: Reilly and Britton, 1916.

Wooster, Robert. *The Military and United States Indian Policy, 1865–1903*. Lincoln: University of Nebraska Press, 1988.

Young, Judge J. P. *Standard History of Memphis, Tennessee From a Study of the Original Sources*. Knoxville: H. W. Crew, 1912.

Newspapers and Periodicals

Batavia (N.Y.) Daily News
Daily Graphic. New York
Daily Morning News (Batavia, N.Y.)
Evening Auburnian (Auburn, N.Y.)
International Review.
Louisville *Courier-Journal.*
Memphis Advocate
Memphis Appeal
National Tribune
New York Sun
New York Times
New York Daily Tribune
New York Herald
San Francisco Chronicle
San Francisco Evening Bulletin
The (Baltimore) Sun
United Service Magazine

INDEX

Page numbers in italics indicate illustrations.
EU indicates Emory Upton; EM indicates Emily (Martin) Upton

accidents, 24–25, 77–78
Adams, Captain, 166, 292n31
afghan, 19, 214–16, 235
Ah Sing (servant), 243–45
Albany, N.Y., 212, 214, 219
alcohol, problems caused by, 80, 85, 88, 99–100, 109, 129, 141, 148, 153
Alexander, Andrew J. (husband of Eveline), 10, 12, 53, 64–65, 74, 86, 97, 114, 116, 205, 208–9, 214, 247–48, 260n28, 276n9, 285n23
Alexander, Eveline Throop Martin (Evy) (EM's sister), 10, 12, 39, 47, 70, 74, 78, 86, 105, 107, 116, 146, 149, 166–68, 188–90, 203–5, 207–8, 214, 219, 231, 260n28, 261n37, 263n6, 274n55; letter from noted, 114, 133, 203, 208–9; letter to, 1, 63–65, 113–15, 208–9, 213–14; letter to noted, 1, 15, 18
Alexander, Myra Madison (Midge) (daughter of Eveline and Andrew), 18, 70, 86, 114–15, 205, 207–9, 213–14, 231, 301n32; name change of, 301n32
Allen, Harrison, 239–41, 304n10, 304n14

Alliance (ship), 114
Almy, Mrs., 197, 298n8
Ambrose, Stephen E., 1
American Bible Society, 140, 299n12
American Chapel (Paris, France), 29, 264n10
Ames, Adelbert, 5, 167, 293–94n38
Anderson, Charles, 247
animals, 35, 42–44, 46, 86, 202, 264–65n24, 276n13
Appian Way (Italy), 53, 267n56
Appleton, D., 251
Appleton, John Adams, 11, 23, 263n3
Appleton's (publishing firm). *See* D. Appleton & Co.
Arizona, 12, 16, 166–70, 182, 186–90, 193–95, 198, 214, 293n36, 295n17; Ute mission in, 206
Arkansas, unrest in, 102, 106, 110, 147, 152, 281–82n61, 290n15
Armies of Asia and Europe (Upton), 237
army, French, 65–66
Army and Navy Journal, 14, 41, 143, 244, 289n9
Army of the Potomac, 6th Corps, 2, 12

Atlanta, Ga., 9–10, 16–18, 20, 195–96, 198–99, 202–3, 205–6, 215, 231, 295n17, 297n27
Auburn, N.Y., 246–47
Austin, Mr., 30–31, 35, 37–39
Austin, Mrs. 30, 35, 37–39
Ayres, Emily (Mrs. Romeyn), 150, 152
Ayres, Romeyn Beck, 77, 105–6, 109–10, 150–53, 273n49

Babcock, Orville, Elias, 99–102, 106, 109–10, 279n45
Bainbridge, Emma Easterly (Mrs. William), 112, 185, 283n6
Bainbridge, William Henry, 283n6
Baker, Anni, 8
Balch, G. B., 197–98, 298n3
Baldwin, Alice Blackwood, 296n19
Baldwin, James Hammond, 99, 278–79n42
Ball and Black (merchants), 130, 162, 288n47
Bartlett, Henry A., 197–98, 298n4
Battle Creek, Mich., 189, 250, 295n18
Beaumont, Gustave de, 3, 257n5
Belknap, William Worth, 230, 302–3n53
Bellagio, Italy, 61, 146, 290n12
Benjamin, Julia Kean Fish (Mrs. Samuel), 92, 129, 132, 275–76n6, 288n46
Benjamin, Samuel Nicoll, 5, 84, 92, 99, 162, 275–76n6
Bibles, distribution of, 17, 140, 145, 181, 199, 200–202, 294n2
birds, 25, 35, 59–60, 92, 263n7, 264–65n24
Birnby [?], Mrs., 93
blacks, attitudes toward, 69, 95, 271n35, 287n36
Blair (Comstock), Elizabeth (Betty) (Mrs. Cyrus Comstock), 86, 101,
129–30, 141, 162, 184, 191, 276n12, 280n50
Blair, Francis Preston, Jr., vii, 276n12
Blair, Montgomery, vii
Bludell, Mrs., 219
Blue Grotto (island of Capri, Italy), 46
Boardman, William E., 11, 24–26, 263n4
Boardman, Mrs. William E., 11, 24, 26
Boman, Mrs. 11, 24
Bowen, George, 66, 270n27
Boyd, Joanna M., letter from, 228–30, 303n58
Brest, France, 12, 26–27
Brittany, France, 27
Brown, Mr. (New York), 200, 204
Brown, Robert S., 30, 191, 264n17
burgundy (wine), 31
Burned Over District (N.Y.), 2
Burnside Bill, 238–39

California, 166, 170, 183
Calvary Church (Episcopal) (Memphis, Tenn.), 87, 94–95, 106, 116, 145–46, 157–58, 200–201, 276n14
Capri (island, Italy), 42, 44, 46–47
Casey, James F., 79, 274n60
Cassie (maid), 220–21
Catholic Church, 11, 14, 48–49, 52–53, 55–56, 141, 289n6. *See also* names of specific churches
Catholicism, conversion to, 95
Catterson, Robert, 290n15
Chalons, 13, 62–66, 270n24
chaplains, 203, 206, 214
Chapman, Mrs., boarding house of, 54
Chateau Bourales (Marseilles, France), 33, 264n21
Cheow Yung (servant), 244
Chickasaw Club (Memphis, Tenn.), masked ball of, 149, 151, 290n19
Chigary, Madame, 63

320   *Index*

China, 135, 154, 203, 289n52
China and the Chinese (Nevius), 17, 203, 299n17
Choat, Miss, 113
Christ Church (Louisville, Ky.), 122
Christmas, 104–6, 108–9, 114, 213–15, 281n57, 282n65, 286–87n32
Christopher, John, 89, 104, 110, 113, 116, 118, 124, 130, 145, 277n21
Christopher, Mrs. John, 91, 97, 99, 110, 113, 116, 122, 130, 143, 145, 149, 182, 185, 277n25
Church, Albert E., 205, 299–300n21
Church of England, 146
Civil War, 2; effects of, 6–7
Civita Vecchia, Italy, 37, 265n26
Clap, Captain, 108
Clayton, Powell, 147, 290n15
Cleveland, Mrs., 217
Coffman, Edward, 7–8, 249
Collins, Joseph B., 124, 128, 287n34
Columbia (ship), 198, 211, 298n10
Comstock, Cyrus Ballou, 101, 137, 214, 280nn49–50, 302n40
Contoocook, USS, 197–98, 298n3
Conway, Mr. (American consul), 35
Conway, Mrs., 35
Conway, Mrs. William, 113, 143, 182, 185, 294–95n4
Conway, William, 113, 284n8, 294–95n4
Cooke, Misses (shipmates), 11, 24–25
Cooke, Mrs. (shipmate), 11, 24
Cooley, Mrs., 57
Corniche Road (France), 33–34, 264n22
courts martial, 109–10, 118–20, 123–24, 126, 128–30, 140, 287n34
Crawford, Samuel Wylie, 122, 286n29, 287n34
"Cricket on the Hearth, The" (Dickens), 215, 302n41
Crittenden, Mr., 46, 266n38

Crittenden, Mrs., 46
croquet, 195
Crosby, John Schuyler, 5
Croxton, John Thomas, 79, 274–75n61
Cuba (steamer), 63, 65, 74, 80, 157–58, 270n21, 286n31, 291n24, 298n1
Cuban war for independence, 108, 282n66
Curtis, Mr., 163
Curtis, Mrs., 163
Cushman, Edwin Charles, Sr. (Ned), 38, 57, 265n28
Cushman, Emma Conn Crow (Mrs. Edwin), 28, 57, 265n28
Custer, George, 10

D. Appleton & Co., 130, 160, 251, 288n48
Davenport, Madame C., 25, 29, 34–35, 62–64, 66, 263n8
Davies, Alice Martin (Mrs. Julian), 98, 278n41
Davies, Francis Asbury, 148, 290n17
Davies, Julian Tappan, 164, 278n41
Davis, Miss, 80
Davis, Mrs., 70
death, cultural views of, 236–37
de Cosson, Dr., 44–46, 61, 96–97, 146, 149, 155, 265n37, 291n23
de Cosson, Mrs., 44
de Cosson boys, 44, 62
de Tocqueville, Alexis, 3, 257n5
Dimock, Joseph J., 298n8
Dix, John Adams, 30, 264n12
doctors, mistrust of, 149
Dodge, Richard Irving, 90, 141–43, 145, 147, 149–53, 156, 163, 169, 186–87, 190, 195, 271n33
Dodge, Mrs. W. E. (Mrs. Richard), 67, 90, 147, 150, 271n33
dogs, 92, 102, 110, 130, 134, 142, 153–54, 280n51

Index 321

Drum, R. C., 239
Dukehart, John M., 75, 123, 286n31
Duncan Sherman & Co., 113, 285n18
DuPont, Henry, 239–42, 246
Dyer, A. B., 243

Eagle (steamer), 129, 135, 137, 156, 158, 162, 288n44, 292n31
Eales, Anne Bruner, 8
Early, Jubal, 2
Easter, in Rome, 38–40, 48–49
Eastman, Captain, 68, 71–73, 75, 271n34
Eldridge, Rev. Dr., 29, 264n10
"Elegy" (Gray), 193
Emory Upton: Misunderstood Reformer (Fitzpatrick), 1
Episcopalians, 17, 94–95, 146. *See also* names of specific churches
Estes, Charles A. M., 95, 105, 113, 278n34
Estes, Mrs. Charles A. M., 97, 99, 113, 116, 143, 182, 185, 279n44, 295n6

Fitch, Mrs., 113
Fitzpatrick, David, 1
Florence, Italy, 54, 57, 204
flowers, 28, 32–33, 43, 46, 54, 57, 92, 199, 203, 213, 217, 232–33, 241, 263n9
Floyd-Jones, De Lancey, 11, 24, 104, 261n32, 263n6, 281n58
Floyd-Jones, Mrs. De Lancey, 104
Foote, Mary Hallock, 8
Foote, Shelby, 7
Fort Adams (Newport, R.I.), 143, 290n10
Fort Hill Cemetery (Auburn, N.Y.), 10, 246
Fort Jefferson (Dry Tortugas, Fla.), 93–94, 98–99, 101–2, 114, 278n32, 278n39

Fort McDowell (Ariz.), 39, 203, 207, 301n27
Fort Monroe (Va.), 241
Fort Wallace (Kans.), 43, 265n36
France: agriculture in, 26–28, 31; railroad travel in, 27–28, 31, 34; sightseeing in, 26–31, 33, 62, 64
Fredericksburg, Battle of, 96
fruit, 41–43, 54, 211

General McPherson (ship), 245
Georgia, unrest in, 205
Gettysburg (ship), 15–16, 107–8, 114–15, 136–37, 281n57, 282n64, 289n57
gondolas, 58–60
Graham, Mr. (N.Y.), 67
Graham, Mrs. (N.Y.), 63, 67
Graham, William Montrose, 77–78, 273n51
Graham, Mrs. William Montrose, 78
Granger, Gordon, 113, 187, 285n17
Grant, Ulysses S., 10, 49, 79, 158, 183, 188, 238, 248–49, 295n7
Greene, Francis M., 197–98, 298n5
Greene, M. R., 135, 162, 289n53

Haines, Miss, 66, 127, 190
Haines, Nettie. *See* Parsons, Nettie [Esther?] Haines
Hancock, Winfield Scott, 246, 248
Harbison, Mrs., 30
Hart, Lily (EM's cousin), 67, 93
Hart, Mr. (husband of Lily), 67
Harte, Bret, 8
Hasbrouck, Henry C., 242–44, 248, 304n14
Hatch, Edward, 77, 273n52
Havana, Cuba, 68, 71–74, 107–8, 114, 123, 126, 134, 137, 143–44, 147, 149, 153, 156, 159, 161, 181, 189, 197–98, 286–87n32
Hazeldon, Mrs., 46

Hazeltine, Mr., 56, 268n8
Heaton, Butler, and Bayne (stained glass), 251
Herculaneum, 51
Hinds, Mrs., 109
Hoff, Henry K., 73, 114, 136, 198, 272n44, 281n57, 289n57
Holman, Silas Atherton, 12, 53, 261n34
Hoskins, Mrs., 217
Hotel de l'Athenee (Paris, France), 29, 264n11
Hotel de Londres (Rome, Italy), 38, 265n25
Hotel la Vittoria (Naples, Italy), 42, 265n33
Houston, William F., 113, 284n14
Hugo, Mrs. William H., 113, 136, 143, 182, 185, 295n5
Hugo, William H., 113, 136, 284n9, 289n56
Hunt, Henry Jackson, 205, 300n22
Hunt, Lewis Cass, 79, 274n59
Huus, Marcus, 110
Hyson, John M., 249

Indians, 7–9, 64, 70, 206
inspections, of soldiers, 87, 95
Irving, Washington, 10
Italians, criticism of, 14, 48
Italy: agriculture in, 42–43, 58; railroad travel in, 37–38, 42, 51, 57–58; sightseeing in, 13–14, 37–42, 44, 46–48, 51–60

John (servant), 160
Johnson, Andrew, 10
Johnson, Mr., 34
Johnston, Joseph Eggleston, 238
jokes, 125

Keats, John, 4, 51, 267n52
Kendrick, Henry Lane, 205, 300n20

Keogh, Myles, 10, 39, 43, *174*, 247, 260n28
Key West, Fla., viii, 14–15, 20, 68–70, 72, 74, 80–81, 84–85, 97–99, 102–3, 118, 120–21, 126, 129, 134, 148–49, 153, 189, 200–201, 271n34, 272n37, 285n20
Kingsford, Algernon Godfrey, 146, 290n11
Kirkwood, A. D. (Mrs. William), 16, 19, 90, 119, 134, 137, 160, 164–65, 169–70, 180, 185, 191–92, 210–11, 216–17, 220, 223, 229, 235–36, 277n23; letter from, 218–19, 262n64
Kirkwood, William, 16–17, 19, 90, 119, 122, 126, 131, 134–35, 137, 140, 156, 160, 162, 164–65, 169–70, 180, 185, 190–91, 208, 211, 215–16, 218–20, 223–24, 226–27, 229, 235–36, 277n23, 288nn41–42, 294n1; letter from, 233–34
Kyle, William J., 113, 284–85n16

Lake Como (Italy), 61, 64
Lawrence, Timothy Bigelow, 57, 269n11
Leander (mythology), 79, 274n58
Leboeuf, Edmond, 65, 270n26
Le Clerc, Miss, 38
Leftwich, John William, 82, 275n4
Liberty (steamer), 197–98, 298n1
Life and Letters of Emory Upton (Michie), 1
Lincoln, Robert, 245
Lindley, Mary E., 67, 220, 303n58; and coughing, 227, 236; letter from, 223–28
Lindley, Mr. (husband of Mary), 67
Liscum, Emerson Hamilton, 194, 296–97n23
Liscum, Mrs. Emerson Hamilton, 194
Lord, Miss, 216

Louisville, Ky., 118, 122, 126, 130, 285–86n26
Lyons, France, 13, 31

Madden, George J., 112–13, 283n4, 284n15
mail service, 70, 74, 82, 93, 107, 115, 120, 122–23, 129, 132, 134–37, 156, 158, 161–63, 169, 181, 183, 189, 193, 195, 211, 213, 227, 275n1, 291n24
Mallory (young), 211
Marseilles, France, 13, 32–33, 35–36, 264–65n24
Marsh, George Perkins, 57, 121, 269n12
Marsh, Mrs. George Perkins, 57, 121
Martin, Bradley (EM's uncle), 207, 301nn25–26
Martin, Cornelia (EM's mother), 3–4, 10, 18–19, 34, 63, 75, 80, 87, 93, 96, 115, 141–42, 146–47, 149, 154, *178*, 181, 196, 204, 208, 212, 216, 231–33, 248, 251, 258n6, 294n2; on Emory Upton, 4, 12, 14; letter from noted, 30, 34, 38, 45, 50, 101, 107, 113, 120, 124, 146, 154, 180–81, 190, 199, 206, 214, 216–17; letter to, 22–26, 34–38, 44–47, 50, 52–53, 61–63, 67–70, 93–94, 120–21, 132–33, 179–81, 190–92, 197–20, 202–7, 209–12, 214–30; and mission work, 145, 191, 206; and religion, 3–4, 145, 191, 221, 299n11
Martin, Cornelia Eliza (Nelly) (EM's sister), 15–16, 18–19, 38, 50, 67–68, 70–73, 75, 78, 84–86, 90–91, 95, 98, 102–3, 107–8, 113, 117–18, 121, 123, 126, 137, 141, 144–47, 153, 157, 162–65, 167, *174*, 180–81, 184, 190–91, 194–95, 199, 204–5, 207–10, 214–15, 217–21, 224–26, 228–29, 233, 235–36, 260n28, 262n64, 286–87n32, 301n37; health of, 218–19, 220–22, 224, 231, 236; letter to, 30–32; nursing of Eliza by, 146, 180, 218, 220–21, 224–25, 229, 235; and reaction to Emily's death, 231, 236
Martin, Edward Sanford (Ned) (EM's brother), 202, 216, 219, 299n11, 299n13, 302n47
Martin, Eliza Williams. *See* Tremain, Eliza Williams Martin
Martin, Emily Norwood. *See* Upton, Emily Norwood Martin
Martin, Enos Thompson Throop (EM's father), 9–10, 47, 60, 80, 86, 96–98, 117, 163, *178*, 190, 199, 204, 207–8, 212, 215–16, 219, 263n2; and injury, 202, 205, 207; letter to, 26–30, 39–41, 57–60, 74–75, 106–8, 183–85, 205–6; and money given to Uptons, 124, 131, 139, 160, 184, 289n1
Martin, Enos Throop (Throop) (EM's brother), 92, 107, 157, 188, 207, 212, 216, 277n28, 291n25
Martin, Fred (EM's brother), 39
Martin, George Bliss (EM's brother), 5–6, 39, 50, 80, 90, 267n47, 277n22; letter to, 207–8
Martin, John Williams (Jack) (EM's brother), 39, 47, 50, 206, 266n40; letter to, 80–81; and West Point, 10, 47, 199, 205, 266n40
Martin, Mary Williams (Molly) (EM's sister), 10, 43, 50, 52, 70, 74, 99, 103, 118, 153, 162, 165, 202–3, 216, 260n29, 265n35, 281n53; letter to, 32–34, 50–51, 164–66
Martin (Wilder), Violet Blair (EM's sister), 39, 80, 93, 216, 219, 302n43, 302n47
Maryland (steamer), 72–74, 120, 156, 272n41, 291n24
masked ball, 149, 151
Max (EU's horse), 86, 145, 276n13

324 *Index*

McClellan, George B., 11–12, 35, 43
McClellan, Mary Ellen (Mrs. George B.), 11–12, 35
McDowell, Irvin, 7, 241–42, 247–48
McElrath, Mrs. Thomson Price, 94, 107, 114, 278n33, 285n21
McElrath, Thomson Price, 107, 114, 278n33, 285n21
McIlvane, Mr., 197
McInnis, Verity, 8
McMahon, Martin Thomas, 103, 118, 281n54
McPherson Barracks (Fort McPherson) (Atlanta, Ga.), 20, 295n17
Meade, George Gordon, 17, 203, 299n16
Mediterranean Sea, 33–34, 37, 42, 46
Memphis, Tenn., 9–10, 15, 78, 82–84, 97, 105, 112, 130–33, 147, 154, 161, 183; citizen's dinner in, 82–83
Methodists, 17, 202–3
Michelangelo, 52
Michie, Peter Smith, 1, 246
Milan, Italy, 61
Military Medicine, 249
Military Policy in the United States, The (Upton), 238, 250
Miller, Morris Smith, 197–98, 298n2
minstrel show, 124–25
Moore, Captain, 136
Mormonism, 150
Moro Castle (steamer), 73, 162, 166, 181, 193–94, 236, 292n31
morphine, 80
Morris, Miss, 163, 284n10
Morris, Mr., 113, 140
Morris, Mrs., 113, 140
Morse, Captain, 72
Mosberg, William H., 249
mosquitos, 153
mourning attire, 236
Mt. Vesuvius (Italy), 13–14, 42–46

music, 39–40, 92, 95, 107–8, 113, 147, 165
Myres, Sandra, 8, 299n11

Nancy (servant), 151–52, 154, 167, 197, 204–6, 215–16, 298n7
Nap (pet dog), 102, 134, 153, 280n51
Naples, Italy, 37, 42–43, 50–51
Napoleon, 13–14, 31, 35, 37, 62, 64, 239, 249
Napoleon III (of France), 48, 266n44
Napoleon III (steamer), 22–26, 34
Nassau, Bahamas, viii, 10–11, 16, 18, 20, 69, 78, 85, 102–3, 109, 113, 117–18, 120–23, 126, 129, 131, 133–34, 136–38, 144–45, 149, 153, 155, 159, 161, 163, 165–66, 169, 179–80, 189, 192, 194, 208–11, 285n20
Neill, Thomas Hewson, 77, 273n50
Nelly (little), 207, 301n25
Nevius, John Livingston, 17, 203, 299
New Mexico, 135 139, 166, 194
New Orleans, La., 77, 79, 163, 198
New Year's party, 112–13, 133, 283–84n7
New York Infantry Regiment, 121st, 2, 246, 250
New York City, 67, 93
Norris, Mr., 116
Norris, Mrs., 116

Oberlin College (Ohio), 2, 4
O'Malley, Charles, 39
opera, 72, 77, 98
Overton (hotel) (Memphis, Tenn.), 84–85, 88, 130, 140, 151, 163

Palmer, Mrs., 87
Pantheon (Rome, Italy), 55, 268n6
Papal States, 14, 48, 266n44, 267n45
Paris, France, 29–30, 32, 62, 64
Parkinson, David, 112–13, 195, 283n3, 284n13

Parsons, General, 61
Parsons, Nettie (Esther?) Haines, 86, 110, 126–27
Peabody, Anna P., 216–18, 235, 303n58; letter from, 220–23
Peabody, Mr. (husband of Anna), 216, 221, 235
Peabody, Mr. (Paris, France), 30
Pettit, Mrs. J. W.A., 95, 97, 112, 116, 185, 195, 278n35, 295n11
photographs, 67, 76–77, 83, 98, 101, 136, 139, 162, 165, 169, *171–78*, 207–8, 213–14, 216, 219, 231, 245
Pickering, Robert, 251
Pius IX (pope), 39–40, 48–49, 55–56, 268n7
Pompeii, 44–45, 51
Poole, De Witt Clinton, 88, 91, 112–13, 195, 277n19
Poole, Miss, 199
Porter, Horace, 99–102, 106, 109–10, 279–80n46
Prentice, Miss, 217
Prentice, Mrs., 217
Presbyterians, 143, 146
Presidio (San Francisco, Calif.), 239, 241–42, 245

quinine, 80, 212
Quintard, Charles Todd, 87, 276n16

railroad travel, 27–28, 31, 37, 42, 51, 57–58
Randall, George Morton (EU's cousin), 100, 280n47
Randall, Mrs. George Morton, 100
Rankins, Julia, 38, 191
Raphael (artist), 51–52, 55, 267n53
Rawles, Fanny (Mrs. Jacob), 72–73, 76, 84–85, 89, 98, 109, 144, 148, 156, 164, 272n40
Rawles, Jacob Beekman, 73, 76, 85–87, 89, 98, 109, 129, 137, 143–44, 148, 153, 156, 164, 272n40, 272n46, 288n45
Reims, France, 12–13, 28
Reuben (servant), 95, 102, 130–31, 134, 138, 152–53, 160, 167
reunions, of Civil War soldiers, 92, 100, 113, 280n48, 285n19
revivals, religious, 2
Rice, Mr., 80
Riggs, Mrs., 32, 63
Roberts, Mrs., 236
Robinson, Miss, 11, 24
Robinson, Mrs., 11, 24
Rogers, Samuel, 58, 269n13
Rome, Italy, 14, 35–41, 50–57
Root, Mrs., 66
Rosecrans, William S., 73, 272n44
Royal Victoria Hotel (Nassau, Bahamas), 126, 215–16, 229, 236, 288n42
Ruger, Thomas, *175*, 199, 204, 206, 237, 297n26, 299n16, 300n19

Sanborn, George C., 249
Sand Beach Church (Auburn, N.Y.), 5, 180, 204, 246–47, 251
Sanger, J. P., 246
Santa Maria Maggiore basilica (Rome, Italy), 56, 268n9
Saunders, William, 240–41
Schlereth, Thomas, 236
Scott, Winfield, 249
sculpture, 52, 55–56, 267nn54–55, 268nn4–5. *See also* Upton, Emily, bust of
Sedgwick Barracks (La.), 78, 274n56
servants, 95, 102, 130–31, 133–34, 138–39, 151–54, 160, 167, 197, 204–6, 215–16, 220, 243–45
Seward, Janet (daughter-in-law of William), 10–11
Seward, William H., vii, 10–11, 47, 266n41

Shakespeare, William, 97, 192
Shaler, Alexander, 246
shawl, 19, 217, 235
Shelley, Percy Bysshe, 4, 51, 267n52
Sheridan, Philip Henry, 5, 7, 10, 238
Sherman, Mrs., 18
Sherman, William T., 7–8, 237–39, 242, 246, 249, 303–4n4
shipboard: accidents, 24–25; food, 23, 27; life, 22–26, 37, 75, 209
Sieur, Dr., 32–33
Simmons, Franklin, 75, 98, 107, 282n62
Sistine Chapel (Italy), 52
Smith, Mr., 140, 151, 163
Smith, Mrs., 140, 151, 163
Smith, T. Ralston, 200, 203, 299nn11–12; letter to, 200–202, 299n12
Smyth, Col., 199
soldiers: and alcohol, 80, 85, 88, 99–100, 109, 129; in France, 27, 31; and inspections, 87, 95; in Key West, 80–81, 85, 99, 153, 276n7; in Memphis, 87–89, 95, 98, 116; reunions of, 92, 100, 113, 280n48, 285n19
Sorrento, Italy, 11–12, 35, 37, 39, 44–46, 51, 64
Standart, Mrs., 227
Stannard, David, 236
Stanton, Edwin M., 238
Star of the West (ship), 73, 272n45
Stewart, Alexander Turney, 188, 295n14
St. Mark's church (Venice, Italy), 59–60
Stoneman, George, 301n28
Stoneman, Mrs. George, 207, 301n28
Storrow, Samuel Appleton, 123, 148–49, 290n16
St. Paul's basilica (Rome, Italy), 53
St. Peter's basilica (Rome, Italy), 14, 38–41, 48–49, 53, 56
St. Philip's Church (Episcopal) (Atlanta, Ga.), 204, 300n15

sugar-making, 79
"Suicide of General Emory Upton, The" (Hyson et al.), 249
Summerhayes, Martha, 260n26
Swaine, Peter Tyler, 124, 287n33
Swedenborgians, 158, 292n27
Switzerland, 64
Swords, Mrs. Thomas, 122, 124
Swords, Thomas, 122, 124, 286n28
Sykes, George, 158, 291–92n26

tactics (military), 95
Tactics (Upton), 131, 140, 146, 160, 192, 203, 238–39, 241, 243–45, 247–50, 288n48, 290n13
Terry, Alfred Howe, 204–5, 299–30n18
Thompson, Catherine, 208, 301n33
Throop, Enos T. (EM's granduncle), 3, 203, 257n5
Throop and Martin Family Papers (Princeton), vii–ix
Ticknor, George, 6–7
Tidball, Eugene C., 249
Tidball, John C., 246, 249
Torbert, Alfred Thomas Archimedes, 5, 130, 160, 288n49
Tortugas (Dry) islands (Fla.), 68, 93–94, 97–99, 101–2, 114, 148–49, 278n32, 278n39
Townsend, Frederick, 47, 246, 266n42
Transubstantiation, 94–95
Tremain, Eliza Williams Martin (Lily, Leily, Lylie) (EM's sister), 12, 70, 78, 85, 105, 121, 160, *174*, 184, 188, 199, 202, 204, 210–12, 265n32, 274n54; and daughter, 211–14, 225; letter to, 42–44, 54–57
Tremain, Grenville (husband of Eliza), 5, 204, 210, 265n32, 274n54, 301n34
Tremain, Helen (daughter of Grenville and Lily), 212–14, 225

Index 327

Tremain, Helen (daughter of Lyman and Helen), 274n54, 277n28
Tremain, Helen Cornwall (wife of Lyman), 77, 274n54
Tremain, Lyman (Jr.), 77–78, 274n54
Tremain, Lyman, 77, 274n54
Tremain, William Scott, 99, 143, 279n43
Tremain, Mrs. William Scott, 99, 143, 185, 295n9
Tucson, Ariz., 166

Upton, Daniel (EU's father), 2, 66, 104, *177*; letter to, 231–32
Upton, Electa Randall (EU's mother), 2, 66, 104, *177*; letter to, 231–32
Upton, Emily: as army wife, 9–10, 16–17, 95, 97, 166–67, 183–84, 191, 199, 218, 294n39; Bible distribution by, 17, 181, 199–202; bust of, 75, 98, 101, 106–7, 115, 136, 139, 160, 162, 165; and colds, 20, 102–3, 118, 179; and cough, 18, 20, 149, 155, 161, 163, 207; death of, viii, 1, 4, 19, 221, 227, 229, 231, 233, 236–37, 262–63n1, 303nn57–58; dying, 18–19, 219–29, 231, 233–35, 303nn57–58; education of, 4; and finances, 203; and French language, 24–25, 28, 80; and gifts to Emory, 19, 80, 88, 109–10, 155, 192, 214–16, 235, 276–77n18; and health, 139, 179, 196, 207, 209, 218–19, 301n37; health advice to, 84–85, 96, 102–3, 117–18, 126, 148–49, 158, 161–62; health of, better, 25, 29–30, 36, 39, 44, 49, 53, 60, 63–64, 69–70, 74, 93, 104, 109, 115, 118, 120–21, 123, 126, 133, 138, 149, 155, 161, 179, 186, 189, 192, 198, 210–11, 215, 217; health of, poor, 1, 4, 8–12, 14, 16–19, 22–24, 29, 32, 37, 45, 49, 61–65, 84–85, 92–93, 102, 115, 120, 130, 207, 211, 213, 217, 262–63n1; and health, worse, 179, 191, 199, 207, 215, 220–21, 223, 227; and housekeeping, 203; in Key West, 14–16, 20, 68–70, 74, 80–81, 118, 120, 129, 189, 285n20; letter from, 1, 22–47, 50–65, 67–70, 74–75, 80–81, 93–94, 106–8, 113–15, 120–21, 132–33, 164–66, 179–81, 183–85, 190–92, 197–218, 302n45; letter to, 65–67, 71–73, 75–78, 82–92, 94–106, 109–13, 116–25, 127–64, 166–70, 181–83, 185–88, 192–95, 234–35; manuscript sources on, vii–ix; in Nassau, viii, 11, 18–20, 165–66, 180, 189, 209–13, 215, 219, 231; and neuralgia, 39, 155–56, 161; photograph of, 98, 101, 136, 139, 162, 165, 169, *171*, *174*, 245; and religion, 4–5, 14, 17, 25, 29, 55–56, 206, 209–10, 217, 221–23, 226–29, 234–35, 263n8; and riding, 44, 46, 81; servant of, 151–52, 154, 167, 197, 204–6, 215–16; and shopping, 29–31, 34–36, 62, 64, 107–8; and tuberculosis, 1, 11, 20
Upton, Emily and Emory (jointly): carriage and horse of, 128, 130, 132, 135, 137, 143, 145, 154, 158, 163–64, 189, 191, 193, 196, 288n50, 289n8; disagreements between, 136; engagement of, 3–6, 21–22, 65, 262–63n1; future plans of discussed, 153–54, 163–64, 166–69, 183–84, 186–89, 194–95, 198; honeymoon of, 11–14, 22–66, 125, 160; house furnishings for (Memphis), 84, 88, 91, 95, 128, 130, 137, 141–42, 154, 189–91, 196, 235, 289n8; separation of discussed, 15–16, 18–19, 71, 74, 76, 78, 80, 84–85, 87–94, 96–106, 111, 115, 117–22, 124, 130–31, 133–35, 138, 140–41, 146, 150–52, 154, 156, 159, 162, 165, 168–69, 181–83, 186–90, 192–93, 208–9, 213, 217,

220–21, 275n1, 297n27; wedding of, 1, 3, 5, 246, 262–63n1; wedding anniversary of, 17, 19, 79, 99, 150, 155, 170, 181, 190, 214, 216–17, 294n1

Upton, Emory, 114–15, 205, 207, 209, 214, 218, 221, 224; and abolition, 2, 4; on alcohol, 88, 99, 109, 129, 141, 148; ambition of, 249; anti-Catholicism of, 11, 14, 48–49, 141; and *Armies of Asia and Europe*, 237; army career of, 2–4, 9, 237–39, 241–42, 244, 246; and Bible distribution, 140, 145, 181, 200–201; biographers of, 1; birth of, 1–2; character of, 4–6, 12–14, 47, 63, 258n11; and church attendance, 14, 17, 29, 48–49, 78, 87, 94–95, 106, 116, 122, 141, 145–46, 157, 161; and Civil War, 2, 6, 274n53; and dancing, 185, 295n10; death of, 236, 244, 247–50; and death of Emily, 217, 220–21, 229–34, 237, 247–48, 262n64, 303n57; and death, theories of, 247–50, 305nn27–28; dental work on, 66, 240; described, 4, 12; doctors mistrusted by, 149; duties of, 88, 91, 97–98, 109, 115, 122, 140, 199, 203, 206, 216; education of, 2, 4; finances of, 84, 124, 128, 130–31, 137, 139, 160, 164, 166, 182–83, 189, 289n1, 296n19; and French language, 24, 125–27, 288n39; funerals of, 245–47; and gifts to Emily, 14, 17, 19, 32–33, 41, 91, 170, 181, 190, 217, 235, 294n1; health of, 66, 80, 169, 193, 239–44, 247–50, 305nn27–28; and Italians criticized by, 14, 48; in Key West, 14–15, 67–70, 272n37; letter from, 21–22, 47–49, 65–67, 71–73, 75–78, 82–92, 94–106, 109–13, 116–64, 166–70, 181–83, 185–90, 192–96, 207, 230–35; letter from discussed, 221, 232, 236; letter to, 233–34; and letters of condolence, 230, 233–34, 302n50, 302n52; manuscript sources on, vii–ix; military orders to, 166–69, 182–84, 186, 188–89, 191, 193–96, 199, 206–7, 237, 239, 241, 297n26; and *The Military Policy of the United States*, 238, 250; in Nassau, 210–13; nursing of Emily by, 11–12, 23, 26, 63–64, 146, 235; photograph of, 172, 176–77; and public speaking, 82–83; quarters of (Atlanta), 203; quarters of (Memphis), 83–84, 86, 88–89, 91, 95, 97–98, 110, 112–13, 115, 124, 128, 130–33, 143–44, 150, 154, 160–61 164, 168, 183, 190–91, 282n69, 289n8; quarters of (San Francisco), 241; and reading, 17, 77, 88, 203; and religion, 4–5, 11, 14, 17, 48–49, 76–77, 95, 116, 138, 146, 158, 210, 230–35, 263n8; and romance, 15, 65–66, 71–73, 75–76, 78–80, 85–86, 90, 92, 94, 99, 101, 103–6, 110, 118–19, 122, 124–25, 127, 129, 142–44, 146, 151, 153, 159–60, 162–63, 168–70, 181, 192–93, 195, 235; schedule of, 88, 157; and seasickness, 24, 37, 71, 75, 79; servants of, 95, 102, 130–31, 134, 138, 152–53, 160, 167, 215–16, 243–45; and shopping, 71–73, 84; and stained glass window, 251; and suicide of, 243–44, 247–50, 305nn27–28; and *Tactics*, 3, 17, 131, 140, 146, 160, 192, 203, 238–39, 241, 243–45, 247–50, 288n48, 290n13; attends theater, 72, 77, 98, 119, 124–25; and Toulon visit, 13, 35; and uniform, 87; United States criticized by, 49; visits European military sites, 12–13, 26–28, 31–32, 35, 61–62, 64–66, 237, 270n24; and West Point, 2, 4, 225, 230–31, 237, 240, 249–50; will of, 250–51; on women, 146–47; world tour of, 237, 250; wounds of, 2

Index   329

Upton, Henry (EU's brother), 104, *177*, 281n55

Upton, James Stephen (EU's brother), 66, *177*, 250

Upton, John Bean (EU's brother), *177*, 189, 248, 295n18; letter to, 47–49

Upton, Julia Sherman (wife of John), 47, 49

Upton (Finley), Louisa Jackman (EU's sister), 66, *177*

Upton (Hanford), Maria Eusebia (EU's sister), 48, 66, 86, 125, 134, 141, 147, *177*, 196; letter to, 125–27, 188–90, 195–96; letter to discussed, 240–41, 304n10

Upton, Parley (EU's brother), 104, *177*

Upton, Sara (EU's niece, daughter of John), 66

Upton, Sara Kelsey (EU's sister), 48–49, 66, 141, 147, *177*, 141–42, 244–45, 248, 250, 271n30

Upton, Susan (wife of Henry), 104, 281n56

Upton and the Army (Ambrose), 1

United States, criticism of, 49

U.S. Army: postwar conditions in, 7–9, 153, 258n15, 290–91n22; reduction of, 166–67, 193–94, 293n37, 295n16, 277n24, 297n26

U.S. Artillery Regiment, 4th, 2, 241–45; 5th, 2, 143

U.S. Cavalry Division, 4th, 2

U.S. Coast Guard Survey, 121, 286n27

U.S. Infantry Regiment, 2nd, 200–201

U.S. Infantry Regiment, 6th, 194

U.S. Infantry Regiment, 16th, 200

U.S. Infantry Regiment,18th, 200

U.S. Infantry Regiment,21st, 207

U.S. Infantry Regiment, 25th, 3, 78, 88–89, 166, 188, 200, 295n16

U.S. Infantry Regiment, 29th, 78

U.S. Infantry Regiment, 32nd, 166, 188–89, 194

Ute Indians, mission to, 206

Utley, Robert, 8

Van Buren, Martin, vii, 3

Van Reed, Mr., 89

Van Reed, Mrs., 89

Van Slice, Edward, 197–98, 298n6

Van Voast, James, 205, 297n26, 300n23

Vatican art, 52–55

Venice, Italy, 57–61, 125, 287n37

Verona, Italy, 61

Vi (EU's dog), 92, 102, 110, 130, 134, 142, 153–54

Victor Emanuel (of Italy), 14, 48

Villa Rispoli (Naples, Italy), 43

Vogdes, Ada, 7, 282n65

Walch, Kitty Dix, 30, 50–51, 53

Walch, Mr. (husband of Kitty), 30, 50–51, 53

Walker, Mrs., 133

Walsh, Aunty, 67

Warrenton, Ga., 205, 300n24

weather: beautiful, 126, 135–36, 142, 144, 213; cold, 32, 38, 75, 77, 85, 91, 93, 98, 102, 163, 169; cool, 193, 210; damp, 69, 74, 120; delightful, 193, 199, 206; disagreeable, 193; dry, 167; hot, 153, 204 206, 210; mild, 155; mud, 112, 126; "Northers," 85, 114, 118, 120, 153, 179, 217; rain, 38, 87, 111, 142, 145, 193–94; in San Francisco, 241; snow, 5, 126; storm at sea, 23, 80, 102, 108, 114, 157; thunderstorm, 42; warm, 155, 158, 161, 167, 199; wind, 50, 74, 93

Weigley, Russell, 249

Weisels [?], Dr., 80

Weisels [?], Mrs., 80

West Point, 2, 4, 10, 47, 100–101, 188, 199, 205, 225, 230–31, 237, 240, 249–50
Whipple, William Denison, 193, 296n22
White, George, 87, 94–95, 161, 200–201, 276n15
Whitehorne, Joseph W., 249
Wilder, Violet Blair Martin. *See* Martin (Wilder), Violet Blair
Wilder, Wilbur Elliott (husband of Violet Martin), 302n43
Williams, Mary L., 8
Williams, Mrs., 212, 215
Willowbrook, N.Y. (Martin home), 5, 9–10, 18, 20–21, 41, 47, 63, 79, 86, 103–4, 115, 126, 131, 141, 146, 156, 167, 185, 187, 189–90, 203–4, 206–7, 209, 211, 213–14, 219, 225, 245, 263n2, 274n57, 295n17
Wilson, Capt., 68
Wilson, James Harrison, viii, 2, 5, 10, 92, 113, *173*, 230–31, 246, 258n11, 277n26, 285n19; letter to, 21–22, 230–31
Wilson, Mrs. James Harrison, 231
wives, of army officers, 7–9, 158, 168, 184, 194, 258–59n19, 259n20, 259n22, 260n26, 296n19
Wolford, Elizabeth Bailey (Mrs. Frank), 163
Wolford, Frank Lane, 163, 292–93n34
Wong Ky Ming (servant), 244
Wood, Mrs., 121

yellow fever, 211–12

Zabriskie, Mr., 203, 206

www.ingramcontent.com/pod-product-compliance
Lightning Source LLC
Chambersburg PA
CBHW020829160426
43192CB00007B/578